FOR LOVE AND COURAGE

Anne Nason is the granddaughter of Lt. Colonel E.W. Hermon and the daughter of Mary ('Mairky') who bequeathed her the letters. Emigrating with her family to New Zealand in 1935 she was educated in that country, graduating with a BA degree from Canterbury University College in 1955. Returning to England in 1956 she worked in MI6 prior to her marriage to an Army Officer and has travelled the world whilst bringing up a family of two sons and two daughters. She lives with her husband in Wiltshire and currently has nine grandchildren.

FOR LOVE AND COURAGE

The Letters of Lieutenant Colonel E.W. Herman from the Western Front 1914–1917

Edited by Anne Nason

preface
publishing

This paperback edition published by Preface 2009

10 9 8 7 6 5 4 3 2 1

Copyright © Anne Nason 2008, 2009

First published in Great Britain in 2008 by Preface
1 Queen Anne's Gate
London SWIH 9BT

An imprint of The Random House Group

www.rbooks.co.uk
www.prefacepublishing.co.uk

Addresses for companies within The Random House Group Limited
can be found at www.randomhouse.co.uk

The Random House Group Limited Reg. No. 954009

A CIP catalogue record for this book is available from the British Library

ISBN 978 1 84809 040 8

The Random House Group Limited supports The Forest Stewardship
Council (FSC), the leading international forest certification organisation. All
our titles that are printed on Greenpeace-approved FSC-certified paper carry
the FSC logo. Our paper procurement policy can be found at
www.rbooks.co.uk/environment

Typeset in AGaramond by Palimpsest Book Production Limited,
Grangemouth, Stirlingshire

Printed and bound in Great Britain by CPI Bookmarque Ltd, Croydon CRO 4TD

CONTENTS

List of Illustration Credits

All photographs and illustrations are from Anne Nason's personal collection, with sketches taken from the original letters, except for the following which are reproduced by kind permission of:

Eton College Archive
Impey's House, Eton, 1892

Victoria Hermon
The Cliffe
Ethel aged sixteen
Ethel with her sister Vio and brothers Vincent and Victor
The family at Inverlodden, 1911
Ethel with Meg at Inverlodden, 1911

Jean Richards
EWH with the Chugs at Brook Hill, 1915
Ethel and the Chugs on the steps at Brook Hill, 1915
Meg with two of the family dogs, 1915
EWH sailing before the war
Betty looking for her dog

The History of King Edward's Horse
Portrait of Lt. Colonel Edward William ('Robert') Hermon

Jessica Hawes
Gordon Offord Buxton
EWH at Aldershot with King Edward's Horse
Troopers of King Edward's Horse, 1911

Hugh McKergow
Brook Hill House in the 1950s

Imperial War Museum
British troops helping with the threshing near Franvillers (Q4331)
British soldiers in billets (Q29051)
Souchez at the foot of Hill 119 (Q70424)
The ruins of the cathedral at Albert (Q1475)
Fixing scaling ladders in trenches (Q6229)
Scene on the road beside the Scarpe at Blangy at Arras (Q6453)
A British tank passing through Arras (Q6418)
The cavalry resting beside the St. Pol-Arras Road (Q3217)
Artillery moving up through Arras
A 9.2 inch howitzer in action (Q6450)
The scene on newly won ground near the Feuchy crossroads (Q5183)
An 18-pounder quick-firing field-gun (Q5171)
Battle of Arras: an advanced dressing station during the battle (Q3216)

CWGC / The War Graves Photographic Project
(photographs by Iain Smith)
Marble headstone at Roclincourt CWGC
Roclincourt cemetery

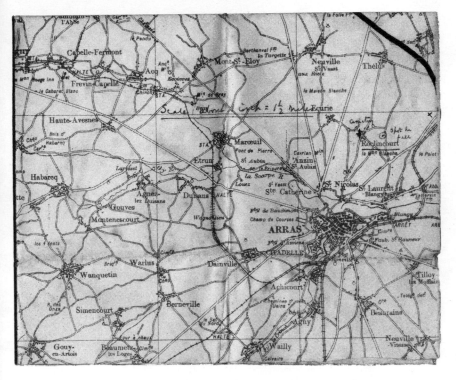

The map sent to Ethel Hermon by Brigadier-General H. E. Trevor
marking the spot where her husband was killed on 9 April 1917.

Foreword

Lieutenant Colonel Edward William Hermon died on 9 April 1917, the first day of the Battle of Arras, leading his men of the 24th Battalion, Northumberland Fusiliers, into the attack. He now lies buried in the Commonwealth War Graves Cemetery at Roclincourt, three miles from Arras. Mentioned in Dispatches three times, he was posthumously awarded the DSO.

This could have been the end of the story, but my grandfather left a testament of his life and ideals in his letters to his wife, my grandmother, written nearly every day from his arrival in France two years before. Though keeping within the bounds of strict censorship, he was able to give a full insight into the day-to-day life of the cavalry officer in France and the frustrations that this caused whilst he and his men were kept on the periphery of the action. Later, when he gained command of an infantry battalion, the daily hardships of the infantry and the awful responsibilities of the commanding officer would become all too painfully apparent, despite a tendency to play down the severity of the situation in his letters home.

Born on 10 June 1878, the son of Sidney and Fanny Hermon of the White House, Balcombe, Sussex, he was known to his family as 'Robert'. Educated at Eton and Christ Church, Oxford, it was whilst he was at university that the Anglo-Boer War broke out and, answering the appeal to 'defend the Empire', he abandoned his studies and joined the 7th Queen's Own Hussars. He subsequently took part in operations in the Transvaal and Orange River Colony, receiving the Queen's Medal with five clasps. By 1904 he was a married man, having wed his cousin Ethel. She joined him in South Africa and the following year their first child, Betty, was born.

The regiment returned home late in 1905, and was stationed in England for the next six years. In the meantime, more children followed: Robert (Bob) in 1906, and Mary in 1908. It was shortly before the birth of his fourth child, Meg, in 1911, that Robert resigned from the 7th Hussars. The regiment was due to go to India and as he could not bear to leave his children behind, as was customary, he left the regular army and joined King Edward's Horse – a Special Reserve cavalry regiment largely made up of men from the old Dominions. Given command of the Oxford and Cambridge Squadron, he was promoted to major.

After the outbreak of the First World War, in August 1914, Robert's regiment was required to undergo months of intensive training, to bring their 'part-time' soldiers up to the active-service standard of a regular cavalry unit. They were then mobilized to France in April 1915. Following Robert into war were his manservant Gordon Offord Buxton ('Buckin'), who had worked for the family since 1908, and who had elected to accompany the man he called 'master', as had Robert's groom, Harry Parsons. Both would remain with him throughout the war until his death.

My grandmother kept the letters from her beloved husband, each carefully replaced in its envelope, in the top drawer of her Georgian mahogany desk at their home in Cowfold, Sussex. These letters remained unopened after her death and, together with the desk, were left to her second daughter Mary – or 'Mairky' – my mother. In 1935 they travelled with us to New Zealand, and as a child I well remember seeing the bundles of letters in the drawer, tied up with ribbon. Mary was only eight years old when her father died and even into her eighties the memory of his death remained almost too painful for her to read them. When she died in 1991, I inherited the desk with the letters still tied in bundles in their drawer, virtually untouched. Once again they made the long sea journey back to England.

When finally I decided the time was right to read them from start to finish, I was struck both by the testament of love that my grandparents showed for each other and by the enormous amount of historical detail that the letters revealed. Throughout, my grandfather remained an optimist. He had a huge regard for the courage of the ordinary soldier who faced the appalling conditions in the trenches with humour and stoicism. The publication of these letters will, I hope, be a testament to them as well.

Anne Nason

A Note on the Text

In the two years before his death, my grandfather wrote almost 600 letters home to his wife. It has therefore been necessary to edit the collection down: some letters are reproduced in their entirety; others have had to be omitted altogether. My grandfather would often write in pencil, on message pads or on graph paper, when in the trenches or living in bivouacs, though my grandmother frequently sent writing paper on request. His handwriting was generally easy to read, though at times it has been necessary to research names and places.

As a commanding officer my grandfather was expected to censor his own letters. Sometimes he used dashes to denote names or places he should not reveal, and occasionally the letters were marked 'Opened by Base Censor'. He never disclosed his locations: these have been derived from the war diaries, regimental histories and Gordon Buxton's own diary, and added to the letter headings. The letters were generally dated, but where they were not I have used the postmark as an indication. Punctuation has been largely kept as in the original.

Anne Nason

Dramatis Personae

E.W.H.	Edward William 'Robert' Hermon
Ethel	Ethel Hermon
The Chugs	their children:

        Bet, Betsy – the eldest daughter Betty
        Bob, Bobbo – the eldest son, Robert Arthur
        Mairky, Pookie – the second daughter, Mary
        Migwig, Wig, Meg – the third daughter, Olga
        Margaret
        Ken – Kenneth Edward, known as Benjamin or
        Ben before christening

Addie, Adeline	Adeline Ryan, an unmarried cousin
Arthur	Arthur Hodgson, a friend and neighbour in Sussex
Brook Hill	the family home in Cowfold, Sussex
Dick	Robert's younger brother, Richard Outram Hermon
Dogs	dogs belonging to the family at Brook Hill: Spoot, Ben, Nell, Teeny
The Governor, Pa	Robert's father, Sidney Alfred Hermon
Juckes, Jucko	Dr Juckes, the family doctor in Sussex
Mimi, Ma	Robert's mother, Fanny née Owtram
Nell	Robert's sister, Nell Hermon
Pike	the chauffeur at the White House
Vic	Ethel's elder brother, Victor Hermon
Vio	Ethel's sister
The White House	Robert's parents' home in Balcombe, Sussex
Woolven	Tom Woolven, the gardener at Brook Hill

Barber	Lieutenant, later Captain, B. H. Barber, K.E.H.
Buckin, 'Buccy'	Gordon Offord Buxton, Private, later Lance Corporal, K.E.H.; formerly Robert's manservant
Chev	Cheviot Dillon Bell, Captain, K.E.H.

D.H.	General Sir Douglas Haig
Harry	Harry Parsons, Private, K.E.H.; formerly a groom at Brook Hill
Henry	Lieutenant Henry Simon Feilding, attached K.E.H.; later Captain, Coldstream Guards
K	Lord Kitchener of Khartoum
K.E.H.	King Edward's Horse, the King's Oversea Dominions Regiment
'Mac'	1. Captain, later Major, J. N. MacDonald, K.E.H.
	2. Lieutenant, later Captain, D. MacKinnon, K.E.H.
Pongo	Lieutenant T. A. Izard, K.E.H.
Steve	Lieutenant, later Captain, P. D. Stevenson, K.E.H.
Syme, 'Slimy'	Lieutenant D. A. Syme, K.E.H.

CHAPTER ONE

MOBILIZATION

On the eve of the First World War, Major Hermon's regiment, King Edward's Horse (K.E.H.), was undergoing its annual training near Canterbury. With the declaration of war on 4 August 1914 the mobilization that Robert had envisaged became a reality, and the regiment was immediately assembled at Alexandra Palace in London, and then sent to Grove Park in Watford and on to Bishop's Stortford for additional training.

Meanwhile, on 22 August at Mons, the British army – the 'Old Contemptibles' of the British Expeditionary Force – engaged in their first battle on European soil for nearly a hundred years. Although the soldiers fought with great bravery, they were forced to retreat. The auspices for a quick British victory were not favourable. Reinforcements for the regular army were urgently needed and in the following April two squadrons of K.E.H., with Robert in command of 'C' Squadron, were mobilized to France as independent commands. He opted to take with him, as many cavalry officers did, his own horse – and his wife's – from their stables at Cowfold. 'C' Squadron was detailed to the 47th (London) Division and 'B' Squadron to the 48th (South Midland) Division. Just before the squadrons embarked on the 21st, a telegram of encouragement arrived from King George V, their Colonel-in-Chief.

31st July 1914, 11.15 p.m. – Old Park Farm, Canterbury

Darling mine,

It seems as if it will be some time before you see me home again, as if mobilization comes & everyone seems to expect it tomorrow, we shall be here for a very long time. However we will hope that things will be brighter & perhaps Prince Henry[1] will work something with the Czar.

---

[1] Prince Henry of Prussia – the Kaiser's brother and a grandson of Queen Victoria. He had recently visited his cousin, George V.

Last night every important bridge in England was guarded by troops & every warlike preparation short of complete mobilization has been made. We are quite expecting to receive orders to mobilize at any minute. Grierson[2] inspected us today & I think the squadron did right well.

Give my love to the Chugs.

Ever your Robert.

3rd August 1914, 11.30 p.m. – Old Park Farm, Canterbury

Just put on all my clo' before going to bed to be ready for a hasty call.

Darling mine,

Just heard that the 'House' has sanctioned a complete mobilization of Army, Special Reserve & Territorials, so I take what opportunity I have of writing you another line as I expect to be on the march early tomorrow to Alexandra Park, & doubt if I shall have a minute for the next few days.

Squadrons are marching up independently I am glad to say. Oh! If I had a squadron of good horses I wouldn't mind but it is not much fun route marching if half one's horses are going lame on the way. What this is going to mean for the nation I do not know.

It really is terrible that all this should come now over so small an excuse, but it seems Germany was mobilizing before Austria sent her ultimatum to Serbia. However let us hope the fleet will give 'em Hades before long just to put our tails up.

Love to you all my dears,

Ever your Robert.

---

[2] General Sir James Grierson, commander Eastern Command. It is believed that it was due to a conversation between him and the acting CO, Major James, that the regiment was allowed six months' training before they were mobilized, in order to bring them up to the standard of a regular cavalry unit.

4th August 1914 – Old Park Farm, Canterbury

My darling Lassye,

Well there's no turning back now, for better or for worse we are committed to it.

We start to mobilize tomorrow sending all our horses back by train at once & going ourselves by train on Friday to Alexandra Palace, where we complete & then I believe we join the 2nd London Div. (Territorial) & act as Div. Cav. to them. You will have to be awfully careful about money. You can't b[u]y a thing in London except for spot cash. They won't even change a five pound note.

I don't know what I am going to do for servants but I think both Buxton and Harry are quite keen to follow master.

Love to you all,

Ever your Robert.

Wednesday 5th August 1914, 6 p.m. – Old Park Farm, Canterbury

Darling mine,

I cannot get down to telephone to you as we are 2 miles out of Canterbury and the P.O. will not guarantee a call under 1½ to 2 hrs.

I hope you got home safe & sound and I wish I could see you, I probably shall next week with luck, but there is such a lot to do & one can't leave for long as so few know their work.

I think I shall have the new horse for a charger but haven't made up my mind yet. I'll see what I can get out of our horses when we get them but it strikes me that if it comes to fighting I should like to be as well mounted as I could be.

Give my love to the Chugs & my dear doggies.

Ever your Robert.

Thursday 6th August 1914, 5.15 p.m. – Old Park Farm, Canterbury

Darling mine,

I have had a very busy day today teaching my men to shoot & with some success. Don't let them take my new horse if you can prevent it. Say it is a registered charger & I shall want it sent to me on Monday or Tuesday.

I am afraid that our boat for next year is off. Will you write to Wally & say that owing to the congestion in the N. Sea I am afraid our cruise must be off.

I shall be at Alexandra Park sometime tomorrow evening when things begin for us in earnest. Buxton is most anxious to go with Master and his wife is all for it too but I don't quite know yet. I think I shall send him back to take care of you. I should be more comfortable if I thought you had someone you could rely upon. Anyhow I shall think it over.

Faversham powder factory was blown up last night & it made a fine old bang & fairly lit up the sky. I heard that several folk were killed. Suppose they were working overtime as it was about 10.30 when it happened.

Best love dearie mine,

Ever your Robert.

18th August 1914 – Grove Park, Watford

Darling mine,

Sorry I haven't been able to write you before but I have had too much to do.

I got in here on Sunday night after a very successful night and am camped alongside the grand junction canal. We bivouacked instead of going into billets as it was a lovely night and all slept in the lines. Exactly at midnight a steam barge came along the canal, blew its siren & the whole of the horses cleared off again. We were all lying on the ground, every man within 4 yards of his horse & the whole squadron except one horse went, & not a soul was touched. One horse broke its neck and several were badly injured. I seem to be cursed with bad luck with the horses but perhaps now all will go well. I have got the whole squadron in farms all over the shop, & one can't look after one's horses personally and it is most disappointing, but perhaps it will be alright.

These two stampedes have taken thirty horses from me & I can't mount the men, which is a terrible handicap. The administration of the squadron under these conditions is also most difficult & valuable time is lost assembling and dispersing to say nothing of the extra trouble of sending rations to six different places.

The C.O. saw Kitchener the other day & he told him he wanted to send 6 more divisions across but that he had fully made up his mind that no regiment should go over unless it was trained sufficiently highly to do credit to the Nation. I was awfully glad when I heard it as I was afraid we should get fired out when I knew we were not fit.

Love to you all,

Ever your Robert.

The first stampede occurred in Alexandra Park. Many of these horses were hunters, unused to being picketed in the open. Unfortunately the commanding officer declined to picket them in the enclosed area of the grass tennis courts, and the racecourse had already been declared off limits. On the night of 13 August, 300 horses were involved in the stampede. All night the terrified animals tore round the park and in the morning, when they were finally brought under control, six animals were either dead or had to be destroyed and thirty more were injured.

14th April 1915, 11.30 a.m. – Bishop's Stortford

My own darling,

God knows it was hard parting when I went to the S. African war, but hard as it was then, this is infinitely harder.

Darling mine you don't know how you have helped me by being my own dear brave Lassie to the last. My work has been very hard these last few days and had you attempted to come to see me dearie, it would have only made it so much the harder. I must be at my very best now to get my squadron off and no personal feelings must be allowed to interfere with the work for a moment.

May God watch over you & keep you & my little darlings till I come back again.

Goodbye my darling love,

Ever your Robert.

On the 14th, Robert also posted a letter to his wife marked 'Open only when I am gone abroad'. With it he included the following poem, written by Sheila E. Braine:

'Farewell'

If, when you think of me in future years,
It brings a pang, and on your pale sweet face
The happy smile is lost 'mid gathering tears,
And grief usurps its lovely dwelling-place,
Then let me be forgot; alone, apart –
Soldier of England, counted leal and true
I shall sleep well 'neath alien soil, dear heart,
Sleep well – and dream of you.

Underneath it he wrote:

Darling mine,

I thought this rather nice in case of accidents.

Ever your Robert.

20th April 1915 – Bishop's Stortford

My own dear Lassie,

Goodbye my darling & may God keep you & the dear little Chugs. Give them all a nice kiss from me & my darling I love you so for being so brave, & I wish I could write you all I have felt these last few days but somehow it doesn't seem to come now, perhaps it will one day later & then I will try & write you a really nice letter my love & tell you why I couldn't see you.

I did so want to write you a letter that would be a comfort to you & it isn't a bit.

Lassie darling, I pray every night I may be worthy of my men & of you. Ever your Robert.

On 21 April, 'B' and 'C' Squadrons embarked at Southampton in the transport ship *Palm Branch*. Major Hermon was 'OC Troops' in the ship, which was escorted by two destroyers. The journey was uneventful with a moonlit night and a glassy calm sea. No submarines were sighted. The ship arrived at 2.30 the following morning at Le Havre, where the squadrons disembarked. From here Robert was able to send a brief postcard to Ethel, which read: 'Landed alright. Robert.'

Robert's squadron entrained at the Gare des Marchandises. The journey to Lillers, via Abbeville, Boulogne, Calais and Hazebrouck, took twenty-four hours, with stops to water the horses and provide coffee and brandy for the men. The men arrived to the sound of gunfire – the second Battle of Ypres was in progress. The War Diary for 'C' Squadron, written in Robert's own hand, recorded:

> *Arrived at LILLERS, raining hard & detrained at once. Acetylene flares of greatest assistance, which was more than RTO [Railway Transport Officer] was, who invaded the trucks with an army of ruffians & threw the saddlery all over the place & it took hours to sort it in the dark while he went off to bed.*

From Lillers, the squadron proceeded to Ecquedeques in pouring rain, arriving at 3 a.m. All ranks rested in a straw barn until daylight when the officers moved into an *estaminet* in the town until they found billets.

26th April 1915 – *estaminet* in Ecquedeques

My own darling,

I got your dear letter today my own darling & I have simply loved it, both your No. 1 & 2 arrived together as my orderlies did not go in to Div. Hd Qrs until today. You can't imagine how cheering your letters are dearie & how they have brightened the day for me, not that it wanted brightening as we are all in the very best of spirits & really thoroughly enjoying every minute of the time. You wonder where I am & at the present time I am in the big room of the 'estaminet' & all the others with me. I think that in a few days I shall be able to give you more news but as I am my own censor I have to be particularly careful what I say & am no doubt erring on the over-cautious side.

Darling mine your letter hasn't blued me a bit & I have loved it. I am glad you felt as I did about the train business. Poor old Bell,[3] he shook hands with me at the train with tears running down his cheeks & his voice so broken he couldn't speak.

We are really doing top-hole at present, Buxton is a top-hole cook, we only want some cakes & you might send me a box of cigars (Harrods Club Stock No. 1).

The staff of this Division are all charming & only too anxious to do anything for one. The G.O.C.[4] came & had a dish of tea with us tonight & was horrified at MacDonald being left at home & has gone off to wire for him to come out to me at once. Poor old Mac he will be delighted. Will you ring him up about 8 p.m. & tell him this & that the G.O.C. told me to write to him and tell him to get his kit together at once. Tell him to bring food for himself for the voyage across as he might get on a ship that doesn't cater for officers. Tell him to keep it dark till he gets his official orders. Also tell him that he will have to act up to the highest traditions of the British army when he does come as I told the G.O.C. that his services were indispensable & that he was the best officer I ever met.

We move to our new billets tomorrow. I will try & send you one of my maps soon if I can & then you will be able to follow in the papers. I cannot of course tell you too much or absolutely promise the map but will do all I can. We are to be 5 days in the new billets & then move into the town to the Division.

There has been a good deal of heavy gunfire today & it fairly shakes the windows of this old pub. They tell me that Mondays are always 'lively' as the French do not shoot much on Sundays so have a double allowance of ammun. to get through on Mondays.

You would laugh at my efforts at French, they are decidedly crude. Those

---

[3] Cheviot W. Dillon Bell, son of the first New Zealand-born prime minister of that country. He eventually joined the RFC and survived the war despite crashing his aircraft nine times. His brother William was killed at Pilkem Ridge, Passchendaele, in 1917.
[4] General (Sir) Charles Barter.

damned verbs fairly boil me. I think you might send me out my French grammar, it is in the gunroom cupboard. The men are doing really very well & I am pleased with them & don't care who sees them now. They are as keen as mustard & working top-hole. Give my love to the family and tell them that I will write to them as soon as I can find time. I must go to bed now dearie as it is late & I have had a tiring day.

All my love to you dearie mine & the dear little Chugs too.

Ever your Robert.

After two days, on 27 April, the squadron left Ecquedeques and marched to Fontinelle Farm, near Béthune. Robert's reference to the fact that Cheviot Bell was distressed at not being fit to go to France is confirmed by a letter from Bell to Ethel Hermon on 21 April, from the New Oxford and Cambridge Club, Pall Mall:

Dear Mrs Hermon,

I have been staying up at Bishop's Stortford to see something of the K.E.H. before they went & this morning saw them off on the train so I thought perhaps you might like to get news of Major Hermon. He has of course been working awfully hard ever since they got their orders & has been looking rather tired, but this morning he was as fresh as he could possibly be & of course delighted to be really off this time & he's looking awfully fit.

Both squadrons looked awfully well & went off without a hitch: 'C' really are top-hole, some of the most unlikely recruits having turned out splendid. With a squadron like that of his own making I'm perfectly convinced he'll do something really big out at the front; I formed this opinion on my first parade under him as a trooper & I'm doubly sure of it now.

I shall miss him dreadfully myself as he has always been so good to me, especially now when I'm stuck as I am, with the doctors telling me that if I join up & start riding I'll probably crack up in a week & making me wait longer & longer. I'm afraid I'm a shocking bad patient but Major Hermon is always going out of his way to cheer me up.

My brother – lucky beggar – went off also this morning with 'B' Sqdn. Personally I'm quite one of the most fed-up men in England at the present moment; to be forced to do nothing except loaf & idle just when loafers & idlers are the last people wanted & not to know when one will be able to get out to the front when one's simply dying to do the latter, is simply the limit.

Please give my kindest regards to Betsy, Mary, Meg & Bob, & whatever you do don't worry about Major Hermon as he'll be as safe as if he was over here for some time yet.

Yours v. sincerely,

Cheviot W. D. Bell

In France, meanwhile, Robert's squadron were adjusting to life closer to the front.

28th April 1915 – Fontinelle Farm

Darling mine,

Just a few lines to tell you I am still well & happy. The G.O.C. came out here this morning to inspect the squadron & seemed quite pleased with what he saw.

I have been in to dine with him tonight. He sent his A.D.C., a gunner captain, out in a covered Daimler to fetch me into the town and sent me out again in the car afterwards. We had a top-hole dinner. Very good soup, fried sole, lamb's fry, apricot tart, cheese & some really first class cigars at about 2/6 a time & I then took 2 frcs 50 out of them at bridge. It seemed so funny to be sitting there just having an ordinary dinner & the guns shelling away like steam just outside the town. There was some talk of a shell having fallen in the town during the day but no one seemed to be quite certain about it.

We are to have our first go in the trenches next week which should be very interesting, a troop at a time just to get accustomed to the shelling & to learn a bit about trench warfare & how it's done, that in case of need, we should know our way about a bit. I haven't been out yet on the German side of the town yet but hope to have a smell round there soon. Today has been simply glorious & the aeroplanes have fairly been on the go. It was almost too hot here at times & one wished one had thin clothes. You will have to send me my thin coats soon as these I have at present will soon be too heavy tho' one fine day don't make a summer & I daresay I shall be glad of them yet.

My love to you old dear.

Ever your Robert.

30th April 1915 – Fontinelle Farm

Darling mine,

I had a most interesting day yesterday as I was told to go & reconnoitre the roads & lanes up to the trenches in case of the squadron being wanted suddenly. The sergeant major & I rode off together & while watering our horses the S.S.M.'s[5] horse stepped into deep water & was quite out of his depth & swam about like a dog but he made for the bank & soon swam ashore, but it was rather funny seeing him swim about. We then rode on towards the trenches passing several batteries in action, which was very interesting. We then reached the line where it was advisable to leave our horses & go on foot, so we tied them up to some trees & walked on, & saw some more guns in action. We went right on till we couldn't go any further without unnecessary risk & sat down & listened to the snipers sniping but no bullets were coming our way & we had lots of time to look around.

I have told you of the absolute tranquillity of the inhabitants, but even here right up within 800 yds of the trenches the ordinary agricultural work is proceeding just as tho' nothing at all was going on. Women and children in all the cottages along the roadside and all the fields around pitted with shell holes. Yesterday the Germans were not replying to our gun fire at all & I didn't see a single shell come over from them which was rather disappointing after a long walk. Today however Barber & Stevenson[6] went over to reconnoitre & while they were having tea with one of the Regts just behind the trenches, the Germans put their shells into the next house.

Yesterday it almost made one laugh to see in the fields so close to the

---

[5] Squadron Sergeant-Major.

[6] Lieutenants B. H. Barber and P. D. Stevenson ('Steve').

trenches, notice boards saying that crops were sown & that soldiers were not to walk or ride in the field!! As I walked out the Germans were fairly letting fly with an anti-aircraft gun at an aeroplane just over my head.

I have just taken over command for warlike purposes 180 cyclists & six officers in addition to my own commando, so in the event of a scrap I have now got quite an army!! Things have been pretty quiet in this sector of the line lately and not much doing. Today we had some field firing in a big sandpit near here & I was delighted with the way the men shot, really top-hole.

I have had some capital letters from the Chugs & enjoyed them very much, will you please thank them & I will try & write them a letter or two soon but one is very busy these times & it is only by burning the midnight oil that one gets a chance.

I asked yesterday how much I might tell you & they said there was no objection to saying where I was so long as I did not mention my unit or other troops in the neighbourhood. I am at present in Fontinelle Farm about 4 km outside Béthune.

I am enclosing you the map I promised you as you can then follow what is published in the papers. Of course I cannot tell you where the trenches are exactly, tho' really I don't see why I shouldn't as the Germans know that already as they are quite close together in places, some places not more than a few yards apart.

You might arrange to send us some good strawberry jam regularly & if you will send me a monthly bill I will send you a cheque from the mess. We want cakes, soup squares, Oxo, Bovril etc., & odd delicacies of sorts. We get plenty of good meat & bread & it is oddments we want at present. Cakes twice a week if possible as they [are] most acceptable.

We have had the most lovely weather you can possibly imagine & the lads are so overcome with the heat that they are absolutely worn out tonight. Extract from old Bob's letter 'Mum & I have been mending a punkture on Bettie's bicycle. We bloo the tar up——'.

We are going to have a turn in the trenches next week for a bit just to see how things are done. I am glad to say in our section it is impossible for either side to mine or sap as there is water only two feet below the surface so that is something gained.

The country here is as flat as a looking glass & is just like the dyke country from Rye to Hythe only as you will see from the enclosed map, small cottages everywhere & willow trees. I must go to bed now dearie mine.

My best love to you all.

Ever your Robert.

Although there was a stalemate on the Western Front in April 1915, there was continual shelling on both sides and daily incursions into no man's land by British troops, with resulting casualties. Just as 'C' Squadron arrived in France the German army used chlorine gas for the first time in the conflict, against French and Canadian Divisions in the Ypres Salient. British army censorship prevented any mention of this escalation in weaponry in letters home at this stage of the war.

During May, 'C' Squadron were employed digging trenches, escorting prisoners and experiencing life in the trenches for themselves. First, however, the squadron needed to clean out the farmyard at Fontinelle Farm, where they were billeted, to reduce the risk of flyborne diseases to both soldiers and horses. The regimental history records that: 'This was at length accomplished to the great pride of the O.C. and the intense amusement of the local inhabitants.'

Sunday 2nd May 1915 – Fontinelle Farm

My dear old Lassie,

I am glad you have begun to get my letters now but I had a terribly busy time getting here & not a moment for writing.

I am taking half my army into the trenches on Wed. night & the other half relieves us after 48 hours. I don't expect we shall do more than one turn just for experience, but I am most anxious to go, simply to see what it is like. Pretty beastly I expect.

I have been into Béthune this afternoon to call on the G.O.C. & see the staff about one or two things. Did I tell you I met old Howe the gunner we knew at Aldershot the other day & also Douglas Haig but he didn't know me & we had no conversation. We had a church parade service here this morning, a padre came over from La Bouvriere, quite a nice little man.

We are all very fit & well I am glad to say & thoroughly enjoying ourselves. Very comfortable in this little farm tho' rather smelly & the water is running out.

Best love to you dearie mine,

Ever your Robert.

3rd May 1915 – Fontinelle Farm

Darling mine,

I got two top-hole letters from you today. Your number 8 came yesterday & I got 7 & 9 today. I suppose 7 got a bit lonely on the way & went off with some casual acquaintances in another bag.

The cake etc. rolled up at lunch time today & as we were having a somewhat meagre lunch the pot of 'pottie' was hailed with screams of delight, especially when we saw the truffles, but what ho! When the maid opened the lid – nearly blew the roof off & we thought the Germans were here with their asphyxiating gases. I am afraid in this hot weather it is no use sending home-made meat things as they don't keep. However the rest of the parcel was most acceptable.

You need not bother any more about cigars as I can get plenty here now that I quite like and the best kind cost 1*d* each!! Many thanks for sending the camera & I hope soon to send you some good photos to have developed.

We are going to have our first dash in the trenches on the 6th for 48 hours & I am going down early on Wed. morning to spend a few hours in the section occupied by Harry Cubitt's[7] battn just to see how things are done first by those who really know.

The men are all very fit & well I am glad to say, & so we are a very merry party, hardly stopped laughing since we left.

I had another nice letter from old Bob today & have got a piece of a German shell to send him when I have time to pack it up. Just a bit of copper from the driving band.

Best love old girl,

Ever your Robert.

[7] Henry Archibald Cubitt, grandson of the 1st Lord Ashcombe, was serving with the Coldstream Guards and was killed in 1916.

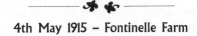

4th May 1915 – Fontinelle Farm

I have been out most of the day up near the trenches arranging about the troops going there on Thursday. I wish you could come and have a look round here & see how everyone takes things, it would fairly astonish you. Even right up in the front people treat it rather as a huge joke, not that I mean that the actual business isn't taken seriously, but that the lighter side is given considerable prominence.

I lunched within a few hundred yards of the front line of trenches with a brigade Hd Qrs & the Brigadier gave me a very excellent lunch ending with a capital pot of Paté & coffee. They were all frightfully amused because the next brigadier at lunch yesterday was shelled out of his house & they had to leave their lunch & off it like steam.

I want you to arrange with Harrods, or someone like that, to send us a £1 box of stores every week. We want potted meats; soup; sweets, peppermint, Mackintosh's toffee de luxe. The jam is essential & must come without fail. We want chutney very badly too as it makes the ration meat go down better, rice & curry powder. Some tinned vegetables & perhaps some bottled Tiptree raspberries remnant. Cherry jam occasionally but the main jam supply to be Little Scarlets. The 'Gentleman's joy' you sent went like wild fire & two or three pots a week would be fine. I met another of my boys today, the 2nd I have met so far & he seemed to be doing alright & looked the part. We have had a lot of wet last night & the horses are now standing in a bog which a very heavy thunderstorm tonight didn't help very much.

However, the worst billet is better than the best bivouac & as they say we have the best billet in the countryside we are all right & still smiling. Henry[8] has come out immensely since we got here & is doing very well indeed & he & Izard[9] are the life & soul of the Mess, & keep us laughing all day. So far life has been most enjoyable & I hope it will continue to be so. Going to spend the day tomorrow cleaning out the farmyard so as to do away with all manure as a breeding place for flies. I fear the fly trouble will shortly be awful as there are so many unburied bodies between the

---

[8] Lieutenant Henry Feilding, son of Lord Denbigh.
[9] Lieutenant T. A. Izard, known as 'Pongo', had been recruited to the regiment on mobilization, had joined at Alexandra Palace and was still serving in 1919.

trenches & the authorities quite rightly are doing all they can to minimize the danger. Flypapers & strings would be good things to send us also any kind of gauze trap that looks like catching them.

Best love dearie mine,

Ever your Robert.

CHAPTER TWO

CAVALRY RESERVE, AUBERS RIDGE

On 7 May, Robert and 2nd and 3rd Troops, 'C' Squadron were ordered to proceed to Beuvry, on the outskirts of Béthune, as part of the Divisional Reserve for an attack between Rue du Bois and Festubert, in an attempt to capture Aubers Ridge. Although the attack, which occurred on the 9th, failed, and the Reserve was not called forward, the squadron came under shellfire for the first time. Meanwhile the 1st and 4th Troops remained at Fontinelle Farm under the command of Lieutenant Barber and then proceeded to Le Touret and Locon to escort prisoners.

The failure of the British attack on Aubers Ridge was largely due to the shortage of high-explosive ammunition and the ineffective barrage. Many shells failed to explode and were known as 'duds'. The French attack on Aubers Ridge was part of the combined Anglo-French attempt to break through the strongly fortified German trenches. They succeeded in advancing three miles but at the cost of nearly 2,000 lives.

8th May 1915 – Beuvry

My darling old girl,

I sent you a field postcard tonight as I have been on the move & am now at Beuvry. Things are very lively here tonight, our aeroplanes are fairly buzzing overhead – dozens of them & the Germans shooting like steam at them but so far as one can see their shells only reach half way. It however keeps the flyers up in the air at a good height & lessens their observing powers. We had 'some liveliness' last night as we are well within range of the German guns & all last night there was a rare old fusillade going on & once or twice today they have sent us an odd shell just to cheer us up, but they have all so far been at the other end of the village.

They liven up before dark a good bit & are just beginning, as I can hear the snipers hard at it now. The German lines run from Neuve Chapelle through Festubert–Givenchy, Cuinchy & on the south of us & I have just had a very welcome telegram to say that the French attacked & carried the German trenches six miles south of us.

Tell Tiptree not to send us any more gooseberry jam, or raspberry. We like the bramble jelly, strawberry, & their Morello Cherry very much. I must stop now dearie mine as I have to get up at 2 a.m.

Ever your Robert. ——10.40 p.m.

10th May 1915 – on pages from a field notebook – Le Quesnoy

I got two nice letters from you tonight as we had no mail yesterday. Tobacco & cigarettes are the chief things the men want at present. They are so well fed & they can buy so much, besides that they are putting on flesh like anything.

They are a lot of dirty swine these Germans but I hope this *Lusitania* business will do them a lot of harm with the outside world.[10]

We have had rather an amusing time these last two days as we moved out to a position of readiness at 4.30 a.m. yesterday, leaving a few sick men & the servants under old Sanderson in the billets. After we had been out a bit we saw the shells popping into Beuvry pretty frequently. We returned there about 10 p.m. to find them all in an awful state of nerves. Old Buxton was awfully cross because we laughed at them but it really was too funny. Their faces were a picture & they had all got bits of shell & stuff. Before I left I warned them of the dangerous places in the town which I knew the Germans would shell if they shot at all & of course old Buxton must go & have a look, with the result that a shell plonked into a house just under his nose which fairly put the fear of what's-his-name into him.

The last two days have been very interesting but I cannot tell you about them yet tho' I shall be able to later on I think when sufficient time has elapsed to make anything mentioned of no value if it went astray.

---

[10] News had just come in of the sinking of the Cunard liner the *Lusitania* on 7 May by a German U-boat off the southern coast of Ireland with the loss of 1,198 civilian lives.

I have got such a nice old man as interpreter, a Baron Floris who was in a cavalry Regt and he rides your old horse & is very happy, tho' he finds him a bit tall!! My two troops under Barber have not rejoined yet, they went away two days ago on a job & tho' I have had messages from them I haven't seen them. They seem in great heart tho' they say their billet is full of very moderately buried Frenchmen & is far from pleasant.

I had a long letter from Bell & he tells me he is going down to see you & that he is resigning his commission in the 10th & is going into an infantry Regt as he will not be fit to ride for another six months.

I must stop now as I am going to bed in a large feather bed & sheets!! Not so bad for war! Tonight we are at Le Quesnoy. I have no orders for tomorrow yet, which means being woken up in the middle of the night, which is a most awful bore.

Best love dearie mine & to the dear little Chugs.

The commanding officer and the 2nd and 3rd Troops remained at Le Quesnoy,[11] a small village east of Béthune, until the end of the month with the 1st and 4th Troops rejoining on the 14th. The squadron remained 'standing to' in a state of readiness, providing prisoners' escorts and straggler patrols for the successful attack on 24 May.

11th May 1915 – Le Quesnoy

I had another very nice & welcome letter from you today & a cake & a capital pot of Marmalade. I was so glad to hear that Mac had had his orders & I most sincerely trust he will come out tho' what the regiment will do without him I don't know, now that the 3rd Squadron is coming out.

We have not done anything yet as beyond hearing the snipers sniping we might be on manoeuvres. They are sniping away now like anything but one grows so used to the noise that I think you would miss it. We are out of range of stray bullets as being so close there is no elevation to the rifles

---

[11] This small village is not to be confused with the major town of Le Quesnoy, which was further south, and behind enemy lines.

and consequently bullets do not come very far behind the lines which is a good thing & also there are a lot of trees & houses in between. Don't be downhearted old girl, & believe very little of what you see in the papers because it is in most cases far from accurate, anyhow that is my experience so far.

Old Mac[12] came over today to see us for a bit & was most amusing. They were all tucked up in their billet on Sunday night when a brigadier who shall be nameless walked in & asked them what they were doing there. He said 'I am a general, I am coming in here, get out.' So they tumbled out of bed & went & spent the night in the field, but they got the better of the man by pinching every bit of picketing rope, water buckets, wire cutters & anything they could get off his horses which were in the same field. Nice sort of general! But some of these territorial generals are a bit swollen-headed.

We still haven't had a go at the Germans and are all longing to have a bit soon. It is very tantalizing to be so close & not to have a shot or two back.

You need not worry old girl I am not smoking too much & in the hot weather I smoke less than in the winter. You seem to have done your guests alright. Anyhow they seemed pleased with their billet & I expect you will get them all back again. It certainly is the exception to be welcomed, most people are getting very tired of having the soldiers.

My men are bivouacking now as it is so very fine. Please address me as '47th (London) Division'. It is getting v. late now dearie & I must to bed, my lovely feather bed in which I slept last night. Had a real good night too.

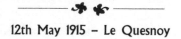

12th May 1915 – Le Quesnoy

I have got your 17 today & all your news about the C.O. Just at present the men do not want anything bar tobacco & cigarettes but there are so many coming over now that they get an issue of them once a week. I cannot help thinking that it would be a good thing to husband your resources for the winter.

---

[12] Two officers known as 'Mac' served with the regiment. The first Mac referred to is Lieutenant (later Captain) Donald MacKinnon who was with the K.E.H Reserve. 'Old Mac' is Captain (later Major) J. N. MacDonald.

We had a great battle here last Sunday. It started with the most intense bombardment followed by the infantry assault – the results of which you will see in the papers. It really was a most wonderful show & the noise was extraordinary. Every kind of gun pooping off for all it was worth. We were not engaged but merely in a position of readiness close up in case by any accident the Germans broke through anywhere. We should then have gone forward & held the gap until more reserves were brought up & I expect that will be our role for a bit. We are having a very slack time now & basking in the sunlight all day. The horses are wonderfully well & the admiration of everyone.

Your old horse is very well & looking grand in his new coat, ditto Saxon & the pony. I want you to buy me a little phrase book of French so that I can learn a few of the ordinary everyday sentences & it might form a foundation to start from. I am making no progress at present.

Tell old Bob that Izard & I went birds-nesting for him. We got a rope & he lowered me down to a sand martin's nest but it was full of young birds & so that wasn't much good. However, I will see what I can do for him tomorrow or the next day. Perhaps that was a very early pair. The cuckoo has been shouting about but I haven't heard it yet. Steve rode over today & saw us & Mac yesterday. I hope they will rejoin soon.

The old French gave the Germans a good knockabout 10 miles from here[13] these last few days & took 3,000 prisoners, 34 machine guns & 11 field guns & are progressing well towards Lens.

I had a capital night last night in my feather bed & this morning Buxton & the two young officers held a conference as to whether to wake me or not & decided not to as there was nothing doing so I slept till 8 a.m. when a barber came to cut my hair. He came from Beuvry & I expected to have to pay 5 francs at least so when he demanded 2½*d* you can imagine my face!

Best love my darling old girl to you and the Chugs.

[13] Near Vimy Ridge.

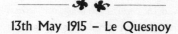

13th May 1915 – Le Quesnoy

I got another short letter from you today which was most welcome as usual, as was also a very nice one from dear little Bet. I wish I could see you all again, but permanently. I don't think I should like to come home for a couple of days or so & then have all the strain of leaving all over again – it would be sort of slow torture.

We are at present in a state of readiness to move at an hour's notice but I do not know why, whether we are to attack or be attacked. This afternoon I rode over to see the other two troops who seemed to be very fit & well tho' doing nothing. You would have laughed if you had seen their faces when I told them that I was being recalled to England! They say if I go & the C.O. comes & wants to get wounded in front, he will have to spend his time walking backwards.

I had a capital letter from Dick[14] today. He says 'it is a pity about the "Lucy Tania"'! It really is a champion letter and I am going to answer it tonight. Our electric light has been cut off tonight which is a bore. I was so glad to hear that old Bobbo is better & himself once more. It has rained all day today which has rather damped things but we have had a good deal to be thankful for.

My interpreter is such a charming old boy & is exactly like someone I know but I can't exactly remember. He gets on fine on your old horse & is most anxious to have a sword as he was a Cavalry soldier. He & Buxton drove into Béthune today in the most ramshackle old cab you ever saw to buy some grub for dinner & I believe I hear rumours of 'soles'! We have had very little except rations so far, so I hope your Harrods case won't be long in coming, it will be very welcome. The French are progressing on our right very fast & doing fine, catching lots of Germans.

Best love dearie mine.

---

[14] His (much younger) brother, Richard Outram Hermon, then aged seventeen.

14th May 1915 – Le Quesnoy

My darling Lassie,

You accuse me of 'fishing' but you are just as bad, if you only knew how acceptable all letters are out here you wouldn't worry. I enclose you a cheque for £9. o. o, you must lump the 1s 5d. I will send you a cheque to cover rates & taxes when I get my bank book. I never pay them till after June quarter day as a rule.

Tonight I got my thin coats for which many thanks & I am sending you my thick ones back again. I got the 2nd consignment of jam too tonight, which was very welcome. If you have any marmalade to spare we should like a pot a week as it is in great demand.

We are still leading the most peaceful of lives & are longing for something to do. You told me that I was not to keep only the nice things for your letters, & that you were to have some of the nasty ones as well.

Well last Sunday in the attack just north of Festubert some of the Black Watch succeeded in getting into the German first-line trenches & owing to their not receiving the expected reinforcements they were eventually overpowered & taken. The Germans stripped them of their uniforms & then told them to go back to their own trenches & half way across they turned their machine guns on them & killed the lot, so I was told by a fellow who was there. Rather a nice act for a cultured nation

Folk out here are getting a little tired with the German & I can't help thinking he will get some rough handling before long.

Two Highlanders rolled in here this morning about 3.15 and bedded down in our room on some straw & had a good sleep. They were fairly worn out having had a very hard week & having led the attack last Sunday. They have got a billet now tho' and go off again tomorrow. Such nice fellows both of them. The Captain quite young & his subaltern 15 years older, but a very fine man, looked the job all over. We have got their company billeted in the yard here.

This afternoon we amused ourselves by chopping up some trees for the men's cooking fires. We found two huge trees and old Izard is a champion with an axe & we really had quite good fun. I want you to get me three splitting wedges either from old Gent or Woolven's[15] brother & send them

---

[15] Tom Woolven, the gardener at Brook Hill.

out to me. I mean the wedges they use to split the oak posts & rails with.

Our old interpreter is full of humour. We have in the house here a very small conglomerate puppy. What it is I defy you to make out but after contemplating it for some time he said 'I think it is a war baby.' That reminds me, how is Benjamin?[16] Have you noticed him yet? My love to you all dearie mine.

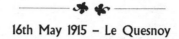

16th May 1915 – Le Quesnoy

Another nice letter from you today. No. 21. The ham is rolling up fine now & we had one case yesterday & another today. We also got your two tins with cake & oddments which have gone down well. Harrods might send us some bacon as tho' we get bacon it is ration & of the meaty kind.

We have had very heavy fighting here this week, commencing last Sunday & continuing today. The Bombardment last Sunday which commenced at 5.4 a.m. & lasted until 5.40 absolutely beggared description & when I tell you that in those 35 minutes one howitzer Battery fired 200 rounds per gun & the field guns up to 1,600 rounds per battery you will easily imagine that this cry for more ammunition is not without due need. What we want is more howitzer guns that fire high-explosive shells, as the shrapnel is all very well for killing men but before an assault can be made it is absolutely necessary to breach the enemy's breastworks & this can only be done by shells making direct hits & violently exploding on impact.

The country here is absolutely flat & the part we are in is only 20 feet above sea level. The consequence is that it is impossible to dig more than a foot or eighteen inches without coming to solid water. The result has been that breastworks instead of trenches are built by both sides out of sandbags & you actually stand on ground level & look over a sandbag wall.

In front of this the Germans have high wire entanglements. Their loopholes, which in the case of machine guns are about 8 inches above the ground level, are most wonderfully concealed & lots of them. Of course you can only attack with any hope of success when the wire & parapet have been destroyed by the guns, which means a lot of ammunition.

[16] Ethel Hermon was three months pregnant at this time; they referred to the baby until its birth as 'Benjamin'.

consequence is that it is impossible
to dig more than a foot or eighteen
inches without coming to solid water.
    The result has been that breastwork
instead of trenches are built by both
sides out of sandbags & you actually
stand on ground level & look over a
sandbag wall.

In front of this the germans have
high wire entanglements

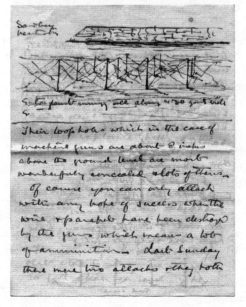

Their loopholes which in the case of
machine guns are about 8 inches
above the ground level are most
wonderfully concealed & lots of them.
    Of course you can only attack
with any hope of success when the
wire & parapets have been destroyed
by the guns which means a lot
of ammunition. Last Sunday
there were two attacks & they both

Last Sunday there were two attacks & they both failed as you will see by the enclosed cutting, which was owing principally to the wire not being sufficiently cut & the Maxim gun emplacements not being destroyed. We have attacked again today & there has again been very heavy fighting here. We have been in support all day & never actually in action & the worst of it has been that we could see very little except the shells bursting about half a mile off & tho' we were well within range they made us no presents today. The day has been simply glorious & one could hardly believe even tho' the guns never stopped all day that only a couple of miles over there thousands of fellows getting killed & wounded.

Tonight one of our flyers was over the line pretty low & the Germans got his range & put 8 shells all round him & he simply dived straight down about 500 feet & then went on as tho' nothing had happened, thus causing them to have to range on him again & set a new fuse only that time he had climbed up again & was away, calmly circling about & spotting all their dispositions & gun positions.

There is nothing out here to be desperately exhilarated over, we hold our own alright & shall continue to do so, but we want more guns & more men before we can take tea with the Boche. I personally don't think that there is any doubt that in the end we shall win but unless the country wakes up to the fact that it is everyone's duty to come, the end will be delayed for a very long time indeed. If we had another K's army[17] it would help things a lot. The *Daily Mail* is taking the right line & if it succeeds in stirring up the nation to a real effort it will deserve our hearty thanks.

Really heavy guns, throwing heavy shells, not necessarily a long way, will win the war. If Germany makes them faster than we do, well it will be unpleasant. Without previous smashing by heavy guns it is impossible to succeed against these breastworks bustling with machine guns & modern rifles & covered by wire.

It is wonderful how they evacuate the wounded in the motor ambulances. Tell Arthur[18] he should come out here with his car & help. Tell him 20 Sunbeams are doing good work carrying 4 lying-down cases & six sitting but the car that is streets ahead of anything is the Ford. They swear by them here, they go anywhere & through anything & where the Sunbeams stick they go on & never mind the mud.

[17] Kitchener's army.
[18] Hodgson, a neighbour in Sussex.

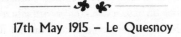

17th May 1915 – Le Quesnoy

I am still in the feather bed billet but I have had to sleep in my clothes these last few nights. I told you a good deal last night & we have done real well today I believe, & taken lots of prisoners, 537 at lunchtime. I am sorry to say we have again not been in the show but I shouldn't be surprised if we got hauled out tonight, but I hope we don't as it is fearfully dark & raining like the devil.

The men really are wonderful, today a fellow came by smoking a cigarette & waving a German helmet to everyone as he passed & had just had one of his feet blown off. We are right on the road along which the ambulances pass on their way to the first collection station & see some pretty 'bluggy' sights occasionally. We are longing to have a go. I cannot describe the present battle to you yet but I hope to be able to when a week has gone by.

I got three nice letters from the Chugs today – please thank them.

18th May 1915 – Le Quesnoy

We have been fighting hard here since Saturday night but we are still out of it & it is most tantalizing. There is, of course, no scope for any mounted action of any sort & I don't think they fancy wasting their small amount of cavalry in the trenches during such an attack as is going on at present. We are making good progress I am glad to say & driving the old Boche back from his entrenchments.

I heard from 'B' Squadron again today & poor little Cooper[19] has been badly wounded. They have been spending their time digging trenches by night about 200 or 300 yards behind the front line & getting a lot of stray bullets into them & as they cannot fire back it has been most unpleasant. They have five of them wounded up to date. These wounded are rather a dismal sight coming past all day long as they do when there is an attack

[19] Lieutenant H. M. H. Cooper of 'B' Squadron.

of this sort going on but when one is advancing like this it is possible to pick them up, but when an attack fails I am afraid that a very large number lie out between the trenches & are never recovered. It is this which accounts for so many missing.

We are all very well & most cheery. Little Henry Feilding & Izard are the life & soul of the place & we seem to live in a constant state of uproarious laughter. We have had a lot of rain. Mud over your boot-tops everywhere.

Best love old dear.

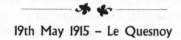

19th May 1915 – Le Quesnoy

I enclose you a cutting from *The Times*[20] & will endeavour to tell you what I can of this last fight. [The letters A–D stand for passages he has marked in *The Times* article.]

A. On Sunday May the 9th the attack was preceded by what they are pleased to call an 'intense bombardment', i.e. 35 minutes with every gun in the vicinity firing at its maximum rate with the result that batteries fired from 1200 to 1600 rounds in the time. By this you will see that accuracy has to be sacrificed to a certain extent to intensity & tho' the effect was shattering the material damage was less than had been hoped for. The result was that the wire wasn't cut & two at least of our battalions were very severely handled, they reached the wire & died there & the net result was that the Germans beat off the attack & we gained nothing except that we held troops to the ground here while the French made their advance at Carency.

B. For last Sunday's [16th May] attack a slower & more deliberate bombardment was made lasting three days & nights, careful artillery

---

[20] The cutting was by *The Times* military correspondent, Colonel Repington. The historian Martin Gilbert states: 'Repington was given detailed information about the shortage of high explosive by Sir John French himself, angered at the Army's inability to maintain the attack on Aubers Ridge. These critical reports, together with the personal representations of two officers sent back by French to intercede with political leaders in London, finally led to the establishment of a Ministry of Munitions.'

observation, correcting & directing the fire, which was quite impossible in the intense bombardment. Considerable damage was done to the German breastworks & wire, allowing the attack to get through & into the trenches. The attack started at 11.30 p.m. & the infantry rushed the trenches & breastworks & established themselves there.

C. This is close to us. About 3.15 a.m. the remainder of the attacking troops advanced & during the day we took about 2000 yards in length & 1000 yds in depth which we still hold & what is more, look like holding. We took close on 600 prisoners. The attacking troops fought for three days & nights without rest so you can see what attacking strong breastworks really means & the immensity of the task. Casualties in frontal attacks on entrenched positions must be heavy & in consequence, the need of more men and more heavy high-explosive shells to make breaches in the breastworks becomes more urgent every day.

D. There is a farm in front of the part we have captured, just such another as Eastlands, where the pony farm is. This is full of machine guns & has so far resisted all attacks tho' large bodies of troops have repeatedly attempted its capture. If we could get this we could advance a lot as we are at this point completely through the German entrenchments & they have apparently nothing fortified behind the line we now hold. But this holds us up at present & is resisting all efforts at capture.

We amuse ourselves in the afternoons by splitting up timber both for firewood & to make racks on which to put the saddles & keep them out of the mud. Yesterday we struck a tree that defied all our efforts in spite of the wedges we had been able to get in Béthune so we then resorted to force in the shape of explosives & I gave my lads a little training in their use with great success. We bored with an auger into the heart of the tree & with the help of some primers & a fuse we fairly took tea with the tree! It really was great fun tho' at one time rather spoilt by the damned Germans firing about a dozen of their beastly shells rather unpleasantly close, tho' so far as I have heard they killed no one yesterday, the day before one poor old woman in the village took it right in the back of the neck. When a shell comes one hardly knows whether they are likely to increase their range with the next or not. It is rather exciting & you hear them whistling along towards you & it is most weird. You needn't worry about my smoking, I am *not* increasing!!

Your new little seaside place[21] sounds charming. I would even consent to bathe if I could come too, tho' really we are having a ripping time & as today is again glorious after three days' continuous wet, all is rosy.

I am sorry to hear Anthony has been wounded, but in a modern attack it is wonderful that anyone shouldn't be. I wish you could come & stay a weekend with us, it is just like Watford only more comfortable. You never told me how Benjamin was. I do hope he isn't worrying you too much? I see a Juckes in the casualty list – is this Juckes' 3rd boy[22]? I fear it is & I am afraid if he is missing there is no hope. Nowadays you can write off 999 out of every 1000 missing as dead. Give old Juckes my love and tell him how sorry I am if it is his boy. Love to you, dearie mine.

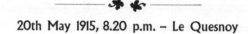

20th May 1915, 8.20 p.m. – Le Quesnoy

As I write there is a rare old battle going on & our own guns are firing like steam. We hope to do well tonight & get some important points & if things really go well it will probably mean a quite decent advance.

After tea the Germans had the lip to start shelling us so we went out to see the fun & they stopped, so we went on to see the captive balloon that I told you was just behind our camp. They had it pulled down & so we went & talked to them & they showed us all their gyms [gimmicks]. While we were there the damned Germans began shelling again and put one or two very close & the man who was showing us round said very meaningly 'If him hit, the hydrogen, him explode,' so we withdrew & sat down & watched the shells bursting from a comparatively safe distance. It is really rather fascinating in a way when they are not too close, as you hear them coming ever so long before they plug into the ground & burst.

One dropped about 50 yards one side of our gate & another about the same distance the other side, right in the middle of the road. As it seemed to burst among a lot of men we went over to see what it had done. It didn't

---

[21] In Worthing.
[22] Son of Dr Juckes, the family doctor.

damage the road very much but a poor old man coming home from working in the fields was walking along & a large piece of the shell struck him on the point of the chin & no doubt the angels are dressing his wound now.

Another bit of it went through a cottage window & hit a poor girl rather badly, but these things are now taken so much as a matter of course by the village that there was no crowd & no excitement, the women all standing in their cottage doors & taking no notice at all. Occasionally one hears some of the old women deplore the horrors of war & break down a bit but generally speaking they are most wonderful & the shells come buzzing along, generally about 6 to 7 in the evening & when the first arrives, folk come out of their houses and have a look & then go back & go on with their washing, too blasé to wait for more.

These shells tonight were high explosives, bursting on impact, and are just the ones we want & which I hope will now be forthcoming according to K's speech in the papers we got today. As we came home tonight one fell in a wheat field & we walked over to see the hole it made which was about six feet in diameter and four deep & when it burst it threw the earth about 40 feet high.

These are the shells we want to fire into the German parapets to make breaches in them as they used to in the walls of the towns years & years ago & none of our field guns have them yet & I cannot understand why they are not forthcoming as they must have known months ago that when we came to attack the breastworks that they would be needed. I am sure they have needed them at Ypres more than anywhere.

We have an intelligence summary sent round this morning and today it contained observations on the examination of prisoners of which the following is rather amusing. 'One officer was taken on the 17th, a lad of 19, tried to be impressively Prussian, and proved himself merely ill-mannered.'

In view of our discussions on shells I enclose you some cuttings from the *Daily Mail* which are good & relevant & which you may have missed. The German shrapnel differs from ours in that the case bursts as well as driving out the bullets; our charge only drives out the bullets and the case remains intact which you will no doubt remember from the old days at Potchefstroom.

Please thank old Bet & Bob for their nice letters which amused me very much. Heredity is a great handicap at times & the spelling is absolutely unique! 'There was two great big crows on the tens cort. I thort one was lame.'

Love to you my darling & I love the Chugs' letters.

22nd May 1915 – Le Quesnoy

I see in the paper today that Laurie Godman is hit again, the old goose, Juckes' boy killed & I see that the Graham-Taylor boy is killed also. He only left my squadron a few months ago. I hear he is buried only a few miles from here & I shall go over & see his grave if I can manage it & write to the old people at Lindfield.

We move very slowly here tho' we do advance which is always something. Tonight we have been out digging for the shell fuses that the Germans sent us free gratis & for nothing two nights ago & I am sending you one by this post. Have it set up as it is the first that the Boche shot at your husband & it is a very good one. It would make a very nice inkpot done as above. We got three tonight & one the other night we went out. I enclose a nice little picture which I hope you haven't seen before.

23rd May 1915 – Le Quesnoy

Great disappointment tonight as I got no letter from you, & was looking forward to it so much as you had promised me several 'bits' in yours of yesterday. However I had four from the Chugs which I liked very much. You don't know how one misses a mail here, especially as we are doing absolutely nothing and there is nothing to occupy one's time. I have to be ready to turn out with my command at 2 hours' notice so I cannot leave my headquarters & the squadron rides round & round a small wood for exercise from 8.30 to 11 a.m. & we do nothing else all day. I only wish we could go & have a dash in the trenches or anything to vary the monotony. We are all very well & so are the men, I am glad to say.

Smith-Dorrien[23] has gone home but I do not know why, but I expect it was health tho' the notice in orders did not say so & old Allenby has got

---

[23] General Sir Horace Smith-Dorrien had been dismissed by Sir John French, under the pretext of ill health, for recommending a strategic withdrawal at Ypres, and had no further important command. He served as Governor of Gibraltar from 1918 to 1923.

his command. It is astonishing how some of our old friends have shot up this last year. I see by the papers that the Cavalry had a warm time a bit ago & several we know hit.

We had a most awful thunderstorm last night. I have never seen anything like it before, it seemed to hang only a few feet over the house & the lightning simply whistled before you heard the thunder crash. It really was terrific. Everyone thought it was some new form of German frightfulness.

I am sorry to say that I shall have to send the camera home as 'it has been found necessary to withdraw the permission given to commanding officers to have cameras'. It is a great pity. Anyhow I am sending you one roll which has no military significance whatsoever.

Best love my own dearie. I would give worlds to have you here for a bit tonight. It is simply glorious, & so still now. It is so funny how you get periods of absolute quiet during all this firing. My love my own dearie.

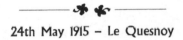

24th May 1915 – Le Quesnoy

After waiting most expectantly for *the* letter I got today yours No. 29 & I am sure that I have missed some.

I have no news & the heat is really tropical & having absolutely nothing to do makes it worse. I am afraid little Cooper[24] got a nasty gunshot wound & I hear it has touched his spine & he is paralysed. Perhaps when they get the bullet he will get better. Damn the war!

Best love dearie mine. Tea now & then blow up trunks of trees for firewood with gun-cotton.

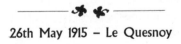

26th May 1915 – Le Quesnoy

We made a bit of an attack yesterday [north of Arras] & I had a most interesting evening as the Div. H.Q. sent for me & I went along to the

---

[24] Lieutenant Cooper's wound would prove to be fatal.

'Fighting Head Qrs'. When I got there, there was great excitement on as there was a 'Taube'[25] just over the house & they were naturally most anxious that it shouldn't learn that it was Div. H.Q. It was really most interesting as I was right in the middle of things which resembled more the conning tower of a battleship. Telephones to all the fighting troops & messages streaming in & orders going out & the whole fight on the maps on the table with flags.

There was some pretty hard fighting last night. Our division attacked & did very well indeed to start with & if we can hold on to the trenches we took shall have made a nice little bit towards Berlin, but one gets the ground by inches in this war & there is no rushing over the country, the cost being roughly one man per foot gained.

We are now going to have a lesson in bomb throwing which is the chief means of evicting the German. The first rush across the space between the trenches puts one in their front line with luck, then the bombers work along the trenches throwing bombs in front of them & using the bayonet. It's a pretty busy time.

We set up some cyclist bombers last night & they had a rare time, not all jam by any means as a lot got hit. One poor fellow who was carrying several bombs round his neck got one set off by a bullet & that exploded the lot with the result that can be well imagined. The Germans made us another present this morning just as the squadron was going to exercise & put it just in front of Barber who was taking them & made him jump a bit. I hear now they are threatening to blow Béthune to bits & have produced one of their big guns for the purpose which will be a beastly shame as it is a nice old place. However in another 12 or 18 months we may be in a position to get back some of our own if not before.

I only hope this conscription will come about. Organization of the workers & all the rest fighting. It is the only way to finish the job, more men & still more men. We must have them. No one has any right now to keep a man who is able to fight & whose retention is not an absolute necessity to the fighting troops. Best love old dear.

[25] The *Taube* ('dove') was a German observation plane, the original stealth plane. There was little engine noise in flight, and, as the wings were covered in clear doped linen, it was almost invisible when flying above 12,000 feet/3,660 metres.

27th May 1915 – Le Quesnoy

I am sending you another map which as it was used as a wrapper to some other maps cannot be of much use to anyone. On it I have marked the position of the trench line during winter in Green and the advance made during the last three weeks' fighting in Blue. I cannot, of course, mention the names of any units engaged but from the recent casualty lists published in the papers you will gather the cost of attacking strong positions such as these trench lines are.

A badger sett is about the only equivalent of the German trench system. Their trenches are a complete & complicated underground town & they fairly want some digging out. They are much better than we are at digging and their ammunition supply seems to be inexhaustible. The other night they seemed to be throwing about 10 bombs to our one so far as I can gather.

Tell old Juckes how fearfully sorry I am to hear about Rowland. However 'C'est la guerre' & that is the only way one can look at it.

You would have laughed today – we were discussing this bombing business & I was talking about organizing a complete bombing party with its own bayonet men, bomb carriers & throwers when there was open insubordination by the young officers. 'If I thought I was going bombing I was thoroughly mistaken even if they had to use force'!! so you see I am being well looked after.

Poor Winston,[26] he has come a proper cropper hasn't he? I am very sorry as I am sure he was a good man & I can't help thinking that he will be missed yet.

Best love dearie mine.

---

[26] Winston Churchill, as First Lord of the Admiralty, had been blamed for the failure of the campaign in the Dardanelles, and was sacked from the War Cabinet by Asquith. After six months he rejoined the army and commanded a battalion of the Royal Scots Fusiliers on the Western Front until May 1916. He returned to government as Minister for Munitions in 1917.

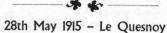

28th May 1915 – Le Quesnoy

Things have been very quiet here today, both sides resting after the attack of this week. You saw no doubt in the paper that a Territorial Division had taken three lines of trenches near Festubert or N.E. of Givenchy. That was our show of the last few days.

All the cyclist bombers who returned were reviewed by the Corps commander today & congratulated on their work. Did you see the Irish Guards casualty list? What they lost was in attacking 'East Ridge Farm'.

I went over to see the grave of the Graham-Taylor boy who was killed the other day. I wrote to his father about it & I want you to send or take him the two prints, *no* send them to me as I must mark his grave before I send them. Your old horse looks better than I ever saw him, fat & round as a ball.

My love to the Chugs.

29th May 1915 – Le Quesnoy

Having no mail one day makes the next day more pleasant than ever & today I got two ripping letters from you, 33 & 34 and one from Pa too. As I was lying on my bed in the garden reading them the damned Germans began shelling us again, rather too close for fun & I had to get up & go up to the horse lines as I thought they were right among them.

They have got, as I told you in a previous letter, an infernal balloon just behind my horse lines. Well they made up their mind this afternoon to have him down if possible, and fired like steam at it with shrapnel & they were making real good practice & bursting their shells right over the horses but the splinters were going over us. I was so afraid that they would drop some short ones among the horses but they didn't. Then a Taube came over & had a real hot time & departed whence he came. The balloon never moved all the time they were shelling in spite of the shells being most awfully close. I must confess I should have hated being in it, it was quite unpleasant enough below!

The Chugs' letters are fine & I like them awfully. Please thank Meg for hers & the postcard which was lovely.

The washing I get done by the folk on the farms. You will find it hard to believe no doubt, that I am well within range of the German guns as I sit in the house & write here & yet the women & children in the house are just as normal as Mrs Grantham, or Mrs Jones at Capons or Brownings. Their garden is better cultivated & cared for than either. The peas are coming up nicely & at the present minute it is a most glorious evening. Not a gun going & if you were here, & arrived at this moment you wouldn't know there was anything going on at all.

I am following your injunction to take care of myself & yesterday when we were practising throwing live bombs and one of them fell short of where it was intended to go & rolled back amongst us, I was among the first to clear out!! Best love to you old dear.

30th May 1915 – Le Quesnoy

I have been in luck today as I went out for a walk & met Hubert Gough[27] who recognized me at once & was most pleasant, & we talked for quite a long time, quite like old times. He was in his usual high spirits & most pleasant. So different from Sir D.H.!! I was so awfully pleased to see him.

Tonight the three of us walked right up to the trenches at Festubert & we stood just behind the line & it was most interesting. The Germans were shelling the breastworks in front of us about 150 yards off & we could see a good bit of the country & our shells bursting just in their lines. Our own guns were shooting over us & the German shells going over us too, searching for our guns.

I saw a 'Jack Johnson'[28] hole as well & you never saw such a hole. It was without any exaggeration just the size & shape of the pond in the front field. I haven't seen one actually burst yet & I don't want to if it is at all close. The absolute ruin of all the houses near the line is awful, both sides

---

[27] General Sir Hubert Gough.
[28] The British nickname for a heavy German shell, named after the famous black heavyweight boxer, 1878–1946.

the same, as far as one could see there wasn't a tile on a roof anywhere, absolute devastation everywhere.

Your Hamel[29] story was most interesting and funnily [enough] I had an R.N.V.R. fellow to tea & I told him this and he told me that two of our seaplanes chased a German at the mouth of the Thames at Xmas. They had to start in an awful hurry and had no time to get in their leather clo'! They got alongside the Taube & were so numbed with cold they couldn't shoot but one of the men knew Hamel well & they were close to the Taube & he swears it was Hamel in it.

I've had to give up my feather bed, there was no air in my room at all & I now sleep in a little arbour in the garden, but it is rather cold but I don't wake up quite such a boiled owl as I used to. Love to the kids.

On 1 June the squadron moved to Vaudricourt Château, on the southern outskirts of Béthune, where the horses were quartered in the park, and Robert and his squadron 'in a very poor farm in the village . . . not half as comfy as we were in our last place'. They remained at a state of readiness in anticipation of a German counter-attack on this part of the front, which did not materialize. No major attack was launched by the British in June; only small-scale raids, and occasional bombard-ments. French troops, however, were fighting in Artois and on the Meuse–Argonne front. Although they suffered heavy casualties, they repulsed the German attack. During the month there was constant fighting by the French at Notre Dame de Lorette and they made some gains in the Souchez area.

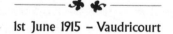

1st June 1915 – Vaudricourt

The French on our right took 1200 prisoners today at St Nazaire which is fine. We can see the German lines from here tho' I think it is almost too far for them to shell, certainly with any accuracy.

Last night those damned Germans started shelling us just after I had

[29] Gustav Hamel, a German national educated at Winchester College, was one of the pioneer aviators in England. His mysterious disappearance over the Channel in March 1914 led to many wild rumours, including the suggestion that he had become a German fighter pilot.

got into bed but they only sent three I am glad to say & as they weren't very close I went to sleep & trusted they wouldn't go on at their games, which I am glad to say they didn't. Vermelles[30] is the most perfect example of a ruined village you can see. There isn't a whole house in it. Everything is destroyed & not a bird or a cat or sign of life of any kind.

My dear old girl I would give worlds for another jaunt in the old boat with little Bet. I couldn't help thinking under what different auspices it was that I left Southampton six weeks ago. It is difficult to prophesy when it will occur again.

Yesterday I had my first experience of the German gas but under the best possible auspices as we had a cove round showing us how effective the preventative measures were. It's awful! You never smelt anything to touch it, it gets in your throat & you cough & cough & without mask or respirator it is impossible to stay in it. The bloke had a very large cylinder of it & let it into a trench & then with his preventatives, walked about in it. It is a thick yellow sulphur-looking stuff & it simply kills the grass the moment it touches it! Foul isn't it.

---- ✿ ✿ ----

2nd June 1915 – Vaudricourt

The mail was very late tonight but when it did come I got some awfully nice letters, your 38 and old Bet's letter with the dog 'locks' in it which pleased me awfully as also did your photos, but old Bet had shaken the camera. Teach her to put it on a chair. Always rest the camera if you can.

Where the Germans are now is all chalk & you can see the straight line of white running all along the front which makes it rather interesting. In the far distance we can just see Notre Dame de Lorette where the French have done so well lately. We heard in a roundabout way that a Zeppelin had dropped 82 bombs on London yesterday. I wonder if it is true?[31] We shall see in the paper tomorrow. You can buy the current day's *Daily Mail* in Béthune on normal days at 5 p.m.!! Rather good.

Best love old girl.

[30] Between Béthune and Lens.
[31] The rumour was correct: the first Zeppelin raid on London had taken place on 31 May 1915. Seven people were killed and thirty-five injured.

3rd June 1915 – on pages from a field notebook – Vaudricourt

I thought the enclosed map might be of interest to you as it shows the system of German trenches in our front & gives you a very clear idea of what it means turning them out even when you have taken their first line. You get in the trenches which are more than 6 feet in most places and it means working up the passages until you drive them out & you can imagine how likely one is to get lost & how companies get split up. This map is made by aeroplane reconnaissance so far as the trenches and wire is concerned.

Talking of wire I heard that one of our flying fellows came down when reconnoitring 'East Ridge Farm' to a height of 600 feet to see if the wire was cut by the guns & returned unhurt. A day or two after, flying at a height of 6000 feet he was hit by a shell & smashed to pieces.

I filled in the necessary papers before leaving Bishop's Stortford & named you as my next of kin so all is in order if I get hit & you should get to know before anyone. Hope you won't have occasion to be notified but judging by the casualty reports the betting seems to be all the other way. My rifle turned up today and I am delighted with it. You were most successful old girl.

I see poor Francis Grenfell was killed but he has been asking for it for some time. Julian[32] also was killed too – do you remember him cutting his hand so badly at Norwich out in the motor boat? Love to the Chugs & I will try & answer Bet's letter tomorrow.

5th June 1915 – Vaudricourt

Very many thanks for all your nice letters which are the joy of my life at present. The only thing I miss is not seeing you and the kids. Otherwise life is absolutely charming. We live in the best of conditions of peacetime. We have a very nice little mess room here. The weather absolutely beggars

[32] Julian Grenfell was the First World War soldier/poet whose most famous poem 'Into Battle' had been printed in *The Times* the day his death was announced in May 1915.

description & is too glorious for words. We are out of range of the ordinary shells & have nothing to worry us at all. Life is one delightful picnic under the best conditions all day long. I am not merely gassing in order to cheer you up, everything I tell you is the truth & nothing but the truth. And the gooseberry tart we had last night with cream the best in the world.

The rest of the tackle is first-chop, especially the tinned peas. Last night for dinner we had soup, fried fish, joint, potatoes & green peas, fresh gooseberry tart, cheese & butter, white & red wine, Perrier, raisins & almonds & cigars. Not bad for active service!!

I was awfully interested in all your war news so don't stop sending it. I am glad to hear that Pike is going & I think the White House folk ought to give all their eligible men notice that they could move off in a month unless they enlisted previously.[33] I am so glad that the shell fuse & the 75 case turned up alright, the latter makes a capital gong for meal times.

Bell sent me the same kind of mask as you but they are not good. The only thing is a thick flannel bag that completely envelops the head & has a mica front. It is soaked in chemicals & you tuck it inside your coat & it is perfectly effective but Oh! so hot!! The Govt supply them and we are to get ours at once. We have other masks too which are equally effective & I have seen both used in the gas where without them one couldn't have lived. We are ordered to have them always on us & have to have frequent inspections & drills to see that the men put them on right. We have no gas plant opposite us tho' they have fired a few gas shells but of course that is nothing like the plant. They have pipes laid up at Ypres just like a town lighting supply & the gas is really awful!

Well yesterday I had quite an interesting day making myself acquainted with the new area & I went down to Vermelles. There wasn't a single roof left, all the upper floors are down on the ground, not a window, not a thing, except the few soldiers billeted in it. It is just the place to take a party of the strikers to see, it would make them buck up. It has been the scene of very heavy fighting, first occupied by French, then by Germans & retaken by French. Some of the hottest fighting of the war has taken place there & it looks like it. We climbed up onto the church tower without showing ourselves & looked down over the trenches which run between it & Loos, the latter being German.

[33] Pike was employed by his parents as a chauffeur. Robert held strong views about all able-bodied men joining the forces as he believed it was only force of numbers that would overcome the German army.

We stayed there a couple of hours & had a bit of lunch & then rode home again & passing through Sailly-Labourse we saw the Germans bombarding the eastern slopes of the Notre Dame de Lorette spur. I never saw anything like it. They were evidently heavy howitzer shells (Jack Johnsons) & for a quarter of an hour they put an average 15 shells a minute on a piece of ground of about 6 acres. The result was a cloud of dust over 100 feet high & as thick as night & the state of the ground must have been awful. How anything could live through it I don't know. I am very glad I wasn't there. We could see & hear every shell burst & it was a most wonderful sight. There has been most awful heavy fighting there lately & it still goes on without either side gaining very much.

We are all delighted over L. George's speech today & hope he will manage to get something done.[34] Everything now depends on England producing shells faster than the guns can use them. What L. George says is quite true & had we had the ammunition in unlimited quantities we could have advanced very much farther than has been done up to date.

I don't expect the bus will let you down old dear, tho' you must get someone taught to crank her for you now, it is very bad for you to struggle with it.[35] Get Jacksons to teach your boy. When the bus is hot give her more *air* & she should start better. With regard to the '75', the French field gun is the best in the world for its weight. It is known everywhere as the '75' or the 'Soixante-quinze' which means the *diameter of the bore of the gun*. The shell fits into the brass case I sent you & looks exactly like a rifle cartridge the whole thing being one. Ours is the same only a trifle larger. I have drawn you a small picture on the other side showing you the difference between a gun & a howitzer. The gun at present fires shrapnel only, bursting in the air & bespattering the trenches with a shower of bullets & by the trajectory you will see how ineffective it is against narrow & deep trenches. It doesn't fall straight enough.

Oh I wrote & asked you to send me some flypapers & fly strings, did you ever send them because they haven't rolled up?

Best love to you all.

---

[34] Lloyd George had stated that it was the absolute duty of every citizen to place his life and labour at the disposal of the state. When the Liberal government had split in May as a result of the ammunition crisis, he became the first Minister of Munitions in the coalition government and later the Secretary of State for War.
[35] In view of her pregnancy.

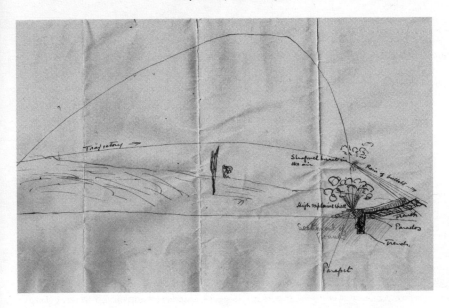

Sunday 6th June 1915 – Vaudricourt

I had a nice letter from the old Govnr[36] today & was very disappointed when yours did not roll up at lunchtime, but when I came in from tea not only had your 42 arrived but 27 was with him too.

The photo is not at all bad dearie & I like it very much. You have got a new hat I see & still wear the 'pres' & the earrings. I loved old Bet's photos but it is so difficult to carry a special one especially as one is moving hurriedly & changing clo' and it gets forgotten & I should hate anyone else looking at it somehow. I'd want it to be mine & mine only. Very stupid, but it would be just you to me dearie & I don't want to share you with anyone else. I do like the photo, old dear, very much, but what I call a weekday & not a Sunday expression!

My love to you my darling & the dear little Chugs.

[36] His father, Sidney.

CHAPTER THREE

THE BOMB SCHOOL

On 7 June, 'C' Squadron moved to Champ des Courses, Hesdigneul, when the division proceeded south to take over a new portion of the line from the French. Bivouacking in a copse, each troop in succession spent forty-eight hours in the front-line trenches in the Maroc area to gain experience in trench warfare and night patrolling. The sector was relatively quiet at this time, but later these trenches were used to launch the Loos attack.

The French army continued to make advances north of Arras and captured trenches around Souchez in the middle of June, whilst the British made small advances at Hooge in the Ypres Salient, but failed to hold the front-line trench they gained east of Festubert on the 15th. The Russians pushed forward on the Eastern Front with heavy German losses but later were forced into retreat in Galicia.

On 18 June, Robert became Commandant and Chief Instructor of the first Divisional Bomb School. This was something of a poisoned chalice because, as it says in the regimental history, 'the bombs of June 1915 were kittle cattle'. Accidents were frequent, but Robert was determined to do what he could to prevent these unnecessary casualties.

8th June 1915 – bivouac at Champ des Courses, Hesdigneul

Darling Mine,

I had a very successful day today with my old gentlemen at the Bomb School & finish them off tomorrow.

Tell Nell[37] I am sorry I can't keep answering her constant flow of letters, I have had no less than two in the last three months – Ditto Mimi!![38] The old Governor has been very good & written me some top-hole ones so you

[37] His sister.
[38] His mother, Fanny.

[44]

might tell him that I mentioned the fact to you & then he will realize that I do appreciate them very much.

Best love my own Lassie.

9th June 1915 – bivouac at Champ des Courses, Hesdigneul

I am at present in a house which consists of three sheep hurdles, with my mackintosh sheet as a roof and my oily coat & large bath towel as a fourth wall, door & window combined. The total area of my house is 6 ft by four & the ceiling at its highest point is about 3 ft 9 inches.

The 9th [Lancers] seem to have done grandly at Hooge, but the others I think you will find did all about the same & a yeomanry squadron supporting the 9th did real well too. I shall be only too glad of the Ammonia tablets as everything helps. I have got a good mask sewn in my coat in a mackintosh bag & shall have a helmet as well in a few days & always both on me. We have instructions not to retire with the gas as then one never gets shot of it. We don't really expect to meet the gas much as we are too far behind the line.

Will you thank old 'Mairky' for her letter & Bob too. I got the dog's hairs and liked them very much & have them in my pocket now with their photos which I was also very pleased with.

We arrived here Monday night & slept more or less in the open & yesterday we had a real heavy thunderstorm & got pretty wet. When I went to bed my feet were in about half a gallon of water which had got inside my blankets!!

I haven't seen a paper today so I don't know what has been going on. I hear rumours of one or possibly two Zeppelins having been destroyed by our airmen. Hope it's true. The heat the last two days has been almost unbearable.

11th June 1915 – bivouac at Champ des Courses, Hesdigneul

Thank you so much for your nice birthday letter[39] which arrived to the tick of the clock. I only hope I shall be at home for the next one but the chances are remote in the extreme. My telescope is on the boat with my other things & I should like it too please.

I don't think you would have enjoyed being with us these last few days as it has rained & thundered like Hades ever since we have been here. However, my hurdle house kept me dry last night alright tho' it rained very hard all night. Today we have built a mess room which is most capacious. Walls of brushwood hurdles and a roof out of a railway truck tarpaulin. Very fine – I suppose tomorrow we shall move!

Béthune has been shelled so much lately that all the shops are closing down & one can get few things there now. The gooseberries were what you sent & were much appreciated. I didn't see Winston's speech at Dundee, but I thought his Lancaster one very good.

I loved the Chugs' letters for my birthday & their dear little presents. Betsy's lighter is splendid & most useful & I have used nothing else since it came. It is so small & handy. I got the pouch & Meg's bullseyes,[40] but old Bob's pipe hasn't rolled up, but don't tell him so as I am writing to thank him for it. I must stop now dearie as it is 11.15 p.m. & I have had a hard day today, wielding an axe since 8.30 a.m. as all our poles for our mess had to be cut from a wood & I want to write to the kids.

Best love my own darling. I long for you so dearie mine & it will be such a terrible long time before we meet again I fear.

13th June 1915 – bivouac at Champ des Courses, Hesdigneul

Yesterday I went down to reconnoitre our advanced lines again & had a very interesting time. We, i.e. Henry & I, rode down through Noeux-les-Mines,

---

[39] On the 10th Robert turned thirty-seven.
[40] A type of boiled sweet.

& then got on the railway and rode along until we came to Grenay where we left our horses and walked on foot to the railway bridge about a mile S.E. of the town where we sat down & watched things. Of course the great disappointment of the war is that one never sees anything. We sat there with our own shells going over our heads from behind & the German coming the other way, but 'divil' a German or English soldier to be seen. The shells of both sides come out of the earth, screech through the air, fall with a bang & send up clouds of dust & that is all one sees.

We were close to the Notre Dame de Lorette spur & exactly end on to the French trenches & could have been very useful to the Germans in telling them how to correct the range of their guns as it was only 3500 yards from us to the spur and the shells were bursting all along this line & we could see which was short & which was over. We left our horses in a farm where there were some French guns shooting & just after we left to walk up the Germans sent one along that fell into the orchard against the farmyard. Even right up where we were there were still women & children living in the houses only 1200 yds from our front-line trench, just taking pot luck whether they were hit or not! As I walked home past a row of workmen's cottages, there was a gun in action in the garden of one firing away & two doors off a woman sweeping her garden path, taking no more notice of what was going on than if a man had ridden by on a bicycle! There is no doubt that one gets used to casual shelling. I know myself that I don't notice it now like I did at first, tho' of course an intense bombardment previous to an attack is quite another pair of shoes.

I got two men from 3rd County of London Yeomanry attached to me. I wanted men as I have 8 away sick & they asked to come to me. Censoring their letters tonight Barber tells me they said to their friends that 'the Regt was thought a lot of out here', which in other words means the Squadron as the others are too far off to be known in these parts.

15th June 1915 – bivouac at Champ des Courses, Hesdigneul

Yes, we have moved West all the time, & are extending our line gradually as we get more troops out I suppose.

So far I haven't heard of any leave for us & I certainly haven't earned it

5 JUIN 1915　　　　　　　　　L'ILLUSTRATION　　　　　　　　　N° 3770 — 571

Le canon braqué à 45°, vu de profil.   Le canon, vu de l'arrière.

LE CANON DE CAMPAGNE FRANÇAIS DE L'ARMÉE ITALIENNE, SYSTÈME DEPORT, A GRANDS CHAMPS DE TIR

Ce canon est caractérisé à première vue par son affût à *flèches ouvrantes*, assemblées de manière à former une flèche unique pour la route et s'ouvrant largement à la mise en batterie. Le berceau porte-canon peut ainsi être orienté dans un secteur de 54°, constituant le champ de tir horizontal, sans que la direction de l'effort du recul sorte de la base d'ancrage. Le grand champ de tir vertical est obtenu d'autre part par l'accouplement de deux berceaux-freins qui donnent une très longue course (1 m. 36) dans le tir voisin de l'horizontale et une très faible course (0 m. 36) dans le tir sous les grands angles. — *L'Illustration* a consacré au canon Deport un article détaillé, avec schéma, dans son numéro du 30 novembre 1912, page 440.

as we have lived the easiest of lives & our trouble is to know how to kill time. Really it is a farce our being here at all! But I suppose we shall have a go sooner or later. I heard something the other day about leave for anyone who had been three months out but I didn't take much interest as I didn't intend to come back unless I was seedy or the show finished.

I am enclosing a picture of the Italian gun – it is exactly the same as the French 75 only a few minor modifications & improvements which are so minor that the French did not consider it worthwhile to re-arm with. The principal feature is the divided trail which closes when hooked to the limber. The great desiderata being the rigidity of the framework, enabling a very rapid rate of fire without re-laying the gun. I thought it might interest you & old Percy.

My love to you old dear.

------- ✿ ✿ -------

16th June 1915 – bivouac at Champ des Courses, Hesdigneul

There is a big attack in progress & last night near Festubert our troops did real well to start with but I have had no news this morning so far, so whether or not they got driven back again I do not know. There has been a lot of ammunition blazed away by the guns and I hope the results will be commensurate with it. I rather doubt the Germans' ability to free half a million men from Galicia. The old Russians are never beaten & they have crowds of men.

There are three Aeroplanes just going over in a covey, they have been very busy these last few days & now two more have come along. We had seven here last night all at once & nine a few days ago. Sopwith seems to be doing a tremendous lot of work. I shall go to midday stables now & will continue this when I get your letter at lunch time.

The attack, I hear, has failed, we took a lot of trenches in the assault & then got bombed out of them again. It is a pity. Neither side appears to be strong enough to drive the other back, each side being strong enough to defend its line & there is a limit to the number of men you can put on a given piece of ground as they all have to be in the trenches before the attack begins.

I am sorry to say my cyclist officer, who runs the bombing school, had a bad accident today, a bomb exploded in a man's hand & killed the man & the one next to him and wounded Leman & his Sgt badly. They are beastly dangerous things, I hate them. However, it is part of the trade, only I wish they would give us a rather safer bomb to handle. No doubt it was the man's fault but we shall never know owing to the fact that the two men actually throwing are dead & Leman and his Sgt are both evacuated to England. Post just off.

17th June 1915 – bivouac at Champ des Courses, Hesdigneul

Your 53, written in the train, rolled up alright today & cheered as usual.

There is a devil of a contest going on near Festubert & the guns are going real hard, the whole sky is lit up with the flashes & the star shells and Verey lights make quite a Crystal Palace display. The French on our right have gone ahead well these last few days & are now well S.E. of Souchez, but somehow we don't seem to make any great advance. They say that it is lack of guns and ammunition. The French seem to have no end of it as they fairly loose off and if you keep it up long enough no troops in the world can stand it, the moral strain even in the best of trenches & dugouts of four or five days' incessant gunning day & night simply demoralizes the other side.

Dearie mine, I am more than grateful to you for your trouble & trek to London about the clothes & things. Your son seems quite a bright lad tho' of course he has a strong dash of his father in him!

I have taken over the 'School of Instruction in Bomb-throwing' & was in——all afternoon seeing them made right from the molten metal. In my opinion under Leman it was very badly run & the amount of instruction derived was very sketchy indeed so I hope to re-organize things & make a really good show if I can and also to, as far as possible, eliminate accidents.

I can't help thinking that Leman's accident was due to faulty instruction in the first place, & not to a bad fuse which they attributed it to. It is becoming now almost as important if not more so, than shooting. It is absolutely necessary in taking trenches to have good bomb throwers & an absolutely unlimited supply of bombs. The factory, tho' only a small civilian foundry, turns out 6000 a day & can't meet the demand in its own area. There is a Birmingham man who has invented a really good bomb & I hope the Govt will have it manufactured in large quantities as it is safe to handle & certain in action.

My love to you old dear. Please thank Bob & Mary for their letters.

Undated, postmarked 18th June 1915 – Champ des Courses, Hesdigneul

I had my first day today as chief instructor of the 47th Div. Bomb School & was much gratified when the class begged to be allowed to remain two more days as they had learnt more today than they had in the four days they had been there. I had rather a stiff job to face, as the only time they had seen a bomb thrown, the previous Instructor was badly hurt & so was his assistant, & two men engaged in throwing the bomb were both killed. So one's first job was to smooth the ruffled waters & try to instil a little confidence. However it is coming back alright I think.

To revert to the war you will find in the big red book *Hamley's Operations of War* that to gain one's end it is not sufficient to take towns or territory. The one objective is the destruction of the enemy's forces. This is the only thing that can bring peace & accomplish one's object. The German forces are far from being destroyed and were a peace to be considered now & entered into, from what she has learnt she could in a few years still build up an army & in my opinion one which would then be invincible. We have only just caught her in time & it is still going to be a very long job.

Must go now dearie, love to you all.

I want two Lacrosse bats please, soon as possible. To catch German bombs in & throw them out of the trench before they explode!!

19th June 1915 – bivouac, Champ des Courses, Hesdigneul

I simply loved your 'rendering of account of your Stewardship'. This financial crisis seems to differ from our biennial crises in that there is still a bank balance. I am only sorry dearie, that I bothered you with it for a minute & that you took so much trouble because it wasn't really wanted. However there is no doubt that for the next few years we shall have to be careful & there will be very little cash I fear for holiday jaunts, & as for a new stable, that will be out of the question.

Since writing the above we have had supper, & now the French on the Lorette appear to be attacking or else the Germans are making a counter-attack. You never saw such a show, the whole sky is bright as day with gun flashes & the noise incessant. They must be firing hundreds of shells a minute. The ammunition question doesn't bother the French. They fire all day & all night & yet can have bursts like they are doing now ad lib.

Best love to you dear lassie & the Chugs.

Undated, postmarked 20th June 1915 – bivouac, Champ des Courses, Hesdigneul

I got a top-hole letter from you again today old dear (56), and after a long day out it was very pleasant to find it waiting in my palace when I got back.

I started out to my school & it was the last day of the class & we spent the morning throwing fully charged bombs as a wind-up to the course.

One damned fool was so frightened of his bomb that the moment he lit it he dropped it at his feet, but fortunately I have a splendid place for throwing, in deep trenches & the man throwing stands in a little room by himself where I can see all he does from a place of absolute safety & from which he can get into safety if anything like this happens – so it was alright, tho' that bloke did move. It takes 5 seconds for the bomb to explode after ignition which sounds short but is in practice ample time to throw it carefully aimed at a distance of 30 yards before it explodes.

After lunch I rode over to the Div. H.Q. & made some arrangements about the school, & I then went on to where the bombs are made to see the R.E.[41] officer in charge & took advantage of being in a town to buy some cakes for tea, & try & get a ball as we wanted a ball to amuse ourselves in the evening. We had a capital game of stump cricket with a box as a wicket & a pick handle as a bat. I played a faultless first innings of 21 & a second of 16, Henry, I & Izard beating the others handsomely. The pitch was a road & the outfield a bit rough, full of small gravel pits & whin bushes!! We really had great fun tonight.

Will you send me one of the *Daily Mail* maps of the Bird's-eye view of our whole line. Today I saw the most ripping panorama photo of the whole of the German front opposite us. I would have loved to have had it to send to you.

It is very sad about Cooper. I wish he had been killed outright. We want candles badly dearie, I have only just enough to finish this letter with & it is the last in camp! I must go to bed now dearie as it is nearly midnight.

22nd June 1915 – bivouac at Champ des Courses, Hesdigneul

Last night I was naughty & didn't write to you as I had a lot of other kind of writing to do as well. It was midnight again before I got to bed.

My business took me near the trenches during the morning and I saw a fine battle between our anti-aircraft guns & a Taube which ended in the Taube thinking discretion the better part of valour & retiring. The enemy's aircraft have been very active in our sector the last few days & there has

---

[41] Royal Engineers.

been a great deal of shooting at them. So far as one can see & distinguish them they don't come very far behind our line, mostly getting driven off by gunfire.

Damn Horsham & its 'fed-up' feeling for the soldiers, I shall have to send a Zeppelin to visit them. I think if they were to come & see Vermelles they would think differently. If the Germans came to England every town & village on their line would be the same.

Old Bob's pipe doesn't smoke very well I am afraid but you mustn't tell him so, dear old boy. I should love to see them all again & I do so miss them. I doubt if I shall be strong enough to say 'No' if I get a decent bit of leave offered me.

I have been down at the Bomb School all day & my new class begins tomorrow so I shall have a very busy week. I wish to goodness I had my workshop out here, I am sure I could produce some very much better engines of frightfulness than they are using in the trenches at present. There never was so much scope for inventive genius as at present. I am hoping to be able to produce something shortly but should like to rope in Percy or someone like that. Izard has gone with his troop to the trenches tonight for 48 hours & the others go in in turn for like periods. They are just going to gain a little experience.

24th June 1915 – bivouac at Champ des Courses, Hesdigneul

At about 5.30 p.m. Mac & I started off to visit old 'Pongo'[42] in the trenches. We rode as far as it was healthy to ride & then walked over the open ground to the Batt. H.Q. to which they were attached. The Germans won't waste shells on small dismounted parties & there was only Mac & I. We got up to the Batt. H.Q. about 400 yds behind the front line when the Boches treated us to some minor frightfulness in the way of 'Pip squeaks' which are a small sort of pompom shell only time fused & about 3 lbs as far as we know. They were concentrating on the particular communication trench down which we wanted to go so we had to wait at the Batt. H.Q. till their evening hate was over. Then we went on and saw old Pongo &

---

[42] Nickname for Lieutenant Izard.

his troop, all of whom were in the best of health & spirits. We went all along the front-line trench & had a good look at the German trenches.

They were a bit smelly in places owing to the amount of Frenchmen who still remain unburied between the lines & the flies are very bad. It's not very pleasant up there but they are really good deep trenches & beautifully kept.

The old French really are wonderful round Souchez, they never let the Boche rest a minute, their guns have been going night & day ever since we came here & are hard at it now. I can't help thinking they are going to make a job of it round Souchez very shortly. This damned censorship is a bore, tho' essential, as I could tell you many more interesting things.

Pongo & his troop come out of the trenches tonight & Henry went off for his turn some hours ago. I hope they will come back before I go to bed as one of our men went out on patrol between the lines & I am rather anxious to hear how he got on. You would be astonished to see how our men stand out among these London Regts composed of men working in offices. They can't get their men to use their bayonets, they don't like pushing them in at all & my blokes would revel in it if I could only get them the chance.

I wish you could see Harry[43] now, he is doing simply top-hole, has smartened up beyond recognition & is awfully popular with the men. I found that he was messing with the Sgt Major & about half a doz others the other day, but I had to put a stopper on that & make them have a proper Sgts Mess for the sake of discipline.

We are not short of shell from a defensive point of view, we haven't enough to attack with at present. No doubt very shortly they will stream over & then we shall be alright. We don't hold our advances, simply because we are bombed out of the trenches we have taken. The Germans are better bombers than we are, but we are learning fast & when we next meet I think things will be better. You see in an attack our guns bash their trenches so that when we arrive they are such very poor protection, & the Germans start on them with shrapnel and it is very hard for our fellows to stay in them, casualties in consequence being heavy. We shall very shortly be better at the Bomb-throwing business & then we shall see. The Germans don't seem to mind dosing their men with their own shrapnel a bit & having settled both our men & theirs in their front-line trenches they just fill them up again with their reserves. I must to bed now dearie.

---

[43] Parsons, formerly the groom at Cowfold.

25th June 1915 – bivouac at Champ des Courses, Hesdigneul

I had a topping letter from you again today. It has rained like Hades all day & been beastly. Have been bombing all day but could do very little. Would you arrange for us to have some good big tins of cocoa sent out as we always have cocoa at nights and can't get it locally very well. The heat tonight is awful, so close that tho' it is 9 p.m. I am sitting in my waist-coat sweating, beg pardon 'all of a glow'! My troop came out of the trenches with a very poor opinion of the Regt to which they were attached. Thought nothing of them at all.

The poor old Russians seem by all accounts to be having a very thin time & it seems to be the weight of artillery the Germans are bringing against them.[44] In this connection I had a very interesting paper sent me tonight, a copy of a secret document captured from a German.

It is impossible to lay down any figures for an authorised daily expenditure, but the Army is prepared to place eventually at the disposal of an Army Corps, on a reasonable demand, the following amounts of ammunition.

Field Guns 800 rounds
Light Howitzers		*up to 400 rounds*
Heavy	"	*up to 300 rounds*
10 cm	"	*100* "
21cm	"	*50* "

Our daily allowance for Field Guns used to be 6 rounds per diem!!! Of course the above 'reasonable demand' means when the Corps has a really good target or preparing for an attack. Our guns fired as much as double this some time ago, but as a *special effort* which had been *carefully prepared* for, but this refers to a daily allowance per gun. I don't believe even if they do transfer men from the East that they will break our line should they attack but no doubt it will be a hot time.

[44] The Russians had suffered a defeat in Galicia and been driven out of Austria. On the Polish front the Germans, using gas, had also driven them back, causing heavy casualties. Russian territory itself was at risk of invasion by the German army. It was feared that the Germans might withdraw troops from the Russian front to increase their capability in the West.

Many thanks for your trouble about the cannon![45] Don't know if it will be a success or not but it is worth trying. I am thinking also of sending a drawing to old Arthur[46] of a spring gun & try and get him to get it made for me. I want a child's ordinary spring cannon that will throw a 3 lb weight 200 yds. Tell him to think it out. A spring piston in a tube 95 mm diameter. Just a piece of drain pipe. If I only had the run of a real good workshop for a few days I am sure I could turn out something far better than we are at present using. The barrel must not be much more than 3 feet. I am quite sure it is a possibility & I will try & get out some drawings for it when I have considered it a bit more. Anyhow it couldn't be rottener than what we have got at present.

With regard to the engine I shouldn't worry at present as long as it is doing its job. Just have the vaporizer acetylene welded & let it go on even if it does knock a bit. If it knocks too much try reducing the compression by a change of some of the compression plates *behind* the big end bearing. [Here he has drawn a diagram.]

Pa wrote me tonight that he had sent the lacrosse bats off. Many thanks for the telescope too. My love to you darling mine.

27th June 1915 – bivouac at Champ des Courses, Hesdigneul

The C.O. comes to visit us tomorrow but he is only stopping a very short time I am glad to say. He didn't fancy the night in the open much, I don't think, so he is motoring over. I got the pamphlet about leave tonight & it says: 'Leave is only granted in very special cases where it is absolutely necessary & in the interest of the Forces in the Field, the object being to give a short rest to those who have earned it by their exertions in the field' – and one must have been out at least 3 months. We have had no exertions, in fact the most restful existence I ever had & can hardly put forward our claims at present, tho' no doubt there will be lots get it who have really done no more.

---

[45] Robert had earlier sent Ethel a shopping list of items to buy to enable him to make a mortar.
[46] Hodgson.

Somehow I feel tonight dearie as tho' I want you more than I have done since I have been out & would give worlds for an evening at home. I shall be damned glad when this blasted war is over & we are all back again but alas I can see no grounds for hoping for an early conclusion.

28th June 1915 – bivouac at Champ des Courses, Hesdigneul

My dear old girl, I am thankful that you have acted with what the C.O. termed today 'exceptional business capability', as the gun was only an experiment & since ordering it I have had time to consider & am now delighted that I can't get it. On going into the question more carefully I find that the trench mortars burst not because the mortar is too weak to stand the charge but because the charge is so weak that the slightest damp in the mortar makes such an impression on it that it fails to drive the bomb out of the barrel and is sufficient to light the fuse in the bomb with the result that it explodes in your own trench & blows mortar & crew to blazes.

My new spring mortar ought to be cheap to make and more reliable, anyhow I will guarantee that it doesn't stick in the barrel.

The C.O. arrived at 12 o'clock, had a hurried talk & at 12.35 had gone back again, just passed the time of day. Had no news & just wanted to see us & was off.[47]

My love to you all dearie mine.

30th June 1915 – bivouac at Champ des Courses, Hesdigneul

I am sorry to say I had a nasty accident at my bomb school today. I had just started my first lecture with the officers, & I always have some perfectly harmless dummy bombs made up for demonstrations. Somehow one bomb made up with a detonator had been put in my demonstration box with

[47] Lieutenant Colonel Sandeman, CO, K.E.H., obviously did not relish spending the night in a bivouac made of sheep's hurdles with a canvas cover.

the result when showing the class how it was lit it exploded in my hand.

Part of it flew into a box of detonators, 20 of them, & exploded the lot with the result that I and three out of the five composing my squad were in varying degrees wounded. I had a marvellous escape & why I wasn't blinded I don't know. When I lit the bomb it was in my hand & not 12 inches in front of my face & bar a slight cut on the bridge of my nose, a small bit in the centre of my forehead & in my left ear, and a piece of detonator through my lip which I got hold of with my teeth & by pulling my lip with my fingers, got out from inside, I have nothing wrong at all. I didn't even want to go & have it dressed but an old colonel sent me to the hospital & I had it dressed & was back with my class again in half an hour. Henry, who was on my left, I am sorry to say got it a good deal worse & his wrist was rather badly bruised but his wristwatch was badly damaged & this saved him from having the tendons of his hand cut I am glad to say. His face too was a bit cut & he went to hospital & two others as well. One had his eye hurt a bit which I didn't like but I don't think it is injured.

It was awful bad luck as I have done everything that is humanly possible to eliminate accidents & then to be sold a pup by one of one's own instructors like that was cruel bad luck. The blow to my pride is far worse than the trifling skin rub I have on my nose. You needn't worry about me in the least, I have had far worse scratches from a 'lawyers humble' out hunting. I have told you the absolute truth & am keeping back nothing for your sake so you need not think I am only telling you half.

I want you to buy me a really good silver wristwatch, which must have luminous hands or figures, as I want to give it to Henry. Have his initials put on it. H.S.F. from E.W.H. June 1915 & I will pay up to £5 for it.[48] His watch looked as if a steam roller had run over it.

I am off bombing again in the morning. I should keep the main portion of this to yourself, old dear, unless by any chance my name gets in the casualty bit which I hope it won't. Anyhow, for your information I am perfectly fit and well, was at duty again half an hour after the accident happened & am as cheery & well as if nothing had happened tho' awfully sorry about Henry. I love that boy now, he is a real good lad. Thank old Bet for her letter & love to you darling.

[48] The watch given to Henry Feilding is still in existence. When he was killed in 1917 it was among his effects returned to the family. In 2005 it was given as a christening present to his great-nephew Peregrine, son of the present Lord and Lady Denbigh.

1st July 1915 – bivouac at Champ des Courses, Hesdigneul

My very superficial 'wounds' are healing grandly & I am perfectly fit & well as also are the other three boys. So all is well I am glad to say. Henry Feilding has bucked up & is doing well, but it was Harry Parsons that I meant. He has done top-hole and all my three horses are a sight worth looking at. Your old horse is twice as fat as ever he was with Bellew at any period of the year & never looked so well before. He is getting very naughty & shies at everything! And when he shies he is very wilful in spite of his tender mouth. I am only going to write you a scrap tonight as I have been bombing all day & winding up my monthly pay accounts as well.

Love to you darling.

2nd July 1915 – bivouac at Champ des Courses, Hesdigneul

I am in the best of spirits tonight because I have had a very uphill fight with my bomb school owing to the fact that they wouldn't give me a proper staff or materials. The G.O.C. came down to see me today & I managed to impress on him my wants and he is now as keen as I am that the school should be a success. He says 'Hermon, anything you want you can have, but don't mind the staff, I'll *order* it and then it will be done!!'

I think the school will soon be a great success, it has started at just the right time & now I can have what I want, should go like hot cakes. I am very pleased with it so far, I want to organize it, get it a thorough-going concern and hand it over to someone else, as I want to devote more of my time to the squadron.

We have got a portion of the Mil. Wing of the Flying Corps next to us & it is really awfully interesting seeing them start off & especially land. Tonight as I rode home one came down within a few yards of me & it really was ripping and looked most awfully jolly though I must say I prefer the bombing [school].

I am glad that old Bet liked my message about the lighter, and I use it always. Of course the two small 'Snippets' are too young to realise what is going on and it is just as well really, but I am glad that the other two miss one. I have nothing more to tell you dearie, and all the lads are talking 20 to the dozen.

3rd July 1915 – bivouac at Champ des Courses, Hesdigneul

You say (69) that I had written you a particularly nice letter but it has also inspired a particularly nice one in return. I have been very busy today bombing all day and then a visit to H.Q.

My patent spring gun has gone on to the Army Experiments Committee & I am very anxious to hear how they deal with it. I hope they will approve of it. There are one or two points I could improve in it even now but it will have to stand its chance.

I am afraid nothing political can possibly stop the War. The forcing of the Dardanelles if it can be accomplished before the end of the month will be a very great help, but I am very much afraid this Russian reverse will put the war back a long time. I hear we have shell contracts out up to well into 1917.

Thank old Bet for her letter and with my love to you dearie mine.

Robert enclosed with his letter of 4th July the following telegram sent by Ethel; it read:

WAR OFFICE WIRES ACCIDENTALLY WOUNDED BUT REMAINING DUTY
WIRE ME NEWS OF YOURSELF   ETHEL

4th July 1915 – bivouac at Champ des Courses, Hesdigneul

My darling old girl,

I have been awfully distressed tonight getting your telegram. It has on it no date or time of dispatch and so I don't know when it was sent off, and I feel now you have had several of my letters and it is no good my wiring you. All private wires go by dispatch rider to Army H.Q. & lie about there until there is a quiet moment on the wires & then take their turn.

I received the enclosed at 9 p.m. on Sunday, i.e. this evening & you must have had my letters telling you all about the accident long before this. Anyhow dearie I am absolutely well & never was better in my life. I have a very small bump on my forehead and a gash across my nose which is for the moment detracting from my beauty but in a week will not be noticeable under the closest scrutiny. There is an order which says that 'Officers however slightly wounded are to be reported' & I had to do it but I was under the impression that it went no further than the Division.

I am most distressed that they should have worried you.

Lass dear it is the most glorious night tonight you ever saw and your reference to Helford river makes me long for such another summer as we had last year. I wish you were here tonight, it is simply lovely and so quiet and still, everyone been in bed some time and the moon just rising. The whole place as still as anything, not a gun firing anywhere, just the moon in one quarter and a constant glare in another of the Verey lights just to remind one that there is a war on. There are so many moths in the candles I can hardly see.

My very best love to you and the Chugs.

5th July 1915 – bivouac at Champ des Courses, Hesdigneul

I am so glad to hear my little Meggie is so brave in the sea – must take after her father.[49] I would give anything to see the Chugs & you, especially if the whole show were over. I am sure my son is not taking after me, there is only one girl in the world for me (at a time) and I quite agree about the third!!

I hear various rumours about 'A' [Squadron] that they all quarrel with their O.C. and have a generally unpleasant time, but it is very funny that they are the only one of us so far who have had a scrap yet and they had a bit of a go in the trenches the other night and succeeded in killing a

---

[49] The family were enjoying a seaside holiday at their rented holiday home near Worthing.

German officer on their parapet. Russell says, I believe, that their actions saved the entire army but we await confirmation of this.

I got a confidential report from the G.O.C. tonight & in his own handwriting a minute expressing his very high approval of the conduct of my men in the trenches which was very gratifying. They did very well I know & on all hands met with great praise. They certainly stood out in the company they were in. They did very well too on patrol between the lines that night, though were not lucky enough to get a prisoner which they wanted badly. They brought in, however, several letters and oddments off the dead bodies of men lying between the lines which are being sent to the owners' relations.

My best love to you dearie & I hope you are now quite reassured that I am absolutely fit and well.

6th July 1915 – bivouac at Champ des Courses, Hesdigneul

I am sorry to say that one of my former pupils killed himself the other day, teaching a regimental class. I gather he threw a bomb and it didn't explode. He went and picked it up and threw it again and it didn't go off, and he again went and picked it up and it exploded in his hand killing him instantly. He was such a nice boy called Wood in the 8th Batt. It was pure stupidity or carelessness, it is never safe to go and pick up a bomb once it has been thrown until a considerable time has elapsed and if folk will take risks of this kind they must take the consequence. The bombs are no more dangerous than an ordinary loaded gun and you must observe the common methods for safety, in the same way.

7th July 1915 – bivouac at Champ des Courses, Hesdigneul

Lassie dear, if we are to beat the Germans we can only do it by bombing them out of their trenches and it is absolutely necessary that someone teaches. As soon as the men have learned what and how to do it they will take tea with the Boche but the training stage must be gone through first and it is more necessary that men should be so trained in Bombing that they will have this ascendancy and a few officers more or less don't matter much in the long run provided we can give them the right training. There is absolutely no other method of getting men out of deep trenches. So much so that the French in the labyrinth, I understand, have armed their men with a large dagger and bombs only, they haven't carried a rifle at all.

I have got an officers' course starting tomorrow and lasting two days only, all company commanders, so as to give them some idea as to the possibilities and limitations of the bomb.

11th July 1915 – bivouac at Champ des Courses, Hesdigneul

We had a most ridiculous parade for 'K' last week. The squadron was ordered to be lined up on both sides of a road at 11.25 & at 12.45 'K' motored through at 20 mph and the squadron rode home. Three hearty cheers were ordered to be given, but long before they were over 'K' was at lunch in the next village!![50] The stock of leaves is getting used up, I have turned over so many now and I am wearying of the pastime.

What a capital letter from old 'Bet'. I sent her a cheque for a birthday present and old Bob a French bayonet, taken by one of my men from the body of a dead man lying between the two front-line trenches when they went out on patrol the other night. Rather gruesome, especially as it is some months now since he fell. However it is a memento. I hope he will like it, but I would suggest it being *firmly* nailed to the nursery wall. We are having some sports here tomorrow, the chief event of interest being a 100 yards race between the senior officers and senior N.C.O.s!! This evening we have a great cricket match on between the officers and the corporals, having whacked the sergeants' heads off.

I start bombing again on Tuesday with another class for N.C.O.s.

---

[50] Kitchener's visit would have entailed a great deal of 'spit and polish' to get the squadron and its horses up to 'parade' standard, so it is understandable that Robert was irritated that 'K' passed by in a flash with 'three hearty cheers' echoing fruitlessly on the wind.

12th July 1915 – bivouac at Champ des Courses, Hesdigneul

I know it is wrong to gype at my dear Mama but I cannot help quoting you the following extract from a letter received today. 'I am sending you a plainer cake this time as we are rather short of eggs, so many hens are sitting.' Are there no farms nearby where eggs can be purchased at a reasonable price or are luxuries of this kind at famine prices in England now?

Now for the piece of colossal memory and my very best wishes to you dearie mine for your birthday. I fear not so happy a one as we spent last year but let us hope the next will find us united once more, but I'm afraid the chances are small.

Old Buxton told me he never wanted to go in the trenches again! He had had quite enough. They had to march on foot to get there, stand for 48 hours and march back so it was hardish work and he feels he is better off where he is!

I won my race v the S.S.M. 6 to 4 laid on the Major.

13th July 1915 – bivouac at Champ des Courses, Hesdigneul

I hear on the best authority that the war will be over by Xmas! This is from outside and not my own deduction or belief, but it was very well told and sounded most feasible. We shall see what we shall see. Many thanks about Henry's watch.

It was capital old Botha[51] doing so well. He ought to come and lend a hand here now. Yes it would have been very interesting to have heard the conference between K, Asquith & party.

I am glad to hear the Chugs are so fit & well. It is cold this evening & I am a bit starved for news. Thank old Bet & Bob & Meg for their nice letters.

---

[51] General Botha, the President of the Union of South Africa, had pledged his support for the Allied cause; on 9 July his forces had received the surrender of the German colony of South West Africa, now Namibia.

On 6 July, French and British leaders had met in Calais to discuss an autumn offensive on the Western Front. The following day, the Commander-in-Chief of the French army, General Joffre, and the Commander BEF, Sir John French, agreed that the offensive was a strategic necessity. Kitchener, however, complained to Sir William Robertson (CIGS) that the generals had given him previous assurances that they would push the Germans back over the frontier and concluded: 'The attacks are costly and end in nothing.'

14th July 1915 – bivouac at Champ des Courses, Hesdigneul

I had two nice letters from you tonight on my return from the Bomb school with your dear brave sentiments which I have loved.

I very nearly got hurt today. After doing the morning's work I went & had a bit of lunch with some of the lads at a shop & then during the lunch interval I rode out to see the trenches where we usually throw bombs as it is an old defence line and they have recently filled some of it in and I feared they had filled in the part I wanted but it was alright. The Huns thought this is a suitable time for a midday hate and started plugging some shells about which rather worried old Saxon. Riding back he took great exception to a high sort of bridge built over the road. There was a very big R.E. wagon trotting towards me very fast, when old Saxon shied violently, crashed into the side of the wagon. I just had time to throw my left heel right up in the air when the crash came, tho' my boot got badly scratched all down, old Saxon got knocked right away and I fell on the broad of my back in the road. I am glad to say that old Saxon wasn't badly hurt and I could ride him home tho' he has got a good bit of skin off in parts. I haven't got a scratch or bump on me anywhere, but how it happened I don't know as I had seen the wagon some way off & noted how fast it was coming. It was most awfully lucky that my leg wasn't smashed to bits. However no damage done at all.

I have laughed over your muddle & *La Vie*. The paper, the Baron tells me, is not read by the best people. In fact it takes the same place in the French family that the *Winning Post* [does in England]. We buy it here, but it is essentially a man's paper and at times has a wonderfully well drawn centre page tho' decidedly French & at times out-frenching the French!

I wonder if you will get over the German submarine. I hear on the very best naval authority that the bag of these now amounts to 28. Official!

Must go to bed now dearie. Please pack marmalade with more stuffing, 3 pots have arrived broken.

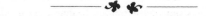

16th July 1915 – bivouac at Champ des Courses, Hesdigneul

I am sorry I didn't write you yesterday on your birthday, but I am sorry to say we had another accident at the school & two officers slightly wounded.

I always used to make up the bombs with my own school staff & while we did that we had no accident of any sort, bar mine, which of course had nothing to do with the manufacture of the bomb. Then I asked for an R.E. man to assist in the manufacture & they sent me two men & a Corporal who were supposed to be experts, which in a way they were, but lazy, & they stripped the whole of the fuse of its outside covering instead of only half.

As they were supposed experts I never bothered to examine their work, with the above mentioned result. We had thrown 70 bombs in the morning & 20 in the afternoon, fortunately they were bombs with the detonator in only, when it came the turn of a young officer & the bomb exploded in his hand wounding him slightly. We took him up the trench & then in a few mins I went back to continue. Old Sir Harry Waechter had come down & in order to restore confidence he threw the next – real guts in an old man & it was the first time that he had ever thrown one only he has taken great interest in the school for some time. His bomb went alright and then a fellow called Chaytor, who is taking over the school from me, threw the next & it too exploded in his hand. Of course then I stopped the throwing & we went back and I found that these R.E. men had fused the bombs so badly that in almost every instance it was possible for this to happen. The flash of a lighter, if the bomb is carelessly fused, passes at once to the detonator without burning the five seconds through the fuse as it should.

To light the bomb you pull out the safety pin, push down the top & turn it at the same time, when the match composition lights as soon as it impinges on the two brass striking points. The flash ignites the fuse which burns for five seconds & then explodes the fulminate of mercury which in turn detonates the ammonal and bursts the bomb with terrific force. Now with this makeshift arrangement the fuse exactly fits the lighter but is too large to fit the detonator, therefore it is necessary to strip the insulating tape off the cover, & then the rubber of the fuse is a trifle too small for the detonator. So long as the fuse (2⅛ inches long) is only stripped for a short way, say ¾ of an inch, it is alright because where it fits the lighter it is full up & the flash cannot escape; where however the whole fuse is stripped the flash comes out of the lighter, follows the outside of the fuse & at once explodes the detonator, with disastrous results. It is much easier & far less trouble to strip the whole fuse. Hence accidents!!

This possibility has been suspected before but never proved & these two accidents have shown it to me without a possibility of a shadow of doubt. I hope it will be taken up now throughout the whole army & all present bombs withdrawn & rendered safe in a way I have shown them. I thank God that the bombs weren't fully charged.

I hope Ralph comes through all right, but the R.E. have some real tough jobs to do out here, wiring between the lines at night & odd little games of that sort. I wrote to old Juckes before, which I hope he got. I am afraid he will take it very hardly.

I've had a piece of detonator in my forehead for three weeks now & was getting a bit tired of it. I was sure it was there the day it was done but the Dr said it wasn't but lately it got runny so yesterday I went to the F.A. [Field Ambulance] & got them to work on it and fortunately they got hold of it first try and out it came and now it is quite healed and doing fine. I'll enclose it for you to see. It's very small but better out than in, about half the size of the piece through my lip. I am now quite sound. There seems to be a great wave of optimism going round just now & everyone's tail is right up. The Huns are to propose peace in Aug. which will not be accepted & we are to have them set by Xmas!! I hope it is true. What a fine response the War Loan had. It will make Germany think yet!

My love to you dearie.

19th July 1915 – bivouac at Champ des Courses, Hesdigneul

I had a very interesting day yesterday as I went down and spent some time in the front-line trenches of the French. We went down to a place that overlooks the lines and is about 1500 yards away & got behind an old ruined house & watched the line through the telescope.

Then we had lunch & after lunch we walked across the open for about 100 yards to the communication trench which leads to the part of the ground we wanted to get to. On the way we found a shell hole and thought we should like to get the nose out but couldn't so we went & got down in the trench. However it was too much for the Boche & they gave us three what we call 'Whiz Bangs!' One of the damn things burst so close to my head that I had a violent headache for the rest of the day. This started a 'strafe' & there ensued quite an artillery duel for a bit. We meandered on down miles of twisty communication trenches & eventually arrived in their front line.

We were much chagrined by the French officer describing the day as 'très calme' as we all were thinking ourselves very brave, the 'all' being Steve and S.S.M. who were with me. Certainly there were a good many shells buzzing about & a French soldier put the nose of one into the S.S.M.'s hand that he had just dug out and it was far too hot to hold even then. Their line where I was ran through a mining village and the shells coming into the houses were certainly rather beastly. The church was an awful ruin, all the roof off, the altar hardly touched & the chairs all lying about anyhow.

On the way home we joined a crowd of soldiers and women in a village watching a French battery getting shelled. The battery certainly wasn't 300 yards away & there were all these women & children looking on just as the folk in the village would look on at the old roundabout that comes.

You know dear, I don't believe our country folk have the guts of these French. Do you think that if half the houses in Cowfold were without roofs and smashed to bits, that with, say, a doz. big shells coming in every day that the rest of the women would go on living in their homes? I doubt it very much & we English think there is no nation in the world to touch us. There is more calm bravery in these women here than in whole villages full of men at home. They go on day after day with no hope of having a shot back & are all the time week after week and month after month exposed to daily shelling & never seem to notice it at all.

Yesterday I left my horse at a farm, where only a month ago I left it in the same way. Then the folk were living in it and a damn nice girl there was there too, yesterday the house had no roof, was smashed to atoms, but their stock remained and they came back to milk the cows.

Tomorrow I have got the C.O.s, Adjutants & company commanders of two of the Battalions coming to my bomb school & I am giving a lecture on bombs & their management & the next day I have another lot coming. I'm very busy there now & have another class coming in again tomorrow night. I hope at the end of this week to hand the school over to Chaytor as I don't want to keep it on as I get so little time with the squadron.

Henry & I had our cake for tea tonight & we both liked it very much, in fact there was enough for us all to have some & a guest too. We've had quite good cakes from White House so far but they haven't rolled up with any great regularity, but I think that very often Buxton unpacks them while I am at the school.

I like the 'K' soldiers, in fact I think they are magnificent & their equipment is the best I ever saw.[52] They have impressed me beyond words.

I liked the photos of the kids very much. Best love old dear to you and all the Chugs.

21st July 1915 – bivouac at Champ des Courses, Hesdigneul

I am so glad to hear that all the birthday letters arrived to the tick of time. What news of old Campbell, where is he now and his army? Talking of Yeomanry we have got the Westmorland & Cumberland Yeo. next to us. They don't wear K.E.H. on their shoulder straps but their other two letters & are known as the 'Water Closet Hussars'. Henry's watch rolled up all right and I am very pleased with it indeed. I gave it to him at 7.30 and before 9 he had broken the glass in a fight with Pongo!

I had a reply from Mimi tonight in answer to mine. My suggestion that

[52] At the outbreak of the war men had volunteered in their thousands to join 'Kitchener's Army'. Many would later lose their lives on the Somme.

Dick should go to Sandhurst has not been taken up. The fact that he did a bit of turning has satisfied them. They forget that any hollow-chested imbecile can turn up a few shells, but that it is only given to a certain class to lead and that class is rapidly being exhausted. You might put this view to Nell & that almost the last words she said to me were that she would see that he did go![53]

My love to you my own darling.

22nd July 1915 – bivouac at Champ des Courses, Hesdigneul

I was just riding along Noeux[-les-Mines] street today to the watchmakers to get Henry a new glass, when who should I run into but old Gibbon. He was fearfully pleased to see me & wished to be remembered to you. Very anxious to know how the family had swelled since he last saw me!

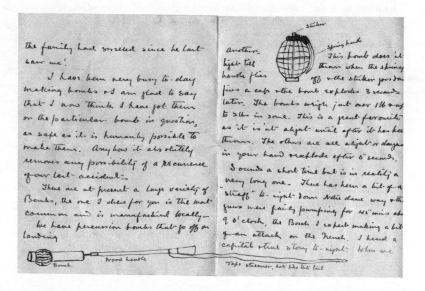

---

[53] Robert was worried that his younger brother, Dick, who was still at Eton, would dishonour the family name by not joining up.

There are at present a large variety of Bombs, the one I've drawn for you is the most common and is manufactured locally. We have percussion bombs that go off on landing.

Another: this bomb doesn't light till thrown when the spring handle flies off & the striker goes down, fires a cap & the bomb explodes 3 seconds later. The bombs weigh just over 1 lb & up to 2 lbs in some. This is a great favourite as it isn't alight until after it has been thrown. The others are all alight or dangerous in your hand & explode after 5 seconds. Sounds a short time but it is in reality a very long one.

There has been a bit of a 'strafe' tonight down Notre Dame [de Lorette] way & the guns were fairly pumping for 45 minutes, about nine o'clock, the Boche I expect making a bit of an attack on the French.

It looks very much as tho' the Huns are going to have Warsaw & if they do it will take [Tsar] Nicholas all his time to withdraw without a disaster.[54] I am hoping great things from Dardanelles in the near future but don't exactly know why.

I heard a capital & true story tonight. When we sank the Leipzig some officers & men were saved & they told an officer that up to a certain point the engineer officer in the stokehold had kept the men at work with his revolver & had shot several. Just as she was sinking they sent down from the bridge 'every man for himself' & before quitting the stokers seized the officer, opened one of the furnace doors & pitched him in. They mutinied on our ship after rescue & had to be kept under by a show of arms & when asked their grievance they said they wanted to kill one of the rescued officers as he had shot another stoker, who was a general favourite on board, because he came up for some water.

Another boat captured a German Colonel returning from foreign parts who was most truculent & eased his feelings by telling his captors that 'thank God his son was fighting, and killing twenty English men a day'. He was landed at Gibraltar & marched to the prisoners' camp & as they marched along the side of a wire fence enclosing it, a young boy ran to the wire shouting 'Hello! Father,' so they had all the active members of that family & the twenty per day was no more.

---

[54] Hermon's prediction about Warsaw came true two weeks later, on 5 August, when the German army entered the city, and Russia lost control of the Polish capital.

25th July 1915 – bivouac at Champ des Courses, Hesdigneul

Yesterday I handed over the Bomb School & am now able once more to devote myself to my own army. The General was down at the school & thanked me most awfully nicely for all I had done for it & left me saying 'I shall not forget it'. Now it's over dearie, I must confess that it has been a most awful strain. Not the fear of an accident to oneself but the responsibility of the whole thing. It even put me off sleeping properly at night & it takes a good deal to do that.

I left the school at 2.30 yesterday and rode home taking Barber with me. At about 6.15 one of my sergeants came back to camp telling me they had had a terrible accident. I went down at once & found that a sergeant in one of the squads, apparently behind the instructor's back, had taken a bomb out of the box, put a detonator into it, taken the safety pin out & struck it off with his hand before anyone could stop him. It killed him instantly, blowing off both arms and head, another man of the squad died as soon as he got to the Field Ambulance & a third last night & the rest of the squad, an officer and five other men including the instructor were very badly wounded indeed.

Fellows are such fools & will mess with things. The other day three of the gunner officers in the Div. took a large live German shell up to their bedroom & proceeded to pick it to bits (it was an unexploded one), it very naturally went off, killed one on the spot, another has since died, and the third is probably done for life. Four gunner men on the same day found another lying on the ground and began kicking it like a football. It got the whole lot!

The old Baron says the same as you do about the French women. They have war in their blood. There has been fighting in these parts since the days of the Black Prince & it's bred in them. I am starting tomorrow on my new bomb-throwing machine which I hope will be a greater success than the last. Old Bet's photos are really top-hole & are quite up to the standard of the Oxford man.

My love my darling.

28th July 1915 – bivouac at Champ des Courses, Hesdigneul

I have been very busy the last two days making 'Bob's Boche Buster' my original weapon 'Hermon's Hun Hustler' having [not] met with approval. The new one is a sort of catapult throwing bombs which I hope will be a great success & I am anxiously awaiting the arrival of the springs.

I am just off to be President of a court of inquiry on the accident at the Bomb School I told you about, and hope to be able to write you a better letter tonight when I have got yours to answer. I am sending old Bob a book of aeroplanes which should interest him & a few uniform pictures. It is a grand day today – bright sun and a strong fresh wind, such a sailing day, but alas no water and no boat.

When the war is over I am coming over here to buy some tools. I have been working these last two days in a carpenter's shop & am simply delighted with their saws. They have a grafter which is the best tool I ever saw.

My love to you all.

29th July 1915 – bivouac at Champ des Courses, Hesdigneul

At last a perfect orgy of letters, no less than 93, 4 & 5 turning up together today. I am now quite happy once more. I am on tenterhooks about the springs as from your letter if they don't send me what I asked for viz the pigeon trap spring, I shall be done as it is for quite a different kind of thing to my original idea which I told you, I think, had met with no approval. I want these springs to pull out & the one in the first idea was a press-in spring.

I have been prospecting for water all afternoon & found plenty which I hope will be a help. The files arrived yesterday, many thanks.

30th July 1915 – bivouac at Champ des Courses, Hesdigneul

I have been digging all day making a dam across a creek so that we can water our horses in the camp without having to go at least a mile to a river which will be a very great help.

I sent old Betsy a little ring tonight which the French soldiers amuse themselves in making in the trenches out of a portion of the nose of one of the German shells. The Germans have been firing shells made in July 1915 which failed to explode on landing which causes much joy. I believe now that the percentage of their unexploded shells has risen to 32. Asquith's speech in yesterday's papers looks like business & I hope they get things going soon. We ought to have a crack at them soon before the weather gets bad again.

I want you to make me a mosquito net. If it is 6 feet long that is enough with a wide skirt. The mosquitoes have kept me awake at night & are very bad tho' they don't seem to bite much.

Today while I was waiting for breakfast I heard a funny little noise & looking up there was a mummy weasel with two little ones just running through the sort of shelter we have rigged up. She didn't seem to notice me & took them into a bush & after a few mins she left them & came back & ran off towards the kitchen. The two little ones played about & presently she came back with two more & then the whole party went off together. They were so awfully jolly. I must go to bed now dearie as I was up early today for a wonder.

1st August 1915 – bivouac at Champ des Courses, Hesdigneul

I know you don't approve of *La Vie* but the enclosed I think is rather nice, especially as the French army are being given leave for four days for the express purpose of seeing that there shall be no lack of recruits in the year 1935.

I am sure you are glad to be back old dear & I wish I was too. I am very tired of this life apart. I too have one thing that is missing oh so badly

at times & I long to have a glimpse – only a long look for preference. The sleep has come back alright now dearie. This is quite true.

My love to you all my darling,

Ever your Robert.

CHAPTER FOUR

DIVISIONAL HORSE SHOW

D uring August 1915 the adverse news from both the Eastern Front and the Gallipoli Peninsula continued to be of considerable concern to the Allies. The Russian army was retreating in disarray from Poland and Austria, and the Allied attacks on Suvla Bay in Gallipoli on the 15th and 21st resulted in defeat. France was experiencing a period of relative calm as there had not been a major attack since Aubers Ridge; however, Kitchener visited the First Army Head-quarters in France on 18 August and told General Sir Douglas Haig that Britain and France must assist the Russians by launching an attack against the Germans on the Western Front in order to draw their troops from the East.

The attack was planned for late September at Loos, a mining area close to the town of Lens. August was therefore a period of preparation and waiting and 'C' Squadron were employed digging trenches, manning the observation posts on the Clarence River crossings, and taking part in the Divisional Sports held at Allouagne.

2nd August 1915 – camp at Bois des Dames

I have been very busy these last two days arranging a new camp & have had little or no time to write. Our new camp will be about a couple of miles away. It is right in the middle of a wood & we have been very busy indeed making waterworks. It is a lovely place & the kids would simply love it. The wood is full of birds and the old woodpecker's note can be heard all day.

The springs will do fine; they rolled up alright yesterday but the Boche Buster has been in abeyance these last few days as I have had other things to do.

I was awfully amused over poor old Nancy's brother-in-law, but I do think it is a fairly good idea to give him leave for the duration of the war.

It is all very well, he may be alright *but* you cannot get over the fact that his father is Krupps & he might correspond with him. Even if he only wrote the most innocent things he might mention things better left unsaid. We don't want alien enemies fighting for us & even with the very best of intentions on their part it is likely to instil mistrust in the minds of others. I don't like your damn Germans, & the less they are connected with the army the better. If he is fighting at all, he has German blood in his veins, he ought to my mind to be on the other side.

I am afraid they won't get much sympathy for him out here, not because he mayn't be all that he should be but when you find a senior N.C.O. crucified & nailed to a door, & a British officer bound and strangled with his own muffler it doesn't make anyone very keen about folk with genuine German names! However I have no doubt that really he is alright, but I think for the sake of his health a sea voyage lasting 18 months would just put him on his legs again. Well dearie I must stop now and go and pull down the mess shelter.

5th August 1915 – camp at Bois des Dames

I am glad you liked the *La Vie* cutting. I thought it was very good. You know though some of the pictures are decidedly risky & some of the subjects too. They are so beautifully drawn that half the moderate part is taken away. It is very high temperature & it is extraordinary how this nation's thoughts travel in that direction. We always chaff our dear old Baron about it & tell him it is the National Sport!

We are 'resting' now, the infantry having been in the trenches for over three months need a rest & are out for a spell. No shells or horribilities for them for a bit which I am sure that they will appreciate.

My love to you all my darling.

8th August 1915 – camp at Bois des Dames

Alas no letter again today, it is a damned nuisance how badly the posts have been working lately, but no doubt I shall get two tomorrow. You might order me another pair of heavy shooting boots from Moykopf,[55] exactly the same as the last he made me with iron toes & heels. Then I want you to get for me & send out the new fly bait that I have read about in the *Daily Mail*. The stuff you mix & let stand for 24 hours before it becomes attractive to the fly & which has been proved so successful by the 'Fly Farm' somewhere north of London. The flies are fearfully bad now and one must do something to prevent them getting at one's food as far as possible.

Tomorrow we have a jumping competition, having been asked by the 7th R.A. Brigade to compete with them. I am going to ride your old horse, he is a rotten jumper I know, but it is a little hard for risking Saxon. We've had it rather cloudy & damp this last week but it blew hard last night & has cleared things up a good bit.

It is a glorious evening tonight and after tea I expect we shall go for a bit of a walk & look for some more water, not that we want it but it is always a good thing to know where it is.

Give my love to the Chugs.

9th August 1915 – camp at Bois des Dames

I got the two expected letters alright today & was delighted that yesterday's hadn't gone astray with its nice little prayer which I like awfully dearie mine & will take it into use right away.

I long to come and see you dearie something awful sometimes that I almost give way & try & get leave & I should love to see the dear little Chugs so much, but I am so frightened that there might be a 'strafe' while I was away & I couldn't let the squadron go into action without me – it would be awful & I would worry like anything all the time I was away.

---

[55] Charles Moykopf & Co., a well-known shoemaker in Piccadilly.

I think the men, too, would hate my going unless there was a special need. I know they didn't like my bombing very much & being away as much as I was. They are so splendid & so awfully soldierly & well-behaved. I have only had to punish two men since I have been out, one for saucing a sergeant & the other for a very minor breach of squadron orders. They are all so willing & ready to do anything & it was rather nice the other night when I read in a letter of one of the men who had come in a draft that 'it is so nice in this squadron, there is no grousing which is wonderful for us'.

I can't tell you about the shells, but I think they are a fair sample all along the line. Germany certainly is on top now but it is temporary only. This huge army of theirs in Russia will not be able to fight on this side this year I don't think & when winter comes the Russians will beat them I am sure. I am certain this time next year should see the closing stages.

Best love my own Lassie & I hope you are not feeling too worried. I was so glad that little Bet liked her ring. I am just going to say your new little prayer dearie.

11 p.m. 9th Aug.

11th August 1915 – camp at Bois des Dames

Today I was asked to judge at the 1st Div. Horse Show & really it was one of the most top-hole shows you ever saw. The turnout of the guns & teams better than I ever saw before & we had a rare old time judging. We were hard at it, except for half an hour for lunch when old Haking[56] motored me to his château & fed me, from 10.30 to 6 p.m. It really was the greatest fun & the jumping, especially the men's, was excellent. I enclose you the programme which is literally true as I went with old Harry Rawlinson[57] to have some tea & we stood & watched a Taube being shelled like anything just over our heads. Every general you can think of rolled up. Douglas Haig, Haking, Harry Rawlinson, two or three French generals & several local ladies, one of whom presented the prizes!! and all within range of the German guns. It seemed incredible that there could be a war on at all. A

---

[56] General Sir Richard Haking.
[57] General Sir Henry Rawlinson.

top-hole band played all afternoon & it was ripping. A glorious day & the show was run most awfully well by Campbell who is Div. Cav. to 1st Div. (Northumberland Yeo). I wish you could have been there, you would have loved it.

I also enclose you one of your naked lady pictures just to show you that the really beautiful drawing takes away what, if portrayed by an Englishman, would probably be coarse & offensive. I found two nice letters from you my darling when I got in tonight 107 & 8. I could very soon find Addie something that would make her hair curl, but I couldn't send them to her! But I like this one I enclose very much tho' of course it is mild to some, one finds.

Yes, I saw the announcement of Cooper's death in *The Times*, but it really was for the best, but poor boy, he suffered terribly I am afraid.

14th August 1915, 9.30 a.m. – camp at Bois des Dames

I am not quite the thing this morning owing to an over-indulgence in honey in the honeycomb, of which I am as you know, particularly fond, but it is fatal.

I got your letter last night alright & was very pleased with it (110). It seems a high number doesn't it, I wonder how many more hundreds it will run into before the show is over. I think by the time it has reached 450, we should be at the end – if not actually at home. However, we shall see & I shouldn't wonder if it were to collapse suddenly still but it is unlikely.

Our diplomacy in the Balkans seems to be looking up a bit & I hope it will.

My love to little Bet & thanks for her tin of Bullseyes.

16th August 1915 – camp at Bois des Dames

I have two nice letters to answer tonight, 112 & 113. I think it is splendid so many men in the village [Cowfold] being out & under training. I wish

EWH as a young man; possibly an engagement photograph.

EWH aged thirteen (*front row, second left*), Impey's House, Eton, 1892.
His cousin Victor Hermon (Ethel's brother) is third row, second left.

'The Cliffe', Ethel's home in Cheshire.

Ethel aged sixteen riding side-saddle.

Ethel (*standing, right*) with her sister Vio and her brothers Vincent and Victor (*seated*).
Vincent was killed motor racing at Brooklands in 1907.

EWH and Ethel in South Africa circa 1905, when EWH was serving
with the 7th Queen's Own Hussars.

EWH, Ethel and a cousin (*right*) in South Africa, circa 1905,
with their staff.

EWH and Ethel with her sister-in-law May Hermon (Victor's wife) and their children at Inverlodden, Wargrave on Thames, 1911. *Left to right:* May, EWH, Ethel; the children: Betty, their cousin John, Bob and Mary.

Ethel with Meg at Inverlodden in 1911, taken on the same day.

EWH, with the 'Chugs' and two of the family dogs, on home leave at Brook Hill, 1915. *Left to right*: Mary, Bob, Meg and Betty.

EWH on home leave cutting the children's hair at Brook Hill.

Ethel and the 'Chugs' on the steps at Brook Hill, 1915, taken by EWH. *Left to right:* Mary, Bob, Meg and Betty.

Meg with two of the family dogs on the same occasion, 1915.

Lieutenant Colonel Edward William ('Robert') Hermon, posthumously awarded the D.S.O.

'Buckin' – Private, later Lance Corporal, Gordon Offord Buxton, EWH's 'soldier servant' and former manservant.

to goodness there were more villages like it. We shall soon want everyone either to repel an attack or make one. One side or the other must make some effort before winter sets in. I only hope that there will be a big push at the Dardanelles soon.

I am awfully glad to hear dearie, that you are not feeling too bad, of course one can't expect you to be absolutely well but it is a comfort to know that you are not feeling things more than usual.

My dear old girl I really am very distressed about Dick, that he doesn't seem to want to take a hand in this show, couldn't you get hold of him and read this to him? Ask him if in a year's time he wants to find that folk won't speak to him. If he won't go of his own free will he must be made to go. Is he doing anything these holidays to fit himself for the job? He is big and strong & he should be getting ready now. It worries me fearfully at times, can't you tackle him on the family honour, surely he will uphold it? We can't have folk pointing him out as the only boy in the county who didn't want to go!

Please thank Mairky for her nice letter, & ask what it feels like 'to become a little garden' which she informs me she has grown into.

Best love to you all dearie.

18th August 1915 – camp at Bois des Dames

D.H. came into the ring [at the Horse Show] the other day & looked hard at me as tho' he ought to know me & I know that he knew it, but there it ended.[58]

I am sorry to hear about the fly stuff as the *Daily Mail* has cracked it up so. The mosquito net has come & is simply grand but there are now no mosquitoes. Where we were before one was kept awake ages with the damned things but here they are very few but it is a good thing to have as it keeps the flies off in the morning and in the afternoon it is top-hole as it is quite impossible to have 40 winks without it.

To revert to the leave question one cannot apply for leave unless three

---

[58] Hermon had known Douglas Haig in South Africa during the Boer War and was annoyed that he pretended not to know him now he was a general.

months have elapsed since last leave, therefore if I come now I couldn't come again before Xmas & I should like best to come when Benjamin has arrived or after you are about again but I have an idea that either the Boche will attack us or we them before very long & I couldn't leave the squadron with any chance of either happening while I was away.

I don't believe Germany is bankrupt yet & besides the internal resources are so great & her imports so few that I doubt if it matters. From the papers things don't look so well with Russia today but the Balkans look better & Romania seems to have had enough of Germany's bullying ways.

We are hoping to have a real good scrap soon but I know nothing really but it is almost as weary waiting here as it was at Watford. The future was ever a sealed book & perhaps it is as well, but I wish sometimes we were doing a bit more to hustle the Hun.

22nd August 1915 – camp at Bois des Dames

I have now got to make a very reluctant confession. Yesterday we had a jumping competition, the Signal Coy running all their own sports for the selection of their candidates for the Div. Sports. I ran Saxon & your old horse & the Judges were ill-advised enough to place your old wretch first & Saxon wasn't noticed. Of course it was all wrong but I had to abide by the judges' decision. I have entered them both for the Div. Sports & when I have schooled old Saxon a bit more I think he will win.

The lads are all making such jokes & what-not that I haven't got half a chance to write you anything decent. I shall be awfully busy this week I am afraid but will try & write. I have spent all day making a most lovely heave gate for the jumping at the Sports & a triple bar but the latter looks horribly high at present.

24th August 1915 – camp at Bois des Dames

I have got two simply topping letters to answer tonight, 120 & 121.

Darling mine, I agree with you that a bird in the bush is the tops & so I will come & see you as soon as I conveniently can. Of course all this is dependent on what the Boche does to us or we to him. I don't believe tho' that you would *really* know if I wasn't enjoying myself, because you never do know when I am pulling your leg, but joking apart I shouldn't of course come if there was any likelihood of anything doing. If I come now, as you say, I could come again when you were up and about again which would be best as we could then do something together & shouldn't have the old gamp fussing about, but you mustn't expect me till you see me.

My dear old girl I'm afraid you will be disappointed but I have never for one moment asked or tried for a staff job – but you have set me thinking & I know that I could get one if I was really to set about it. My trouble is at present that I am away down on the extreme right of the line & I haven't a single friend of the old days anywhere near here who I ever see. I can't quite make up my mind if I should be right in asking for a job. If it were offered I should take it if it was a worthy one, but I have such an exceptionally good lot, both of officers & men and they so absolutely trust one & look up to one to do the right thing that I don't feel that I ought to try & work a job. I see fellows getting jobs as Lieutenant Colonels on Staffs who I know I could compete with & beat & do better work. To tell you the truth there is nothing in the Div. Cav. work that can't be done by a man, and is being done & well done, who has had no military experience. I've a good mind to write to Allenby & put the case to him in a way & see if there is anything going that I could do but I don't know whether I should be doing right by the squadron.

I should hate to feel that they thought I had carted them, but really anyone could have done what I have done since we came out. Darling Lassie, I know that I could do more for the country and be better employed elsewhere if I could get it but so far as I can see there is no chance at all of getting on without scheming and I hate that – simply because I should hate these boys to feel that I had left them.

What I should like is G.S.O.2 of a Division or Brigade Major of a regular Cav. Brigade. I could do either well, but I don't want to get on the Q side of the staff except that it would be a start & would lead to something in time perhaps but one never knows.

Lass dear I must stop now. Love to you all & many thanks to old Bet for her nice long letter. 11:15 p.m.

27th August 1915 – camp at Bois des Dames

I meant to write to you early this morning but got prevented as I got a message from Pongo, who is away on a job with his troop, that his kiddie had not been a success & I tried to get him off on leave but I cannot get him away before Sunday. I am so sorry for them as he had set such store by the kid.

It is awfully sad about poor [Graham-]Taylor, but that girl will be able to do things which will employ her thoughts & help a bit. There are, I am afraid, a great many similar cases & there is no doubt the soldier shouldn't be married during a war, tho' without it the nation would melt away. However you will soon be able to give your quota to lessening that 298,000 shortage last quarter.

I am going to let Barber come home on Monday Sept 6th & all being well will come myself so as to get home on Tuesday morning Sept 14th. I believe the leave train arrives in town about 5 a.m. & would come by the next one from Victoria. Sounds odd talking about a regularly organized leave service when the greatest war on record is going on but when I tell you that on Wed. we had our Div. Sports & that I won General Barter's Silver Cup for Officers' Jumping on *your old horse* before a crowd of 10,000 people of both sexes & nationalities & that two brass bands played throughout the entire afternoon, & that yesterday I played in an ordinary station game of polo, you will cease to wonder at anything.

I was greatly amused at your 'double' story!! That reminds me of another story. 'A man wounded at Dardanelles was in hospital & said to the Nurse "I want to——" (using a man's term). She said "You mustn't say that, say No. 1 or No. 2." The next day the Dr going round the ward found a man under his bed clothes simply shaking with laughter & he pulled them down & asked him what it was all about & he said "The man in the next bed wants to——most awfully badly but he's forgotten the number; I know it, but I won't tell him!!'"

I am so sorry that it wasn't me in your dream but perhaps it will be shortly now. My dear little Meggie, tell her it wasn't at all intentional, far from it, & give her my Steward's rosette as a 'quid pro quo'.

Now for the sports. I enclose you a programme with what we did marked on it. I had a great deal to do with it & therefore my natural modesty forbids that I should acclaim it to be anything except what it was, but everyone who was there says it was top-hole. There must have been between eight & ten thousand folk looking on. Douglas Haig came & I went & spoke to him & I saw him at the polo yesterday & talked to him again & he was quite pleasant. I wasn't going to have him ignoring me any longer so I went & shook hands with him when he came into the ring & all is well! All the boys from all round were there.

Will you send me a bottle of aspirins as I have used most of mine on other folk. Can you arrange for us to have some china tea sent out to us. There are six of us & we drink tea three times a day. You will know best how much to send.

28th August 1915 – camp at Bois des Dames

Many thanks for your 126. Chuckle on! Your vulgar old horse is quite coming round under my tuition. I am sorry that old Bob has wanted a letter but I have had much too much to do to write to any of them lately. I loved their photos & the one of Maddy & the dogs is topping.

Poor Pongo's kid came tail first so he tells me & there were all sorts of complications besides. She was such a poor frail little thing, quite young & didn't look as if she ever ought to have had a kid.

Short letter tonight dearie as I have a long day before me tomorrow in reconnoitring the front line. Best love.

30th August 1915 – camp at Bois des Dames

I got your two letters 127 & 128 last night when I got back from a trot round our front. We lunched off sandwiches & cake outside an 'estaminet' where an old woman made us some coffee & within 100 yards of her door we had to creep under a wall & go along the back of it because one was sniped at there. There was this old woman carrying on her little business all alone, right up practically in the front line.

Really the courage of these folk passes all belief. The top storey of the house had a shell hole through it & the ceiling of the room we were in was all smashed to bits with shell splinters, where they had come through the windows from a shell bursting in the road outside.

Lassie mine, I have taken heart & written to G.H.H.A.[59] this morning & am now off to post it. The only thing is tho' that he is not in very high favour just at present, I am afraid, so far as I hear, but I may be mistaken.

Henry Feilding is going as A.D.C. to old Horne[60] who I expect you remember at Aldershot. I am rather glad as now they can't say that it was I who went first. I must stop now old dear, as I must go out & it is still early. (11.30 a.m.)

3rd September 1915 – camp at Bois des Dames

They have found some jobs for the squadron to do which will last at least a fortnight so you will have to possess your soul in patience for a bit longer old dear.

Today I went down in a motor to visit our front line again, it seemed so funny motoring down there quite close to the old Boche in perfect comfort

[59] General Allenby.
[60] Henry Feilding had been appointed ADC to the GOC of 2 Division, General Sir Henry Horne, and later served with the Coldstream Guards. He wrote to Major Hermon saying he was travelling to Marseilles via Paris to the 'sunny south' (Egypt). He was killed in action in 1917.

with our own guns shooting over us as we went along. The Boche was very quiet again today & we were doing all the shooting, which was pleasant.

This afternoon I spent making a brick fireplace in our mess tent & am now sitting in front of a most glorious fire which is simply topping. It is a screaming success & has cheered us immensely after two days & nights of continuous wet & bitter cold. I wish I could take it into my tent with me. I am going to move my camp again now which is a bore, but we shall go inside for a bit I think. Get the men in barns or somewhere & ourselves into a very nice house indeed if we get the one we are after.

Again I had hoped to write you a better letter but what little I would like to tell you touches the military side of one's life and I cannot put it on paper. Will you post me that new mackintosh of mine please. The summer seems to have quite broken up at present tho' I still hope for another six weeks' fine weather.

Best love old dear.

4th September 1915 – camp at Bois des Dames

This camp is most unpleasant of an afternoon. We are just behind the rifle range & a good many ricochets come along here & rather a nasty whistley one came then. I don't know where the Guards Div. are to be but they are a long way off at present. Many thanks for the aspirins.

You mustn't be too excited old girl over me & my affairs, I am not sure myself whether I regret writing [to General Allenby]. Not much harm can come of it. I would rather be taken on the Division here on merit alone if I possibly could, only now the bombing is off I see them much less frequently. I am going to lunch with them tomorrow & then on to arrange a bombing competition for the Division.

Thank old Bet for her nice letter.

5th September 1915 – camp at Bois des Dames

The enclosed from Allenby tonight. Very nice & kind, but as he says not a very good job. As it happens since writing him I have had work galore thrust upon me & for three weeks at least I couldn't in common fairness leave this Div. I have written to him tonight telling him that I couldn't leave the Division now without letting them down & as they have been so kind I feel I shouldn't be playing the game with them.

There it stands, & I have been offered a job & refused it. Whether another will roll up or not remains to be seen, but right or wrong I don't feel I have any right to leave the Div. just at present. I have had a very long day today dearie, & must stop. I will try & write tomorrow but you mustn't expect too much as my present job will keep me very busy.

A cartoon sent to Ethel by EWH as they were expecting their fifth child.

CHAPTER FIVE

THE BATTLE OF LOOS

Early in September 1915 an artillery duel took place between the Germans and the Allies in the Arras area lasting thirteen days. In the meantime the Allies prepared for an offensive at the end of the month with the intention of diverting German troops from the East where the Russians were facing the possibility of defeat. The French army were to attack at Champagne and the British at Loos.

Sir John French had serious misgivings about the choice of Loos for a major assault as it was a heavily populated mining district, obstructed by slag heaps and mine shafts. However, Kitchener ordered him to attack in support of French troops, and a concentrated artillery barrage began several days before the attack. On the 25th the battle commenced with the British army using chlorine gas for the first time, in retaliation for the German use of gas at Ypres in April. One hundred and fifty tons were released in no man's land from 5,243 cylinders, but as Robert here observes, some of it blew back across the British lines, so its effectiveness, although initially allowing the British troops to advance more than 4,000 yards, was debatable.

For 'C' Squadron it was a time of intense preparation for the attack planned for the end of the month. They were in demand for duties such as traffic control, trench construction and as guides for the transport of gas cylinders to the front line. The latter occupation was carried out with the utmost secrecy – Robert refers only to a special 'job' when writing to his wife. Fortunately she would have had no inkling of the real nature of his mission.

8th September 1915 – camp at Bois des Dames

Sorry I have not written you much these last two days but I have been very busy indeed marking out traffic routes & controlling it. I got old Steve to write you a postcard last night for me asking for refills for my lamp which I am using a good bit now as I have a lot of night work to do.

I did so enjoy the Chugs' letters, will you please thank Bet & Bob for their nice long ones & also dear little Meggie for her very touching post-card. Our family party has been rather broken up as Pong hasn't come back from leave yet & I cannot understand why. He should have been back on Monday and he hasn't returned nor have I had any word of any sort. I expect his wife is very bad & he has managed to get leave from the W.O. I am afraid we shall never be quite the same happy family again & every-thing has been so very jolly so far.

Benjamin is to be called 'Charles' if he is Benjamin. If he isn't Benjamin well then he isn't.

Best love old darling.

From 10th to 18th September, 'C' Squadron was employed digging a communi-cation trench from Mazingarbe to the front line, known as 'London Road', in preparation for the Loos attack. This work involved cutting a trench nearly 2,000 yards long through solid chalk, sometimes under enemy fire.

❧ ❧

10th September 1915 – Haillicourt

We started digging today. Left here at 7 a.m. & began digging at nine, some 9 miles away in a bit of ground close up to the trenches but not actu-ally in view.

I wish I could tell you more but I am afraid it is impossible. Yes, Buxton is going to have a dash home soon & may start on Monday but I am not quite sure yet. We didn't move on or go to the place I said a few days ago but we left our lovely camp last night. We were all very sad at leaving. We are now in a four-roomed empty cottage. The weather has been grand lately.

My old oilskin was made by the Beacon Oilskin Co. & their Advt is in the *Yachting Monthly*, which by the way I should like occasionally.

I enclose you Allenby's letter in answer to my second refusing the job but he seems to be alright. I think things are looking up here a bit as I am getting to know the brigs a bit more & old Harry Rawlinson seems to have taken a bit of a fancy to the squadron & was up at our last camp & tonight I have been over to dine with him & had a very pleasant evening indeed.

Pongo hasn't returned; his wife was so bad that his remaining was the only hope & it seems to have done the trick.

11th September 1915 – Haillicourt

You would have been rather amused today, after I had got back from the trenches today old Foote came riding round here and looked rather glum & asked me if I had got a mysterious note, & when I said no, he told me that a wire had come asking for me to go to 2nd Army as Town Major of Hazebrouck, the copy of which came later & which I enclose. Old Barter promptly said No! as you see, which got me out of refusing & which I can't help thinking will do me good, as one sometimes doesn't know the value of an article until some other bloke wants it, & it will let old Barter realize that there are others who would be glad of one's services.

We had another day's digging again today and are for it I expect for some days to come. I am sending Buxton home tomorrow & he will tell you all about me & that I am fit & well. He has been in a much better temper lately as one of the other servants has been doing the cooking lately & he has more leisure.

I got a topping good letter from you old dear when I got in tonight (141). The Turk has always been one of the very best of fighters behind entrenchments but no good in the open, & with German instructors to help in the planning & digging he no doubt has some real good ones to fight in.

Allenby's letter was very nice wasn't it. I shall try & go & see him but it is very hard to get up that far & I don't know if I could arrange it. However it is well worth thinking about.

The men have been doing very well digging & I think surprised folk a bit by the amount they did as the powers that be hadn't seen anything like it in this Div. before, & they were very pleased.

I wish I was in Buxton's shoes but it is quite impossible just now as I have so much doing. I expect Buxton will tell you all the news dearie & buck like steam. However believe about $^1/_8$ of what he tells you.

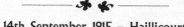

14th September 1915 – Haillicourt

It is only 8 p.m. now & I have a little time to write to you tonight at last. So much for that, 'tempus fugit' & it is now 9.45!

I wish you could have had your Ma's chauffeur but as you say those sort of men should be making munitions of war. The colossal expenditure of ammunition if there is a big fight nowadays wants some keeping pace with. I see the Crown Prince got rid of half a million shells in two days.

I had a boy in here tonight who was only 16 & he took his part in the attack at Festubert. It's a pity Dick doesn't do something. I wrote to the old Govnr very strongly a short time ago but he has never referred to it.

I am glad your servants are doing you alright now & that you are more or less fixed up for the event.[61] I wish I could be with you dearie.

One of my men was home on leave when the Zeps came[62] & he heard the shooting & quite forgot he was at home & never took any notice of it at all till his wife rushed into the room frightfully excited.

I haven't had my clothes off for two days & as I am full of chalk I have got a drop of hot water tonight I must stop & have a wash.

15th September 1915 – Haillicourt

Just a few lines tonight as I am going to bed; got worked rather to a stand-still today so I am taking a day off tomorrow. We have been digging for six days now, riding out 9 miles, marching two more & then digging in pure chalk for 4 hours & back home again. It is rather a stiff day's work. We have now completed 800 yards of this trench but still have another 1500 to finish. Trench 3 feet wide & 6 feet deep. It is a pretty big

[61] Their fifth child was due in November.
[62] German Zeppelins had again attacked London on 7 and 8 September, causing a huge fire in the City of London and damage in Holborn and Bloomsbury. Anti-aircraft barrages and searchlights were subsequently deployed around the capital.

undertaking. Many thanks for the Oilux. I expect it will turn up tomorrow alright.

I am glad the Chugs enjoyed their day at Leonardslee[63] but it was a pity you couldn't get someone to explain more to them.

Hope Buckin is enjoying his leave. Love to you all.

16th September 1915 – Haillicourt

I am sending a little ring for Meggie, which Sergeant Kock[64] brought me in tonight 'for my little daughter'. Will you get either Betty or Mary to write and thank him, his No. is 706 Sergt Kock, & the rest of the address you know, but I should like one kid to write to him as it was very kind to think of it.

I have got a most poisonous bilious attack, I think from digging in the chalk & bending down or too much toffee. I don't know which. I was lunching at a farm the other day & a little girl to whom I had given half a franc produced some lovely honey in the comb & I simply had to eat it.

I am glad you are pleased with your room & I hope it won't be long now before I see it again but one never knows from day to day what may turn up. I am glad you have got the sofa, & perhaps with a fire I might be induced to stop now & watch you dress.

Old Pongo came back yesterday & his Mrs is mending well. We are all in the best of health & spirits except for my temporary tummy derangement which I hope will be alright by the morning.

My love to you all my darling.

---

[63] The woodland garden in West Sussex laid out by Sir Leonard Loder in 1889, renowned for its rhododendrons and azaleas, and wild wallabies that were introduced to the park over a hundred years ago.

[64] Sergeant Kock was a South African NCO in K.E.H. of Boer descent.

17th September 1915, 9.30 a.m. – Haillicourt

I am anxiously looking forward to getting your letter today & hearing what Buckin has to tell you. Very busy these times & two nights out of bed to come tomorrow & the next day. Alas it is now nearly 8 p.m. & I haven't got your letter, so I must wait – they will be a pleasant welcome when I get back on Sunday morning as I am off on my special job that I told you about some time ago & shall not be back until the very early hours of the following morning. There is nothing more to tell you dearie mine, except that I am quite fit again & have been out all afternoon on the pony. [Here he has torn off the last inch of the page.]

I shall not be able to write you at all tomorrow dearie I am afraid & so you will have to possess your little soul in patience & I will try & write you a decent letter on Sunday afternoon. Did I tell you I was talking to a boy in a horse battery the other day & I asked him who commanded his battery & he told me & then he said Hermon-Hodge & I said where is he & he said inside the house here & I went in and found Guy.[65] He seemed very hearty & well.

My love to you dearie.

17th September 1915 – Haillicourt [This letter accompanied a parcel containing a fur coat, sent from London.]

My darling,

I send you this little present with all my love to you & Benjamin just to keep you warm when you are able to get up & about again, because it will be cold. I thought I would send it now & then you could wear it if it was cold & both of you could benefit by it. With my very best, & all my love to you my own darling,

Ever your Robert.

---

[65] Guy Hermon-Hodge, his cousin, son of Baron Wyfold, later Lord Wyfold.

On the nights of 18 and 19 September, 'C' Squadron troops were employed as guides to ensure the safe conduct of gas cylinders from the detraining point at Verguin to the unloading point behind the front-line trenches at Maroc, ready for the impending attack on Loos. It was recorded in the War Diary that '36 waggons passed through and unloaded without accident or casualty'. Enormous care was taken to maintain the secrecy of this transport of gas cylinders. The boxes were marked 'bacon' and the wagon wheels muffled with old motor tyres. All metalwork on the harness was wrapped in rags to cloak any sound that might alert the enemy to their presence.

20th September 1915 – Haillicourt

I am afraid that there has been a great hiatus since my last letter but I have been working day & night lately.

Buxton arrived back alright today & seems to have enjoyed himself no end. Didn't you think he was looking awfully well? I am very glad he didn't grouse, but he has been very much better lately since he gave up cooking for a bit. Where Buxton got the fact that I thought it would be over by Xmas I don't know, because I cannot see how it can be. We shall be very lucky to get the next birthday party together but I do think that there is a chance. I think that winter will make the old Huns think a bit in N. Poland. I don't think they can stand it & I shouldn't be at all surprised to see them come tumbling home about May very much faster than when they went out.

Very many thanks for sending the Oilux mackintosh which arrived quite safely.

We had an exciting morning yesterday tho' I didn't see it, but one of our blokes here got two aeroplanes in the morning. The two, the pilot & observer, did awfully well & tho' several times wounded, succeeded in downing two Boche planes both falling with a crash to the ground & tho' wounded ours got back safely.

I am so sorry to hear of Charles Godman. I do hope he isn't very bad. Heaps of people have the most wonderful recoveries after being hit in the head. I saw a French officer yesterday who had had a bullet right through his head behind the eyes. He said he felt the vibration of the guns a bit now.

Don't say anything to Pa about Dick if you can help it as it might lead to a row & one doesn't want that. As you say it would be a sad day for us if Bobbo was his age & wasn't straining every nerve to go. Tell old Nell that I hear on the most reliable authority that since she wrote to me the Blarney stone has shrunk to half its size, it had such a smacking kiss.

Well we had our two nights, last night & the night before, at our special job & everything worked like clockwork. We were very lucky as we got through without any kind of mishap & no one hurt. As we were walking up in the dark the old Boche dropped a good big shell into a house about 10 yards in front of Mac's troop but hurt no one & they had several shrapnel [shells] over us but they were bursting them about 200 yds further on & so we got our job done without any bother at all & the next night there was hardly any shooting & we got finished in perfect peace.

I got a draft of fine men today, such splendid men but they are so big that I don't know how I shall mount them. Certainly not on the runts of ponies they sent me as remounts today. I am very fit & well again now dearie. Best love to you old Lassie. Love to the kids & thanks to Bob & Mary for their letters.

21st September 1915 – Haillicourt

We finished our digging today & the enclosed came from old Barter tonight,[66] which was very nice & has given great satisfaction. Even tho' I say it; it was well merited.

Today we were digging where, tho' hidden by a small rise from the German trenches exactly opposite, we could nevertheless see their line stretching away on our left. There was at the time a very heavy bombardment going on and it was one of the most wonderful sights I ever saw to see the huge shells bursting all along the line. It was a very noisy business

---

[66] General Barter, the GOC, congratulated them on 'the excellent way in which the entrenching work called for from your squadron has been carried out. The C.R.E. reports upon the work & methods as exceptionally good – please inform all ranks.'

as we were in front of all our guns right in between the two. I should love to be able to tell you more about it but of course I can't. My letters will be very sketchy for a bit now & I doubt my ability even to send service postcards. Love to you all.

The bombardment was the prelude to the Battle of Loos when the British artillery shelled the German lines for several days to cut through the wire defences and damage their trenches before the assault, which Robert knew was imminent.

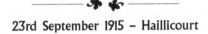

23rd September 1915 – Haillicourt

I am most awfully sorry to hear about poor old Betsy, it is a pity, tho' if it is ordinary human ringworm perhaps it will be alright. I hope she won't have to have all her hair cut off. Iodine is the only thing that will really settle it so far as horses are concerned but I expect it would be a little too strenuous for her.

After all I got dragged down to do another day's digging yesterday. The Huns however started to shell with 9-inch shells the very 50 yards of ground that I wanted to dig. I got down about 9 a.m. & wandered out onto the ground to see what I had got to do & get the tasks worked out when the first shell arrived & after about half a doz., they were rude enough to increase their range a bit & they put one so close to me that until the dust had cleared away & one found oneself on one's feet it was very difficult to realize that one had escaped untouched. I withdrew then for a bit & we sat & watched the shells burst & tho' they were then falling nearly 500 yards away every time we got hot pieces of shell dropping all round us. The crater of one of these shells in hard chalk is about 12 feet across the top & five or six feet deep so you can imagine that it makes a bit of a blast.

They put 25 of these on to about an acre of ground in an hour! Then they stopped & we went on digging alright. One of the shells pitched on the side of our beautiful trench & blew the whole side in for 15 yards filling it up to the brim & it has taken 8 men 8 hours to clear!!

There is no doubt that what we have done is about the best work that has been done in the Div. & I am glad to say is recognized as such. We dug 2000 yards of trench 6 feet deep & 3 feet wide through the worst digging you ever saw. Every inch had to be picked out & not one single spade full was got without previous picking.

I think my biliousness was attributable to café au lait in unlimited quantities after digging and the glare of the white chalk, but I am now absolutely fit again. I wish you were out here with me as you say & up to now there has been no reason why both you & the kids couldn't have been.

Best love to you dearie, I must stop now.

23rd September 1915 – Haillicourt

I am going to move tomorrow to the little house which is marked in square L21. This salubrious spot is an old knacker's yard & smells accordingly. I am sorry you have lost the companionship of old Betsy but I am sure it is for the best. I expect by the time you get this you will have got your 'pres'[67] but I haven't seen it & so if it isn't nice will you please send it back & tell them to keep the money to the credit of my account & go and choose yourself something you would rather have.

There is just a chance of my getting a real good job & getting a more or less independent command, by having the three squadrons of the Corps and the three cyclist Coys & a battery of guns, a command of nearly a thousand men. It depends on so very many things about which I cannot tell you but it would be a most top-hole show if things turn out alright. Don't say a word to a soul about it as it more than likely might not eventuate, but it is on the cards!

Well dearie, good night & God bless you all. Don't expect very regular letters. I will write when I can.

[67] The fur coat.

At 6 p.m. on the evening of 24 September the squadron moved to battle positions at the prisoners' depot at what the troops aptly named 'Smelly Farm' – the farm had previously been a knacker's yard – midway between Noeux-les-Mines and Les Brebis. The War Diary for the following day records: 'Attack 6.30 a.m. by 1st Army capturing Loos, about 2,000 prisoners and much material.' The Battle for Loos had begun. Had the attack opened a gap in the German lines, the intention was for Major Hermon and his squadron to follow the cavalry division through the gap and act as advanced guard mounted troops. Orders for the cavalry advance were issued but in the event no gap was established so they were countermanded and the squadron was detailed to escort and guard prisoners of war.

Although Loos began well for the Allies, the superior German machine guns proved decisive. Among the dead was John, the only son of Rudyard Kipling, who was declared 'missing in action'. His body was never found.

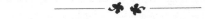

26th September 1915 – bivouac at 'Smelly Farm'

We had a bit of a battle here yesterday. I have been very busy handling prisoners for the last 24 hours & have so far sent to the base 1502 & 33 officers. Our special mission that I told you we had been on was convoying cylinders of 'frightfulness' up to the front-line trenches at night.

We commenced the attack yesterday by giving the Boche a taste of his gas for fun. He didn't like it a bit. I can't help think that our old friend Kaiser Bill slept badly last night with all his troops so far off in Russia. They are hard at it now & I hope soon to hear that we are making as good progress today as we did yesterday.

It is really most amusing how appreciative the Staff has become & the very high opinion everyone seems to have of the squadron. They are all after the squadron now if they want anything done.

How I laughed when I tore that bit off the letter. I knew you would be as curious as an old cat!! As a matter of fact it was a reference to the 'pres' & then I thought I would like it to come as a complete surprise so I tore it off!! I had a very nice letter from old Vio[68] & am going to answer it now

[68] Vio was his sister-in-law.

if I have time, but I am so bothered with prisoners who keep rolling up every minute.

We have had two damnable nights. We are at L21d where there is a little house marked & have our prisoners' camp there. We came down here night before last at 7 p.m. & camped in a ploughed field behind a stack, no cover & it rained incessantly for 30-odd hours. Mud up to one's knees, but it is now glorious sunshine & warm & we are basking. No more now dearie mine,

Best of love.

The first phase of the Battle of Loos lasted for four days, from 25 to 28 September, at the enormous cost of nearly 50,000 British casualties. The Germans called it the 'Field of Corpses of Loos' as once again the German machine gunners had proved deadly effective, in spite of the British enjoying numerical supremacy. Loos itself was captured, but, crucially, the lack of reserves on the first day proved to be a major factor in the failure of the British to make further advances. The French made some progress at Champagne and Vimy Ridge but the German defences prevented any long-term gains being achieved.

28th September 1915 – bivouac at 'Smelly Farm'

If you send me such nice letters I shall have to send you a present once a week. Lass darling, in the midst of all this awful death & destruction a letter like your 157 with your thanks for the coat just makes life bearable.

The fighting here these last three days & nights has been desperate & many a splendid officer who I knew so well only a few days ago I shall never see again. Our Div. has done grandly & the only fly is that tho' right up among it we haven't been actually engaged, tho' last night I was sent for as had things been as we hoped I expect we should have seen enough fighting by this morning to have lasted a lifetime.

Please send me my thick undies. The cold last night was bitter & we are still out under a haystack. Rained like Hades all night. However I am very well & enjoying life so far as is possible under the circumstances.

There is no doubt we have given the old Boche something to think about these last few days & took nine guns & several Maxims from him. Poor old Goochie, it's terrible losing him but one can't moralize one must just be callous or one couldn't go on. I hope to go up to Loos today & try & catch a few Huns in the cellars there. It's too cold to write much more.

That same day Major Hermon received a signal ordering him to clear Loos of war material – shells, rifles, bombs, etc. He took with him Lieutenant MacKinnon and a party of six men on the hazardous mission into Loos – which was still partly under German control.

On 30 September, Robert received a second signal:

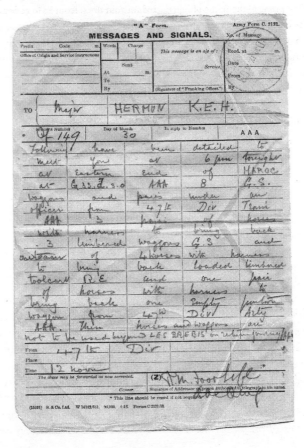

Following have been detailed to meet you at 6 p.m. tonight at eastern end of MAROC at G33.d.s.o aaa 8 G.S. wagons and pairs under an officer from 47th Div. Train aaa 3 pairs of horses with harness to bring back 3 limbered wagons G.S. and one team of 4 horses with harness to bring back loaded limbered toolcart RE and one pair of horses with harness to bring back one empty wagon from 47th Div. Arty aaa. These horses and wagons are not to be used beyond LES BREBIS on return journey.

The squadron rode to Maroc and then marched into Loos to continue the removal of war material. The War Diary records: 'No casualties'. During this time Robert wrote to his wife using field postcards, crossing out the lines 'I have been admitted into hospital, sick, wounded, I am being sent down to the base', leaving only the phrases as below. If anything personal was added these cards would be destroyed by the censors at the Field Post Office.

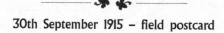

30th September 1915 – field postcard

I am quite well.
I have received your letter dated 159.
Letter follows at first opportunity.
Robert. 30.9.15 – 9 a.m.

2nd October 1915 – bivouac at Gosnay

My Darling,

I will try now and give you as good a description of the events of the last ten days as I can as my time for writing up to now has been meagre in the extreme. We are snatching a day or two's rest now & are welcoming it after a rather strenuous time.

The bombardment commenced on Tuesday the 21st Sept and continued for the rest of the week, day & night incessantly, until Saturday morning.

At about 5.30 a.m. on Saturday we loosed off the gas & it went rolling away opposite us over the German lines, & was, opposite our front, very successful but in some parts of the line it came back instead of going forward & was far more hindrance than help.

About half an hour later the assault began and our infantry leaped out of their trenches & rushed across, swept over the German front line & on to the second. I learnt from prisoners that they had expected the attack & had been standing to arms all night. In the morning the wind not being right for the gas, the attack was delayed for some time after daylight and thinking that we were not going to attack they went back to their second line, took off their equipment and began breakfast – it was just at this time that our attack was launched.

At 10.15 a.m. I took over the first batch of prisoners consisting of 1 officer and 10 men & after that they came in thick and fast, as I was collecting them from three Divisions, until by Monday night I had handled 33 officers and just over 1,600 men. I kept these & sent them off to railhead under escort of two troops of 'tins' who were detailed for the purpose. It is these prisoners who are referred to in the enclosed D.M. [*Daily Mail*] account. The 500 already entrained I sent off from L21d, on Sat night & the 750 on Sunday morning.

We were all naturally very tired at getting a job of this sort, which tho' useful & necessary was far from being what we wanted. However, I was sent for & told that I was to prepare at once to be ready to be employed in my true role,[69] I was dragged out of bed for this & returned highly excited, but unfortunately things didn't eventuate & it fell through. The next time I was sent for I was detailed as per enclosed telegram of 28th.

I had a motor placed at my disposal & came back to camp, stuffed my pockets with food & taking with me two of my best 'toughs' I went to H.Q., picked up my other officers & we started off to Loos in the car. We went through the Marocs & then across the open where we had made some very rough bridges across ours & the German trenches & half way to Loos we thought it advisable to leave the car & walk. It was now about 9 p.m. & we walked on to Loos. It wasn't very pleasant. A modern battlefield is not pleasant I can assure [you]. The dead of both sides were lying very thick on the ground.

Loos itself is at present very close to the German line, & it is a place on which they concentrate a good deal of their heavy artillery & in fact all

---

[69] As divisional cavalry.

their artillery have a blow at it when there is nothing else to do. Buchan had been in Loos all day & had got three guns & a Maxim out in the street already & so we got them hitched to the limbers we had brought with us & sent them off. Buchan was wet to the skin & completely worn out & so I sent him home in the car. Meanwhile Mac & his troop had arrived to help me.

The first thing I did was to scout about among the houses for a really good cellar where we could be reasonably safe. You would have laughed if you could have seen me creeping down the steps with a revolver in one hand and my electric torch in the other but the late occupants had left & we had great fun going through their equipment & getting 'souvenirs'. We then left our kit there & proceeded on our duty. There were two guns in a chalk pit in M 6-A on the Lens road about 300 yds from the then German front line & close to Hill 70. I am glad to say we got them both out and ran them by hand down the road to Loos where two limbers were waiting, hooked them in and sent them off. All these guns are on view today near here, for the men of the Div. to go & see. By this time we were all pretty beat so we retired to our cellar to sleep. There were three feather beds in one of the cellars & Mac & I slept in one, the old Baron who most gallantly came with us on the other, & two men on the third – the rest of Mac's men being in the other cellar & two on sentry.

In the morning we got up & the men began nosing around & soon found a shop & some women. They made us coffee & we had some breakfast in the rooms upstairs. We had just finished when a huge shell came into the house wrecked two rooms & covered the remains of our meal with so much brickdust & mortar that it quite spoilt the butter we had got which was an awful blow. Incidentally it smashed one of my men's rifles to pieces. We then split up into parties and began to search the town for guns & amm & stores of all sorts.

The town is just about the same size as Cuckfield[70] with what remains of the church in a big square in the centre. Throughout the previous night & all through the day shells were arriving at the most alarming rate, twice the previous night I had escaped by the skin of my teeth – one shell passed only a few feet over my head & completely demolished the house on the other side of the street, & we were all covered with falling bits of bricks & mortar. The shells are bad enough in the open but when ever you are

[70] In Sussex.

out in the street & you have the houses falling all around you it is absolute hell. Loos is about the most unhealthy spot you can imagine just at present. I don't mind admitting I was terrified.

We spent the whole day going round collecting things & then went & laid low till dark & waited for the wagons & horses to come & take the stuff away. What with shells & stumbling over dead Germans we were getting a bit worn out. Then just before the wagons came the Boche succeeded in putting a 'Jack Johnson' right in the middle of the road & the only road we could use. It made a crater 8 feet deep and 20 feet across & as it was between two houses it was impossible to get a wagon across. I was by then completely worn out & so when the wagons came I sent them back & we all walked back to our camp.

On the 29th we had the house brought down on us three times during the day with very heavy shells & the poor women who I told you made us coffee had nine rooms in their house when we arrived and when we left they had only half a kitchen left & a cellar. One shell that hit our house brought a big four-post feather bed out of the upstairs room & put it in the dining room only to be shortly covered up by the rest of the upstairs storeys coming down on top of it.

OK! there was sufficient excitement in Loos to last a lifetime. We evacuated over 80 women & kids running in ages from 87 to 3 & all the women are out now I am glad to say. When we arrived they begged & cried to be allowed to remain in their homes, but our friends, after losing seven out of their nine rooms, said they would go. If it wasn't so unutterably sad it would have been ludicrous if you could have seen me at dead of night, with the aid of a small boy of Bob's size pushing a pram full of 'lares and penates'[71] through thick mud, with old Pongo cursing a poor old donkey with twice as much in the cart as he could pull, who was stuck in the mud at one of the bridges over the trenches.

Five or six old women all shouting directions & making enough noise to get us all shelled like Hades. Then another old girl upset her pram and all the lares went into the mud & then they had got cows tied on behind their carts. My darling old girl when you have seen scenes such as I have seen these last few days it makes one's blood boil to think one belongs to a nation amongst whose population there exist male beings, I can't call them men, who could come & yet do not come.

[71] 'Household goods', roughly translated from the Latin.

Never as long as I live will I employ a man married or single who was of military age & who didn't come, when he could. The very thought of Pike makes me so angry I can hardly sit still when one sees men wounded, lying on the ground in mud so deep they can hardly keep from suffocating. The Govt simply crying for motor ambulance drivers & repairers. Talking of ambulances the Ford cars were practically the only ones that could cope with the mud & get to Loos to evacuate the wounded. They are magnificent.

I have seen some cavalry lately & have had the shock of my life when I realized that compared with my squadron they were awful. The very best of our regiments have been here & I was ashamed that my men should see the Cavalry that I have always held up to them as an ideal. Their horses look awful.

You ask if the 'excitements' make me feel shaky. Well to start with I didn't mind them a bit & tho' not liking I didn't feel them so much, but the man who says he likes shells is a damned liar. Well of course my first 24 hours in Loos was beastly. I had to meet a man there to show me where the guns were. He was in such a state of nerves that I had to send him back, he had certainly had a bad day there & there was every excuse, then I had another fellow with me who was too awful too & he kept on explaining to me all the time that it wasn't that he was really a funk, but that it was his nerves. I must say that at the end of the time I was myself feeling pretty much the same. I simply hated the idea of going near the beastly place again & when I had to go on the 30th I disliked it very much.

However this time I only had my own men & officers to deal with & whether it was that or because I had so much to do I don't know, but I never felt a qualm the whole evening. I was very frightened about myself as I didn't at all relish the idea of my nerve not standing the strain & was simply delighted when I found my fears to be groundless so far.

There is no doubt that you don't know what is in a man till you try him & one of the most unpromising of my pupils at the Bomb School, from appearances only, died most gallantly trying to rally some men under very heavy fire, on Saturday. He was the poorest thing to look at, sort of mediocre village school master.

Our farm was certainly well within range of the German guns & a man was killed while we were there while the horses of a battery were watering at our trough & one or two other men camped close to us. I am afraid old dear that you poor women who sit at home have a bad time. The waiting and anxiety are worse than the up & doing. Yes, please send me the air bed & I will try it.

With regard to the prisoners, there were some very fine men among them, they were well clothed, & well fed, & many brought bread, brown sort of wholemeal bread which I tasted & it wasn't half bad. Two boys said they were only 16 but the tales of them being in rags & starving is the greatest rot & one store in Loos was simply piled with the very best food you ever saw. Tinned salmon, very good fresh vegetables, tea, coffee & everything you can think of. There wasn't what you would call an old man among them. The German officers weren't Hunnish a bit & I talked to some but not much. I talked to the men most. I had one or two very good interpreters.

Mac is without doubt the best boy I have & is one of the very best subalterns I ever met. Old Steve is certainly the next best & is a very good officer. Pongo, conscientious to the bone, but oh so slow & has not the initiative of a sausage. Can't do anything without having to ask one a thousand questions & always got yards of excuses for every little thing that goes wrong but he is doing alright & is a great tryer but he is too old to be a subaltern & hasn't the knowledge to be anything else. Tulloch[72] will be really good, he has great initiative and plenty of self-confidence.

I wrote & asked for Tulloch & [Major] James worked it alright for me. I had a splendid letter from old Bet today, really top-hole. What do you think of the enclosed drawing done by a French officer on the Div. Staff, just from memory as he has only seen me about four or five times & then only in the office. I've nearly written myself silly dearie.

My love to you all,

Ever your Robert.

4th October 1915 – Chartreuse, near Gosnay

We have had it bitter cold & wet today & tho' we have been in a house it hasn't seemed much warmer than outside. It is on these sort of days that one longs for home & the whole thing to be over & done with beyond words.

---

[72] Lieutenant H. M. Tulloch.

I must say that I have very great hope of this winter. I think that by April & May they will be in a very different position & I shouldn't even now be surprised to see the whole thing collapse. I think the Russians will soon begin to bother them like anything now & if winter catches them where they are, Napoleon's retreat will be nothing to it. Everything is in our favour – time especially, & it is now merely a question of waiting on for the final bump.

I am afraid this is an awful 'pessim' tonight dearie mine but I want comforting tonight more than I have done before & I should so love to be home with you that I hardly dare let myself think of it.

Best love my dear,

Ever your Robert.

CHAPTER SIX

A VISIT FROM THE KING

During October the French continued to gain ground in the Champagne area, with the British and French holding the front at Loos after a German counter-attack on the 8th – reported by Robert as 'very heavy gunning' in his letter of that date. 'C' Squadron were now in reserve after their exertions in support of the Loos attack. For the next few weeks they shuttled between a bivouac at Gosnay, and billets in Chartreuse, Haillicourt and Noeux-les-Mines.

5th October 1915 – Chartreuse, near Gosnay

My darling old girl,

Dearie, our old friend Freddie Wing[73] has been killed, he was standing behind a wall with his A.D.C. & an absolute chance shell came through the wall & killed them both.

I have just got your 164. Loos as you say showed one quite enough & it is most amusing, every single soul you meet who has been in there says he hopes he will never go there again & that it was quite as bad as Ypres at its worst.

The cold has been beastly & even last night in a house it was bitter. I will let you know about the marmalade as soon as we have tried it.

There is no doubt old dear that once one has started this game it does make it hard to come home to all one's comforts & dear ones and then to start all over again because thank God one forgets out here that one has belongings of any sort at times. One couldn't carry on, I don't think, if one lets oneself think too much. However, if things quieten down for the winter later on perhaps I may be able to come home for a bit, & if Benjamin has arrived it will be too lovely – but I shall hate leaving it all again. Darling

---

[73] Major General Fredrick Wing.

mine you must arrange to send a wire with the announcement to *The Times* as we get the papers here before we get wires or letters so that is the quickest way I could hear.

My very best love to you all dearie mine,

Ever your Robert.

The War Diary for 'C' Squadron records that in the afternoon of the 7th there was a rugby match against the 32nd Regiment of Infantry of the French army.

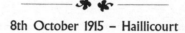

8th October 1915 – Haillicourt

I got your letter & the bed pump, sounds funny but isn't really, no ulterior meaning.

There has been some very heavy gunning this afternoon & we can't make out here if we are advancing or if the Boche is trying to regain Loos. I can't help thinking that if he does try it he will have a pretty warm time as having once taken it our fellows won't give it up without giving some very hard knocks first. I am hoping however that it is all the other way & that we are giving them a bit of a poke.

I went over & saw 'A' Squadron today & the old men of 'C' who were there all begged me to get them back to 'C' again, but I am afraid that it is impossible as I doubt their squadron officer doing much to help it out. He is not very amenable to such transactions.

This is a rotten letter dearie I am afraid but all the lads are talking & the men are having an issue of rum & the window is open & talk about Magpies!! We are hoping against hope that we are going to be left in peace here but one never knows, but if it is to be an advance, well it doesn't matter what we have to stick.

Best love old darling.

9th October 1915 – Haillicourt

Today we had a ceremonial parade while the Corps Commander[74] congratulated the Div. in general & the infantry in particular on the very fine work that they have accomplished. Rather boring, but nevertheless well deserved by the latter.

For all there has been in the papers you might not have thought that there was such a Div. in France but it is a fact that out of all the troops that were engaged it is the only Div. that reached its objective, consolidated it and held it for four days. I could tell you several other tales but they are best left till we meet again. You don't always read the truth in the papers by any means.

The Huns attacked us last night near the 'Quarries' and also just W. of Loos & took it in the neck. It was a very heavy and strongly pushed attack and they paid the price alright, but got no front seats in our trenches I am glad to say. The French caught three of their battalions in close formation and turned their guns on them and the French gunner is pretty hot stuff when he is pushed. I hear they lost a fearful lot of men & a good job too. Old Boyd told me there was only one thing to do with a Hun & that was to kill him & then look for another & kill him too, & there is no doubt that it is right.

One can't take chances with them. Only one of the many instances one hears of, a boy in one of our Battalions was just running up to take a Maxim gun when the officer in charge jumped up & put his hands up. The boy at once lowered his revolver, whereupon the Hun shot him, only however to be immediately bayoneted, I am glad to say. They play every low trick that one can imagine & it isn't safe to trust them even tho' one can see them. The boy wasn't killed tho' he lost an eye, the bullet going into his eye slantwise.

[74] The inspecting officer for the divisional parade on the 9th was General Sir Henry Rawlinson, GOC, 4th Corps.

Sunday 10th October 1915 – Haillicourt

I went to church this morning at 10 a.m. We had a Communion Service instead of the ordinary service. It took place in an empty room in the mine buildings here where there was a large water tank that was hissing away like anything, nearly drowning the Padre's voice. There wasn't a chair & only a tiny table in the corner for an altar. The room was packed & one could only just find standing room. It really was one of the most impressive services one ever attended. There was only one Padre & so while he was going the round of the front line, the others standing behind sang hymns, without music and sang most awfully well too.

'A' Squadron is now close here & is in fact in the same Corps as we are. It is most amusing to hear the comments of my crowd on 'A'. At present the men in 'A' are offering '100 francs' to anyone who will transfer, and there are no takers at present.

Lass dear, there was a shade of failure in a way,[75] in that tho' we broke the Germans we didn't actually penetrate their line, nor did we reach the objective that we set out to gain. That we very nearly did you can judge from the fact that we intercepted a frantic wireless message to Berlin to the fact that 'the British have broken through' so you see things were very close indeed. We failed undoubtedly in the full realization of our intentions & tho' the success was greater than Neuve Chapelle it wasn't the crushing blow it might have been.

Had we had the same number of troops composed of the troops we knew in the old Aldershot days we should have smashed them without a shadow of a doubt, but the new officer hasn't the training and consequently the leading is inferior to what it used to be. The men are quite magnificent but the best troops in the world must be led. It is the same of course for both sides, but they being on the defensive have the easier task with partially trained troops. It is quite another matter attacking. The attack gets split up and then it wants leading. You get men of various units intermingling. If you get a good officer who knows what is wanted he will at once reorganize these men and lead them on. Especially in village fighting this is the case & Loos came right in the centre of the attack.

75 At Loos.

One large body of troops dashed on & nothing could stop them & instead of consolidating as they should, on reaching certain predetermined trenches they carried on over them, absolutely mad with success, with the result they got thrown back and confused & then became a little unsteady. Other troops had then to be thrown in, who were wanted for other jobs & the sting was then out of the advance & we had to be content to hold what we had.

It is quite wrong that we lost Hohenzollern because a whole brigade had surrendered. There was no such incident on the whole front. We never had the whole of the Hohenzollern Redoubt at any time & were only hanging by our eyelids at times. At one time we held both sides of it & they had the middle which they never lost & eventually we were bombed out, but this was a long way on our left, & we had no part in that portion of the attack.

You say you don't know how I find time to write you so long letters but the war is [like] this: both sides look at one another from behind a continuous line of sandbag breastworks varying from as little as 30 yards and even less apart, up to as much as 500 yards, according to the ground. Each side has barbed wire entanglements in the front and in places they are as much as 8 metres wide and even more at special points. Now the supporting troops of both sides are in second lines two or three hundred yards behind the front lines and live in dugouts etc. The reserves live in the villages behind this & then the towns etc., further behind still, are occupied by still more troops to reinforce with.

Now one lives like this, the front line continually being shelled, practically no rifle shooting at all by day, except sniping. At night there is a varying amount of rifle shooting & all night Verey lights going off to light up the ground in between the trenches, neither side wishing to be surprised by the other. This looking at one another is the normal. Then comes a time of attack, the shelling grows by degrees more intense & continues in intensity until the appointed time for the attack. The opponents' wire having been blown down by batteries specially told off for wire cutting, the infantry assault takes place.

Then comes the fight, lasts two or three days, the troops in front are relieved, and pass back to the towns in the rear where they refit, get drafts & rest, during which time they might as well be in barracks at Aldershot. For the most part one is just far enough back to be free of the shelling or very occasional shells wander over just to let one know that there is a war on. You can of course hear the guns plainly all day & all night & that reminds you of a war. The towns even 3 miles behind the front line are full of women & children, shops open & doing a roaring trade & in fact exactly the same as in peace manoeuvres.

Steve was standing talking to an old woman the other day when a shell just came over her house and went into the next garden. All she did was to roar with laughter and say 'Allyman, souvenir. No bonne, no bonne'! You would be awfully amused how the language is being corrupted by contact with Thomas Atkins. All the locals now say 'Allyman' & 'No bonne'.

In this last attack when one of the Battalions of our Div. went over the parapet they took a football and kicked it in front of them right up to the Boche trench!! Shows the spirit of the men. Muriel's story of the brigade surrendering is absolute tosh!!

I am most awfully glad dearie that you are going to have Addie for your days of trial, I wish I could be there to help & share in a mild way so far as I could in what has been largely my fault.

Well goodbye for the present dearie mine.

O n 11 October the squadron moved yet again, to billets in the town of Noeux-les-Mines, which had to be made habitable as they had been left in an appalling condition by the exiting troops. From here Robert sent to Ethel translated extracts of two letters found on the bodies of two officers of the German General Staff, killed in a recent battle. The first read:

> *Please give instructions that a large number of proclamations be issued to the Russian soldiers. I rely upon the secret order of the Emperor William on this subject being executed. It is necessary to do everything possible to weaken the Russian Army, which is escaping from our grip and withdrawing to an unknown destination. Time is not far distant when our situation will become impossible & it is possible that we may be compelled to sign a peace treaty of which the terms will be dictated to us by our enemies.*
>
> *Men who formerly had dreams of conquering the world no longer think today of taking London, Paris or Petrograd. This task will be reserved for our grandsons & not for the heroic German warriors who are now sacrificing their lives on the endless fields of Russia.*

The second, taken from a letter written by a senior German NCO, read:

It is terrible. We have no more men. You know what it means. The Russians have guessed our plan in time & without accepting definite battle have retired to the depths of their country inflicting terrible losses on us in the course of their retreat. [Emperor] William has taken from Germany all that she can give & now you only see old men, women & children in the streets of German towns. We have no more reserves. Our losses are enormous & soon we shall no longer be in the position to make them good. There was a time when the Russians were short of munitions but this is no longer so.

The attack by the British at Loos was renewed on the 13th with an assault against the Hohenzollern Redoubt, but bad weather and further heavy losses caused the offensive to be called off. Gas was again used in the attack, but this time the wind was blowing towards the enemy trenches and away from the British lines.

14th October 1915 – Noeux-les-Mines

Buxton had an afternoon off yesterday & spent it going round the cemetery. He tells me he came across poor old Freddie Wing's grave & so I must go & see it I think, but cemeteries are such unsavoury spots these times.

Dearie mine, I do say 'Your job is at home!' I don't in the least mind you munitioning but your first duty to your country is the efficient upbringing of your children to be useful members of society. Let the 'spinsters with unmarriageable faces' make the shells[76] & the good-looking widows like Mog. I want you to look after 'Ben'.

My love to you dearie mine. I shall begin numbering my letters, I think, now tho' with my awful memory it may lead to even greater confusion!!!

---

[76] With the war going badly the British government were preparing for a long fight and needed a continuous supply of shells. The new Minister of Munitions, Lloyd George, was urging women to work in the munitions factories to keep up with the demand while so many of the male labour force were on active service.

15th October 1915 – No. 100 – Noeux-les-Mines

The air bed is top-hole old girl, & I have had some very comfortable nights on it indeed. Talking of the men wanting to come back to 'C' one of my new draft wrote down to the base last night to a friend advising him to come here whatever he did as 'it was a very nice squadron'.

It is impossible to publish more in the papers than they do as we have a book of the German forces & when we take prisoners one can at once identify the regiment & formation that is in front of one & from that calculate the force opposed to you to a man. We knew exactly what we were up against in this last attack. We reckon the Boche lost 25,000 killed & wounded in his attack on Loos the other day & this in addition to anything he lost in the attack on the 25th. I quite agree with you that it is a pity that our misfortunes should not be equally clearly stated as the successes but you see the Boche knows exactly the extent of our successes & he may not always know the reverse & it is a pity to inform him.

It is most difficult under these conditions to get accurate news & in these last three days it has been very hard indeed to find out in what trenches we were. You see, in an attack the infantry go forward & take a trench, they disappear from sight into a trench 8 foot deep & until you get messages you don't know where the devil they are & consequently in the first rush they carry on & take a lot that eventually they are unable to hold. Then when they gain a trench they at once endeavour to extend their gains to the flank & go bombing along it as far as they can, all out of sight & so in reality it takes some days sometimes to sift out of all the reports where they are. The official reports are not doctored; when mistakes occur it is due to inaccurate reports by Regiments or Brigades actually in the operations.

I am waiting very anxiously for Edward Grey's statement which ought to be in tomorrow's paper, but I think you will find we haven't made so much of a mess in the Balkans as one is led to believe.[77]

I expect the Chugs will have grown an awful lot when I next see them

---

[77] Early in October the British Foreign Secretary, Sir Edward Grey, stated that the situation in the Balkans was of the utmost gravity. On the 15th Britain declared war on Bulgaria, as did France the following day.

& I am looking forward to seeing them soon. I am sorry you have got colds in the house. My men have got a sort of influenza cold too.

Best love old girl.

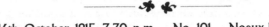

16th October 1915, 3.30 p.m. – No. 101 – Noeux-les-Mines

I am bound for a burying party tonight, a most unpleasant duty especially as all the bodies that we are likely to find were killed on the 25th Sept.

You were saying you wondered how so many could be buried, well they aren't. They just lie until such time as opportunity offers, which in the case of an advance comes soon, but in the case of an attack that fails & is driven off such as the last German attack at Loos, there is nothing for it but to leave them. There is no armistice for the purpose as there used to be in the old days. There are Frenchmen lying out here now who have been dead since May 9th. They are alright now but you can't move them & can only throw earth over them. However it is one of those jobs inseparable from war & must be taken as such.

There will be a good deal of spare lead tonight I expect as it is very close behind the trenches. However it's all in the day's work these times & the more one looks the less one likes it. It doesn't do to think too much. If you are for it you're for it, & if you ain't you ain't & there it is.

Best love my old dear.

17th October 1915 – No. 102 – Noeux-les-Mines

Well, I got back at 3 a.m. this morning alright after a very unpleasant night. Clearing a battlefield is not an amusement I can recommend except that it has the effect of making one perfectly callous to everything connected with life and death.

I cannot believe that this is the end of life. After what I saw last night I am convinced that the soul of man must be so to speak 'detachable'. It is impossible that if there is a Divine will ruling all life, I cannot believe that that is the finish. The soul must leave the body & go elsewhere. I saw it last night as clearly as if it was written in capital letters. I buried 41 poor fellows including a subaltern officer.

My party consisted of 'kilties' with which should have been four officers but only three turned up & one of them got shot after we had been at it only about half an hour & so as they had neither maps, nor electric torches or compasses, had never been on the ground before & it was so dark one couldn't see the ground you were standing on & had the above mentioned officers had all the articles required I doubt if they could have used them. We were working on a huge plain absolutely honeycombed with trenches, barbed wire etc. I had never been on the ground either before & it took me all my time but the result was on a par with our entry into Dartmouth.

I had to lead the party home across country 4500 yards & by the aid of a good map & a compass we fetched up to the inch. I tried to launch my party off on their own when we were nearly back but they weren't having it at any price & insisted on clinging to my coat tail until I had brought them back to a place they knew. We were really very lucky in only losing one out of the whole party as it was rather a lively evening and bullets were going by like wasps on a summer evening.

I don't know how to express what I said earlier on except that I am convinced beyond shadow of doubt that there is a future life. Not that I ever doubted it for a moment, but it has been one of those things that without actually knowing one has believed in but I somehow feel now that it's a snip. I can't tell you what one saw, but the deaths occurred on the 25th which will give you some idea.

18th October 1915 – No. 103 – Noeux-les-Mines

I am becoming a regular Jack of all trades & am now back at the Bomb School again for a week. It got bust up just before the last attack and everything seems to have been lost & the whole show wants re-organizing. However the Guards Division came over here yesterday & asked if we would show them how to run a school & so I said if they would send their proposed staff over I would instruct them. Rather amusing that the Guards should come to a mere Yeoman for instruction.

I have found a gold mine. It is quite simple – you earn £40 a month & spend nothing. I should put old Bob's money *on deposit* with the Bank of England. I am glad you will have a fire for me when I come home, as I like a fire & we have just about the biggest fug on in here now that you ever saw – or felt.

21st October 1915 – No. 105 There! – Noeux-les-Mines

After your rude remarks about my numbering I don't think you deserve a letter at all.

As for the 100 it seemed so stupid after all this time to start at 1, so I split the difference and started at 100. Wasn't the *Observer* good last Sunday, I thought it a really capital article, it is a downright good paper that?

I much resent my squadron being called a rough lot!! There isn't as well behaved a crowd in France. They are no trouble at all, they go down with the country folk like hot cakes. Where they won't have anything to do with other soldiers my men go in & they cook for them, & wherever we go the folk call them 'bons soldats'.

The lamp has gone out & I am going to have a much needed bath. Haven't had one for a very long time!! This is a capital place to be in as Buxton calls me every morning at 6.30 and brings me a cup of tea & bread & butter & the previous day's *Daily Mail* which I read till 7 a.m. & then get up, breakfast at 7.30 & off to dig 8.30. Home again 4.30 and Dinner 6.30 & to bed 9.30.

Best love to you my darling.

23rd October 1915 – No. 105? – Noeux-les-Mines – marked 'Opened by Base Censor'

This letter should have been dated 22nd but last night I got no opportunity to write as we had a bit of a concert just to celebrate our six months in France. Some bits were really quite good and it was very good fun.

Yes, in our burying job one has to get all identity discs off & tie up everything in the pockets with the cord of the disc & register the position of the grave & the whole thing has to be most carefully done.

We have got a lot of sort of influenza colds running round here too & Pongo is in bed again which is a nuisance. Barber went home for a week yesterday and I hope by now has rung you up & told you that I am still pretty hale & hearty.

I am just off to go & finish the trenches for our new Bomb School. It is very satisfactory to know that our Division held its gains simply & solely through the sound instruction they had had in the bombing. They did awfully well with their bombs & took the scrub which runs from the chalk pit on Hill 70 by bombing along it.

The boy who is now in command of the Bomb School, because I am only sort of advising & supervising its re-start, got a Military Cross for his work on the Double Crassier[78] in the last attack. Shennan, one of my lads of Watford days, got a Mil. Cross too for laying a telephone cable to Loos. Several of my original lads have been killed, I am sorry to say, in the recent fighting. Well I must go now dearie mine.

Love to you all.

25th October 1915 – No. 108 – Noeux-les-Mines

After the awful day we have had today I don't think I shall come home on leave – it would be too beastly coming back again?!! It really has been a damned day today. It started heavy rain last night about 6 p.m. & has done 24 hours solid with a bitter N.E. wind. The whole country, roads & all, is a vast sea of mud & the horses standing in a pond. Everything wet through & what the poor devils in the trenches are going through must be a thousand times worse. It has been too bad to do anything much.

I walked down to Mazingarbe this afternoon & got covered in mud splashed up half way above my knees. The road had 2 inches of liquid mud on it. I never saw anything like this country – it turns to mud in an instant on the slightest shower. What it will be later on I don't know.

---

[78] A twin-peaked slag heap near Loos.

I am wondering if things have been early this time & that is why there was no letter & I am looking forward to my paper in the morning in case.[79]

Best of love old darling.

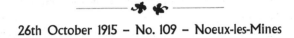

26th October 1915 – No. 109 – Noeux-les-Mines

I got your 188 at breakfast time, & it was written & posted 10 a.m. 24th so it was very quick. Many thanks for sending the socks for the men – they will be much appreciated I find as the wet work in the horse lines makes a change or two very necessary.

No, if they send conscripts out to these men here I fancy they will have a few home truths told them before they settle down. I wish they would shoot a few strikers – it would have a very good effect. It ought to be made impossible for men to strike on a mere quibble of that sort. It is bad enough when they have a genuine grievance but at a time like this it is too much altogether.

I hope it will be Benjamin too, but one must take what Providence gives one these times & be thankful but we will hope for the best. Tell old Mairky to stop barking. I am glad to hear the others are losing their colds.

We are just starting a regular daily, or rather nightly, digging party & old Mac goes off with 20 men at 6 p.m. to dig and I am going to ride up & have a look at them about 9 p.m. I shall not stay long as it is to go on every night for a considerable time and one can't do it every night & all nights. They dig till midnight & then come home. I am going to take Buxton up tonight as he wants to see the Hun front-line trench & it is a chance for him. It is freezing cold now & there is no doubt that winter has set in tho' today was beautiful after yesterday's rain. I was lunching with the staff today & it was lovely in their garden which, tho' well up among the guns, has its lawns mown like peacetime.

---

[79] Newspapers arrived in France only a day late, so Robert was hoping to read the announcement of the birth of their baby in *The Times* before a telegram or a letter reached him.

On 28 October the division received a visit from the King, George V. Because the horse lines had deteriorated into a sea of sticky mud, the troopers selected to line the route for the King were left in their billets to don their uniforms whilst their comrades groomed the horses. They were then 'piggybacked' to their horses to keep their riding boots clean. The squadron's War Diary recorded: 'Appearance of party highly creditable considering conditions of mud & wet.'

29th October 1915 – No. 110 ?????!! – Noeux-les-Mines

We left at 8 a.m. & policed the roads from Marles-les-Mines, through Bruay-la-Buissière for [King] George to come & go. He came & saw a few soldiers who had marched in from all points of the compass. He looked worried but was to me much the same as usual. He motored to La Buissière & there got on his horse & rode round the assembled masses. It blew bitter cold & rained like Hades all the time & was just about as unpleasant as you could well imagine.

We got home about 1 p.m. & at 4.30 I rode out with the digging party under even worse climatic conditions than in the morning. Got back about 8.30 p.m. & had dinner, a hot bath in the pig tub & to bed. Today I have done very little really, trying chiefly to keep the horses' heads above water & mud in the lines.

I see the enclosed in *The Times* today. The two 85 mm I got out of the chalk pit on the Loos–Lens road & I brought in also the 19th Battalion gun and two others that were in Loos as well as a Maxim.

It's funny how few letters the Censor has opened & I am glad there was nothing in it to which he could take exception. [The following insert in different handwriting then occurs, possibly written as a joke by one of his 'young gentlemen'.] *NB. The above has been passed for publication, but the censor, while not objecting to its publication, gives no guarantee as to the veracity of the statements contained therein.*

Once more the squadron was employed for its digging skills — to construct the Lens Redoubt. Each night a party of one officer and thirty other ranks went out when darkness fell until 2 a.m. constructing the redoubt in the old German second line in front of 'Quality Street'. In full view of the enemy, the position was constantly shelled, but as there was a regular pattern to the shelling, it was possible to avoid casualties. Five battery rounds were fired at fifteen-minute intervals, so work stopped after fourteen minutes while everyone took cover, five rounds were counted then work resumed for the next fourteen minutes. The work was particularly unpleasant as it was the burial ground of many German soldiers.

30th October 1915 – No. 111 – Noeux-les-Mines

After breakfast today I got two nice letters from you old dear. When I got your 190, I was very glad that it was not my 'grouse' letter that the censor had opened.

One's doing nothing now & yet there is a lot to be seen to in odd little ways.

Take this digging I am doing now. I am having no R.E. supervision at all & am constructing a strong 'redoubt'. Well the C.R.E. [Commander Royal Engineers] just tells me what he wants & I can go and do it & it saves him sending an officer there to superintend. It is all very useful for the Division & they know the work will be well done. We found a gent buried in the trench we were tidying up last night & he had to come out. I wasn't there myself I am glad to say but I realized he was there alright the night before & old Steve found him & Tulloch had to re-plant him last night.

How funny old Vic[80] being near Loos. I heard no tell of the Carabiniers tho' he may have been near, the only brigades I saw were composed of other Regiments. I am glad to hear you have got old Addie & that all the arrangements are complete. I wish I could be there too dearie, to give you what moral support I could. As you say, it only remains for Benjamin to be Benjamin for all the world to be rosy. I hope the 'pres' kept you &

[80] Victor Hermon, Ethel's brother.

Ben warm. I think he will have to be called 'Ben' even tho' it is tempting Providence perhaps!!

Give my love to the Chugs.

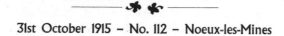

31st October 1915 – No. 112 – Noeux-les-Mines

Last night I was round the Hun trenches that they were turned out of and really their dugouts were wonderful.

They have a completely boarded tunnel with steps leading down from the trench to dugouts as much as 30 feet below the ground level, the ceiling and walls being shored up with 1 ft boarding & pit props used to give extra strength. I found one tunnel that was 80 feet long but had no time to explore but hope to go down it one of these nights. The trenches had had a rare old hammering and in places were fairly bashed in. I am sending you a sample of their barbed wire which will open your eyes a bit. I don't know if it is the normal wire of peacetime or a special wire for war, I should think the latter.

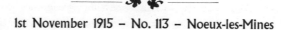

1st November 1915 – No. 113 – Noeux-les-Mines

Time's nearly up & I do so hope you won't have to wait that extra fortnight. My dear old thing, I would love to be with you if I could but it was no good risking it. We could have so much nicer a time a bit later when we could be more alone together. My leaves start on a Friday & one is back the following Sat. morning at daybreak. The trains get into Victoria about 3 a.m.!! It's an awful hour.

I got another lovely letter from you today & I unpacked two boxes of socks, about 50 pairs; these will be much appreciated.

We are fearfully pleased with ourselves as tonight we got a water cart which had been strafed by the Huns. We have been badly in need of one ever since we came out & this one belonged to the party of 'German guns' that I sent you the *Daily Mail* photo of. It was left on the road & is, I hope, going to be very useful to us. It's got a shrapnel hole or two in the tank but I can get that fixed up alright here.[81]

Best love old dear.

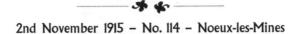

2nd November 1915 – No. 114 – Noeux-les-Mines

Your 194 to cheer me on the most damnable of damnable days. It seems to have rained for the last week without stopping for a minute & the state of the land is simply awful. The horse lines simply beggar description. We have dug a certain number of drains through them but the ground is more like the mud bank in Bembridge Harbour than anything else.

It is bad luck about the King. His horse came over backwards with him & I heard he had a rib broken but am not sure. I was standing in the road as he left the first parade on the way to the second & he passed me quite close & then I went to a corner where I had some men & was just getting them mounted when to my horror I saw the Royal Car coming towards me as hard as it could go. I'd got some damned fellow in a car just turning round & right in the way, but I got him out in time. I thought H.M. was lying back very far in his car & I knew he couldn't have fulfilled his programme but I thought it was perhaps the wet that had stopped things & being so wet & cold myself made off for home the moment I could, & I did not hear until later in the day that he had had an accident.[82]

I think getting £400 at the [charity] sale was marvellous. I am so glad the Chugs did so well with their part.

---

[81] The water cart made the work of watering the horses far easier; it remained with the regiment until the Armistice.

[82] King George's horse had taken fright at a sudden burst of cheering, reared up and fallen backwards on top of the King, resulting in his suffering a broken pelvis.

3rd November 1915 – No. 114 – Noeux-les-Mines

I got your most stimulating epistle, No. 195, today & if it has done nothing else it has driven the rain away. No! H.M.'s accident happened about 10 mins after he had left my piece. He motored from his Hd Qrs to La Buissière & then rode onto parade & then on to the next parade & towards Hesdigneul where it happened.

Poor old Pongo has been sent to England, but it is a blessing that I could spare him the best of the lot tho' I fear it would break his heart if he read this. The rain has taken up I am glad to say and tho' we have had intermittent showers all day it is now a glorious starlight night.

We heard a very good story against the Staff the other day. A Turkish sniper was caught & interrogated & he told them that he got 3d for every man he shot, 6d for every N.C.O. & on a sliding scale. Then they said 'What do you get for a Staff Officer?' & he said '28 days confinement to Barracks'!! It's very easy to criticize a huntsman but the poor old Staff do come in for a good deal of criticism. In certain cases it is merited.

Now the French, whose horsemanship we laugh at, have all their horses roofed over & on dry standings. Nothing at all has been done for ours, they stand in the open up to their bellies in mud & shiver. Now I am ordered to make standings for them by laying bricks on the ground with no foundations at all & after the first shower of rain these same bricks will be 3 feet down in the mud. They have waited to make even this until the ground is absolutely soaked with water & you can't get to the hard under about 2 feet digging!! Do you know that not a single water trough for horses, hardly, has been put up in this area. That thousands of horses water daily at a trough where four can drink at a time!

We have a lot to learn yet & what's more the French can teach us. I used to laugh at them when I first came out but the more I see of them the more impressed I am. They waste no time on 'show', everything they do has a really sound reason & they do little that isn't thoroughly sound. I'm a little fed up tonight but I had a pill last night & shall be alright tomorrow!!

Thank old Bet for her nice letter.

Ever your Robert.

CHAPTER SEVEN

HOME LEAVE

Late autumn 1915 was a time of continuing setbacks for the Allies. French troops were involved in fierce fighting in Champagne, where several villages were totally destroyed. Both Serbia and Montenegro had fallen to the Austro-German alliance, and the whole of Russian Poland was now under German control. Allied forces in Gallipoli were facing defeat and the serious possibility of evacuation.

On the Western Front there was no major British attack, but constant shelling and night raids continued on both sides. Relentless wet weather contributed to the general discomfort of the troops and conditions in the trenches were now appalling.

For Robert personally, it was an anxious time waiting for the birth of his fifth child, although this was tempered by the anticipation of his forthcoming leave after seven long months in France.

4th November 1915 – No. 115 – Noeux-les-Mines

Your 196 duly to hand today. Go on with you about my numbers – they're hot stuff!!

I hoped the Chugs liked their time in town & saw the guns?

I am much happier tonight as I have at last persuaded the Staff of the fact that to lay bricks on soft mud for horses to stand on is the act of an idiot & have managed to get out of making them for the present & hope later on to be able to make some cover for them which is what is wanted, as if you can keep the wet from the standings you can keep the horses fairly dry.

This afternoon was very fine & nice & I went up to see my redoubt[83]

---

[83] Lens Redoubt.

in daylight. I had the most wonderful view of the fight I have yet had since I have been out & saw the whole German & our lines from Hohenzollern Redoubt right round to W. of Maroc & it was really a splendid sight as one could watch the shells of both sides bursting all along the lines.

I heard tonight that the Germans had shouted across from their line 'If you fellows can hold out for two months more you have us cold!' I don't know how much truth there is in it but Mac heard it while I was out and he had gone up to dig before I got back as I was taking a dish of tea off the General.

Asquith's speech seemed to be to be rather 'a collection of enterprises badly bungled & half-heartedly begun'.[84] However we shall muddle on no doubt & muddle to a successful conclusion as we have muddled to the end before.

6th November 1915 – No. 117 – Noeux-les-Mines

For once old darling you are quite wrong. I never was in better health in my life & have been up-to-date ever since I was out & hope to continue in that same.

I am addressing the parcels tonight & they will go tomorrow. I have put in another unloaded bomb known as the ball bomb & used extensively in the last battle. I will unload some more & send you them as soon as I can, as an example of the various kinds would no doubt interest folk very much. Your letters have turned up alright recently. How much longer are you going to keep me on tenterhooks!

I don't for a moment think the war can last two more years. Germany is now using her 1917 class which means boys of 18 yrs & that is too young to stand much either in Serbia or Russia & for that even here. If our push in Serbia is strong enough we have her stone cold as we should then get Romania & Greece & her last outlet is closed.

---

[84] In his speech the British Prime Minister had referred to the possibility of conscription, which was introduced two months later, in January 1916.

8th November 1915 – No. 118 – Noeux-les-Mines

We are now being sent by Havre & the boat gets into S'hampton about 4 a.m. so I think the best thing is to get the family to send the car to the Docks & I ought to be home by 7 a.m. My dear old girl you would look your best at any hour now, you would be so new!! I've no more news old dear & am off to an early bed as I am orderly officer tomorrow!!

Best love dearie mine to you & Ben.

9th November 1915 – No. 119 – Noeux-les-Mines

If I remember right I have had letters from you bearing the same number. Don't scoff or I shall stop writing!! I don't want you to try & write while you are seedy & shall be very angry if I get even a line from you for 10 days so you needn't worry a bit about me. Make the Chugs write & Addie can send me a p.c. each day.

It was most amusing about the pheasants. We had just eaten one when your letter came to say they were only half cooked. So we left the second & are going to have it tonight. They travelled very well and you would never have known they weren't shot in the next field. The one we ate was certainly a little underdone for me! I must go now dearie as I have to go to evening stables as I am doing Orderly Officer today.

We have invested in a most lovely gramophone & it arrived at lunchtime today. It really is a topper so a few nice tunes will be acceptable if Mimi or any of them are going to London shortly.

Best love my own old darling.

9th November 1915 – No. 119a – Noeux-les-Mines

I have written you one letter already today but oddly enough & I don't know why but I feel I want to write you another. I think it must be the effect of the newly arrived gramophone stirring up home thoughts & making one rather homesick. Just a great longing to be shut of the whole of this wretched business & once more be back with you & the Chugs.

It is raining like the very devil & I am afraid that tomorrow my horses will be up to their necks in mud once more. I moved them all onto a dry piece of ground the other day & we have all been enjoying it & now I am afraid it will all be bad again. Poor old Steve is most awfully unlucky in his nights for digging, he always strikes the wet ones & tonight is worse than it has ever been I think. I am hoping he will bring his men back early tho' I fear it will not be in time to prevent them being drenched. I wish this damned German nation would crack up, but they certainly don't look much like it hereabouts.

I hope all the doggies are well, but as you don't mention any untoward happenings I conclude that such is the case. I wonder if old Spoot will have forgotten me?

Tonight would be a fine night for the waders, I think. The Government are issuing the men with the most splendid field boots you ever saw. I got 25 pairs today and the men are delighted with them. They really are splendid boots & it is astonishing how well they fit the men. Far better than puttees this kind of weather. I don't wonder the war is costing a bit if they are giving them to everyone which of course they must.

I must go now dearie & look at my poor drowned rats.

My love to you dearie mine.

10th November 1915 – Noeux-les-Mines

I got the enclosed letter today from Chev[85] which is most amusing. We marched into camp on the day before Loos in the dark and latrines are always dug as one of the first duties on getting into camp. Well we dug ours in the usual way. When morning broke we found that they had been dug right in the middle of a 'Cavalry road', these were marked out 30 yds wide by signboards & lead to the front clear of telephone wires so that the Cav. could go through if wanted.

About an hour after daylight a young, or rather to be correct, oldish

[85] Cheviot Bell.

2/Lieut. comes along & his horse puts his feet in the holes, nearly falls, thoroughly unseats said Subaltern. The men were all standing about and I expect laughed. Then he set about cursing the squadron in general & got the men fairly wild, ending up with 'That's the worst of having to go on service with "dud" regiments' & rode off. Just before dark this same officer returned & complained to me that he had lost his patrol, had had nothing to eat all day & was starving. Well he had been so awfully rude that I just asserted 'That it was bad to be hungry' & let him go!

I was damned if I was going to feed him (as I knew he could get food in the village if he liked to go & look for it) after he had been so rude!! I have never seen the men so upset before & I really believe if he had stayed much longer in the morning they would have had him off his horse & given him a real good hiding! That is enough explanation for Chev's letter.

Your old horse is still doing very well & is still looking hale & hearty. He stands outside in all weathers!!

Best of love dearie mine.

11th November 1915 – No. 121 – Noeux-les-Mines

There is a little story about a pot & a kettle which if I remember right ended in some very sharp words that both sides regretted in their cooler moments. Why you should cast aspersions at my system of numbering when you dart into No. 103? Dated Nov. 8th!! However let it pass!

Now oddly enough Barber has a Beacon oilskin catalogue here – it is called 'Weather Comfort'. The leggings are L-13 black clog. No. 325. Wellington Clog No. 165 7/11d. Have, say, two pairs of each of these three sent out to me at once will you please & I will then let you know. Size 10 in clogs.

There was a most magnificent air fight over this house this morning. An old Hun flew over & was set upon by four of our planes & the anti-aircraft guns. He got clean away & then he turned & came back right through them all & by that time a big French warplane had joined the fight & then the Hun made off getting lower & lower & I hear tonight that he failed to reach his lines & we got him. I was sorry really that he didn't get back because he was a bold man & took on very great odds. His machine was much faster than ours tho'.

Best of love dearie mine.

O n 11 November, Ethel gave birth to their fifth child, a son. Robert would not hear the news until two days later.

12th November 1915 – No. 122 – Noeux-les-Mines

They have now increased my leave to 3 per week so I can come on any Friday that suits. I am sending Steve today so that clears all officers out of the way and I can then just suit myself & Ben. Tell Addie she had better make arrangements to stay on as second fiddle where she is, she's so useful about the house!

I've finished our digging for the present I am glad to say. It started to rain again yesterday about 6 p.m. & it has rained something awful ever since. The wretched horses standing out in a sea of mud & water.

I'll get old Steve to ring you up if he has time in London, but he can't tell you much more than I can as there's nothing to tell tho' he can ease your mind a bit as to my position. Do you remember the name of the place where we went to after detraining? I am still at the 'Pork butchers & boulangerie'. Well I am off to the lines now to see if I can do anything to drain a little more water away from the horses.

Best love old dear & hope to see you all very shortly now.

13th November 1915 – No. 123 – Noeux-les-Mines

I suppose the strain of writing 1901[86] letters in 24 hours was so much for you that you have broken down. I haven't had a letter today & no papers from

---

[86] Ethel Hermon had added 100 to her numbering by mistake.

England so I am properly in the dark. By-the-bye you must hurry up now as the time is fast approaching when I shall have been away a long time!!

I have lived in my long boots ever since they came and they arrived absolutely in the nick of time. The men are looking forward to getting their leggings & clogs as winter conditions are very trying. If we can keep them with dry feet it will be a tremendous help. I am writing to Morrish[87] tonight to see what can be done about allocating some of our annual income to providing useful things for the men. I believe the income is nearly £600 a year & I can't help thinking that a lot of this might be spent on the men. My men haven't gone to bed with dry feet for 10 days.

Best of love old dear.

13th November 1915 – No. 123a – Noeux-les-Mines

The weather conditions today have been too awful & most dispiriting. I had had a long day in a motor & got back to find no letter from you, & no newspapers & everything was rather rather. In the throes of a move too & everything thoroughly upset.

Was having dinner when Buxton brought me in a wire. I opened it wondering which it was to be & when the glorious news dawned on me everything changed at once, & incidentally the weather took up, the storm has blown itself out & the new moon is shining in an absolutely cloudless, starlit sky & the whole world seems at peace. There isn't a gun firing & if Ben wanted a better augury he couldn't possibly have it. Oh! Darling mine that I could be with you to join in your joy because dearie it must be worth all the weary waiting and anxiety now.

You don't know what a difference it has made to me. It's simply grand. Well done my old dear. Now about my coming dearie. I make out from the wire that Ben arrived on the morning of Thursday 11th & if I come next Friday that would make me arrive on Sunday morning 21st which would be a bare ten days.

I don't want the excitement to put your temperature up or anything stupid of that sort & I feel I would be wiser to put it off until the following

---

[87] The regimental accountant in London.

week when you would have had another week & I could then see you up before I had to come back again. Dearie mine isn't it splendid, I can see you looking at him as proud as anything. Poor little Bobbo! I do so want to hear all about him & his arrival.

Dearie mine, I feel this is a rotten letter on such an occasion – it hasn't half in it that it should, but I am just the happiest man in France tonight & it will smooth away all difficulties for a long time to come. So dearie mine, in fourteen days from tomorrow, all being well, I will be with you about 8 a.m. Don't worry about me old dear, just lie still & get well.

On the 14th 'C' Squadron moved from Noeux-les-Mines to Hurionville, where they were now part of the Corps Reserve. Construction of brick standings for the horse lines began on the 17th in an attempt to keep the horses clear of the deep mud.

14th November 1915 – No. 124 – Hurionville, near Lillers

I hope by now that you are beginning to feel a bit more like yourself & that Ben is behaving himself as a 'War Baby' should. We are now at a little village one mile S.E. of our first billet on arrival in the country. For the moment we are out of the awful mud & have got a nice clean field to put the horses in which I hope will remain fairly decent tho' I see little or no prospect of its doing so.

I wonder what the Chugs think of Ben? I expect they have nearly torn him to bits by now in their anxiety to hold him. I expect Mairky's remarks will have been the funniest. Well, I hope to have been with you for twelve hours by now in a fortnight's time. Something has gone wrong at Calais & Boulogne, rumours of German mines having drifted in owing to bad weather in the N. Sea.

Anyhow little or nothing is coming through & I haven't seen a paper for three days now. Had it not been so I should have known your good news 12 hours earlier if I was right in timing Ben's arrival to Thursday morning. As at 6 a.m. the previous day's paper was on sale in Noeux & I went to get the *Times* & *Daily Mail* with my early morning tea.

As it is we hear rumours of 'unmarried conscription' but know nothing definite. Tomorrow we only get the *Observer* but really I believe it is the best paper of the lot now. Had rather a strenuous day today as I am minus subaltern officers, two being on leave, one sick, and Tulloch at the Bomb School with 11 men.

I hope Ben is a credit to Pa & Ma but gather from the wire that he is alright & worthy of his membership of the family. I expect you are feeling as proud as an old Peahen! I wish I could see you just for a bit but it won't be much longer now, tho' I don't expect time flies with you as it does with me.

Best of love my mother of five.

15th November 1915 – No. 125 – Hurionville

Again no mail & beyond the telegram announcing Ben's arrival I know nothing at all.

However no news is good news & so I must possess my soul in patience once more tho' it is beginning to get a little impatient. We had some papers today so I hope that we shall get a regular budget tomorrow.

We are expecting Von Mackensen[88] back in an hour or so. He has got a room in a farm where the man is a most awful talker & there is a small baby too! We are not half so well situated here as we were at Noeux. We have got one room for a men's room & I sleep on a stone floor on about three straw mattresses piled on one another. Quite comfortable really but nothing like so good as my last room. The only crab about the last place was 'Jane'.[89] The French as you probably know are a little casual in their sanitary arrangements.

Well Jane occupied a very central position in the house. Jane was most unpretentious. A large square hole going down into what might be the cellar. Over this the ordinary conventional seat & the whole taking the form of the earth closet, but minus the earth. I suppose it was emptied once or twice a year. Personally, on active service one in the garden was

[88] Von Mackensen was a German General, but he is referring to 'Mac' (Donald MacKinnon), one of his officers, to whom he had jokingly given this nickname.
[89] The 'Jane' was a commonly used term for 'lavatory'.

more to the liking of yours truly but inside, well! What ho! when they opened the lid. Why there was no plague, goodness only knows, but can you imagine anything more awful. It amounted to nothing more or less than an open cesspool right in the middle of the house!! I attacked it with copious draughts of carbolic which somewhat reduced things a bit but it wasn't very quiet even then. Truly they are a wonderful race. However, we none of us took any harm and so all part of the job. 'C'est la guerre' as they say here to everything they don't like.

What the devil are we going to call Ben? Personally I have rather a leaning to Kitchener, Jellico, Joffre as being seasonable but we will discuss matters when we meet. Our leave day has been put back to Saturdays now & so I have applied tonight for leave from 27th to Dec. 9th which I expect will be sanctioned alright.

There is nothing more I can tell you now old dear but if I get some letters from home tomorrow it will, I hope, start me off & you will get a head splitting epistle that will put you back months!!

My love to you my own darling, just lie still & get well as fast as you can old dear & we will have a right jolly time when I get back. What a family it is now & times so hard.

16th November 1915 – No. 126 – Hurionville

At last I have got a mail but not so big a one as I have hoped for, as I only got Addie's letter written on the birthday morning but it is quite possible I shall get another bunch tomorrow. I got one letter from a Chug saying that the little brother was only one day old. Betsy says he has 'lots & lots of hair for his age' & 'it is a very dark baby, sometimes dark babies turn fair'. 'Isn't it funny you left England with four of us & now when you come at the end of the month you will find five of us.' Old Bob says: 'We have got a little baby brother & he is so sweet a few minutes ago he was crying like anything.' He also says 'it is a foul day!' I can hear the intonation of his mother's voice in the last remark!! Isn't Woolven's[90] a nice letter. I was so very struck with it & surprised too!

---

[90] Tom Woolven, the gardener at Brook Hill, had sent a formal congratulatory letter.

Best love to you dearie mine & I do so hope you are mending rapidly & in no pain now. 'Ben' must be a topper from all accounts.

17th November 1915 – No. 127 – Hurionville

I was very glad to get Addie's letter card today. I couldn't quite make out from her first letter whether you were really alright or not. It wasn't a very good letter & I rather fancied that I read between the lines that you weren't quite as well as you might have been, but her card today dispels that idea completely. Especially when she raises the possibility of your writing a short line yourself.

I had two very nice letters from the family who seem most awfully pleased about Ben. Mimi says 'With regard to Dick and Sandhurst we have the matter in hand. Cattley says certainly not before Easter so there we shall leave it.' I put it pretty strongly to her last time I wrote. I am writing today and am going to ask them to send to S'hampton for me as I could then be home in the time it would take to get up to town. The boat is due at 4 a.m. Monday so with luck I should be back by breakfast time.

We have been out today doing a little squadron training which probably sounds funny in these times of war but is never-the-less true. I have just had my hair cut so as to be looking quite my best when I arrive. The boats appear to be most irregular in their crossings.

The weather is damnable, cold & snow showers & our grass field that was so nice to start with is fast becoming a bog again. I must go now & erect my chaff cutter.

Best love to you old dear, hurry slowly & take care of Ben & don't drop him!

17th November 1915 – No. 127a – Hurionville

To my great surprise & delight quite unexpectedly I had a perfect budget of letters from you at 5 o'clock tonight. I don't know what to say to you as you ought not to have done it, but I have loved them old dear. Really darling mine you are a dear brave old rascal because you have never let on that you were in pain all the next day, it's very, very naughty of you not to tell the truth as I always do to you. I would love to be with you dearie, as you say.

Somehow dearie mine, I have never been able to write you a decent letter since Ben arrived. In the first place I never can write decently with other folk in the room and my own bedroom has been so awfully cold that it was impossible to raise even a warm thought except when one was in bed with one's head under the clothes. Barber has just started the gramophone so now I don't know what this letter will end like.

Darling mine you have been a dear brave old thing over this, not a word of all your pain, & your nice cheery card only a few hours afterwards makes one feel but a very poor thing when one thinks how one dislikes these damned shells which if they do hit one makes the job instantaneous.

Really the bravery of the woman is something far finer than the ordinary man's in some stirring moment. I shall never forget the calm bravery of these women out here. It is what the parson would call 'beautiful'. The 'sit still & never show it' kind, the hardest of all. Any damned fool can run along in a crowd but it's the 'all alone' that wants the sticking & my very own dear I can see you have stuck more, and more bravely than ever this time my darling, & my love and admiration dearie is more than it ever was before. Goodbye my darling for the present. My love to you all & buck up the time when we meet again.

20th November 1915 – No. 130 – Hurionville

My darling old girl,

Your 210 duly to hand & your remarks re the 'completeness' of the family equally duly noted for future guidance.

I have got a new pair of boots sent me by Pa, they came day before yesterday. I am so glad, my darling, that you are doing so well & it has eased my mind a lot.

I enclose you Bingham's letter. I will talk to you about it when we meet, but tho' I wouldn't mind going to an infantry unit out here I do not know that I very much fancy one at home tho' I could very possibly get one. I think I shall have to stay on in that position that it has pleased Providence to call me to & await events. However, I have only myself to blame because if I had really worked & passed into the Staff College no doubt I should be far better placed than I am.

As long as I can satisfy my own conscience & know that my own show is a good one, it is something at least. I am certainly not going back to the cavalry as a captain, after having had a Majority for five years nearly & having a squadron that will hold its own with any squadron I have seen out here yet.

Best love old dear, next Saturday at this time I shall be impatiently pacing the station waiting for the train to start.

21st November 1915 – No. 131 – Hurionville

We are having a very 'cushy' time here at present & thoroughly enjoying ourselves. Lass darling, you are quite right we have a very great deal to be thankful for & as you say I wish we could go & say a combined 'Thank you'. However as you say, as long as one is grateful it is the main thing & we both are that I am sure. Harry's boots turned up at Midday today and he is awfully pleased with them.

We are just close enough to hear the guns going and since I began this they have been having a sort of birthday treat & shaking my little cottage badly. The window rattles well when the heavier ones go, but one can put up with the noise as long as one is without its usual accompaniment. I've liked this week's rest very much & shall come back quite fresh which will be splendid. It's a great thing really this holiday & does one any amount of good. I must go now old dear, as I am Orderly Officer today & must see the skins[91] put to bed.

Best love to you all, my little half-dozen.

---

[91] Horses.

23rd November 1915 – No. 133 – Hurionville

I am suffering also from excitement & I don't feel at all like writing. I got your 213 today.

I am glad your cow is doing Ben well. Sorry he only weighed 8 lbs when I know for certain Dick weighed 3 cwts 1 qr 27 lbs. Very poor effort indeed. I am sorry the kids don't like Charles Henry but we will talk it over amongst the many other things that we shall probably discuss.

My love to you all.

25th November 1915 – No. 125 [sic] – Hurionville

I was rather worried when Addie said in a later letter you had had bad pain the following day but I believe our old friend Chavasse says that it is to be expected as the family increases & so I took it as normal tho' very unpleasant for you old dear. Anyhow, the family is now complete.

I am awfully glad that Ben is so good & I like the Charles Edward very much & am quite agreeable to let it stand at that. Pity that we can't spell Charles with a 'K'. How would you like 'Kenneth', only name with a 'K' I can think of?[92]

Best love old darling.

Towards the end of 1915, the first full year of the war, the Central Powers were in the ascendancy in several theatres of war, with Serbia under Austrian and Bulgarian occupation and Belgium and Poland under German control. Evacuation of Allied troops from the Gallipoli Peninsula had begun on the 8 December. A week later, on the Western Front, the Commander of the BEF, General Sir John French,

[92] Their second son would soon be christened Kenneth Edward, sharing the same initials as the regiment, K.E.H. Ironically, he would celebrate his third birthday on Armistice Day.

resigned because of the continuing failure of British attacks. He was replaced by Sir Douglas Haig.

With the approach of winter there was less activity on the Western Front and with 'C' Squadron of King Edward's Horse in Corps Reserve, Robert felt able to go on home leave. Leave boats sailed from Le Havre to Southampton, crossing the Channel in darkness to avoid German submarines; the journey took thirty-six hours. Robert remained in England until 9th December, meeting his newborn son for the first time.

9th December 1915 – telegram sent from Southampton

GOODBYE MESSAGE OPENED ONLY ON ARRIVAL HERE TOO LATE LETTER BY THIS POST. ROBERT.

9th December 1915 – Southampton

My darling,

I have only this moment (S'hampton) opened your note. It never occurred to me what it was. Lassie mine that I should have gone & left you with that request in my pocket grieves me beyond words.

Darling mine you know that had I seen it I would have come at once. Old Bob will have told you that I put it straight into my pocket without opening it & as we had agreed as to our parting, I took it to be just a sweet message to carry with me & I dare not have opened it then. Lass dear I was sorry I was so stupid & just broke down for a minute, but I am alright now, but I couldn't have read a message from you & then said goodbye to the kids afterwards without breaking down. You say it was hard going before, but this dearie beats anything & to think that I have left you with your request unfulfilled makes it harder still.

Lass dear, I have been treasuring that last message to read on the boat & when I realized what I had done & gone & left you like that it makes me feel an awful beast.

However darling, it is too late now. We have just got here (4.30) & I am going on board after tea.

God keep you all my darlings,

Ever your Robert.

11th December 1915, 12.30 a.m. – Hurionville

Here I am at last in our little mess & Buckin is making me a cup of cocoa before going to bed. Weary & worn & sad, inexpressibly sad, dearie mine that I didn't see you again as you wished. I am absolutely obsessed by it & can simply think of nothing else, it grieves me beyond words. Your food stood me in good stead & had it not been for it I should have been in a bad way.

Only this short note now dear, but I simply couldn't go to bed without writing.

There is a large aching void Lassie mine, that will take a lot of filling. My lovely time at home ending with little Ben's nice service will last me tho' some time.

Goodnight my own sweet darling & my love to the Chugs.

11th December 1915, 4.30 p.m. – No. 4a – Hurionville

Have just got your nice letter my darling, written on Black-Thursday morning. You dear old thing to think of it & it has cheered me up wonderfully. I loved getting it as I hoped to get a letter from you by today's post & then realized that it was an absolute impossibility. Then coming in just now I found your No. 0 lying on the table. 'Ken's' duplicate was also much appreciated! It is so like him!! I never realized how much my holiday had done for me until I got back & feel absolutely different to what I did when I left & ever, ever so much better.

I am now quite settled down old girl & you need not worry in the least about me, I am only so concerned about you my love, lest the parting has put you back at all in your recovery. They talk about parting being such 'sweet sorrow' but they can "ave parting' for all I care. The Chugs nearly defeated me on the doorstep by reminding me that I hadn't said goodbye to 'Mum'. I wish to God I had only known how true it was. It was a bit of a shock when I opened your note at S'hampton & realized what I had done, but I can't imagine what it must have been to you dearie to hear the car drive off & your dear request so very callously disregarded. I only pray that old Bob saw me put it straight in my pocket & has told you so.

Give my best love to the dear little Chugs after skimming the cream for your old self. Dearie mine, I'm so ashamed of breaking down at the last & making things so much harder for you especially when you aren't strong, but I simply couldn't help it. I was leaving everything in the world to me, & it was so terribly, terribly hard.

Ever my love, my own.

12th December 1915 – No. 5 answering No. 1 – Hurionville

Lass darling, if you only knew the store I have set by this, how I have longed for Ben to be Ben for this one purpose; your sentence has told me the one thing I have wanted more than anything. To feel that should anything happen to me that you have a substitute that is me & of me so recently, especially when old Bob is so soon going to school, takes all the pain out of the thought & is what I have longed for, ever since this beastly war began. It is too glorious that you have said this old dear & the greatest comfort. You say you have all the comforts but I thank God that you have.

What a lovely time we did have dearie, every minute was priceless under present conditions & the memory of it all will keep me going for months.

The General came over today & is at present proposing taking Barber as Staff Captain for the 141st Infy Bde but I don't know yet if Thwaites will approve of him. 'Cherchez la femme.' All this has come about because he has a pretty sister. She knows a General, gets him to write to his old pal Barter, & it all coincides with a vacancy occurring. I am going to let him go if Thwaites will take him as he has done very well indeed since I have been away, & he has had a lot of work & responsibility.

I am enclosing you 30/- to buy the Chugs some small things from Dad for Xmas & you must add something to it if it won't go round out of my money you will get at Xmas.

My love to you my own dear Lassie.

13th December 1915 – No. 6 in answer to No. 2 – Hurionville

Darling mine,

I have quite cheered Lassie dear & am as fit & well as ever I was. What a lovely time it was. I keep thinking & thinking about it and long for the next time. You will have to be very severe next time. It was so very safe this time.

I am fearfully pleased with the 'pres' & it writes beautifully I think. I was afraid when I first got it that the nib was a bit too soft but having used it I like it very much indeed & I don't think it could be improved upon. I shall treasure it like anything because like one's watch it seems somehow to be a very near medium.

Shall be pretty busy these next few days so you will only get scrappy bits. I want a couple more pipes & some more paper & envelopes. The typewriter paper would do well.

My love to you my darling.

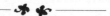

14th December 1915 – No. 7 in answer to No. 3 – Hurionville

In some ways I do feel that I have never been away, just as coming home again made one feel the same, but there are times when one misses something & things seem dull & blank & one gets sort of fed up & wonders how it will all end. I'm feeling a bit that way tonight.

The Balkan news is very bad according to the papers but perhaps things will cheer up later on.

It's a great blessing being able to write like this as if it wasn't for your letters dearie, I don't know *how* much more poisonous it would be. The pen still 'Marché bien' & I like it most awfully – it brings one somehow nearer to you dearie than at any other time of the day & I am very lonely now. The home influence & associations haven't worn off yet & at times I want you very badly my dear.

My love to you my darling.

On 15 December the squadron moved again, to Drouvin just south of Béthune, where they were forced to share billets until the 19th when they moved to nearby Vaudricourt. Here they immediately began to construct stables to provide cover for the horses for the winter months ahead, using saplings for timber and three sailcloths from the Royal Engineers for roofing.

17th December 1915 – No. 9 in answer to your No. 6 – Drouvin

Rain, rain & still more rain!! I very much doubt if it will ever be fine again. We are living an awful hole & corner existence at present, haven't been able to unpack or settle in any way & move about 200 yards only on Sunday morning.

I am so glad that your bit of comfort still comforts. I am sorry to hear you are without light especially as I am writing by the best electric light now. Barber went & fiddled with his switch last night with the result that he put out half the lights in the house, but by the aid of pins as fuses I have been able to mend switches and restore everything tonight.

I had arranged such a nice Xmas dinner for the men in the Château here & now they are going into hovels that are nothing like so good as the hovel at home, tho' I hope to get the school for them if I can get them all into it. We are still smiling but it is a bit of an effort at times. What price our old friend D.H. now?

18th December 1915 – No. 10 in answer to your No. 7 – Drouvin

A lovely letter from you today & a great blessing and help these times as conditions of living are pretty bad & seem worse every day, the mud & wet being beyond a joke.

I am so glad to hear that Ken & his 'vache' are going on so well.

How funny Effie having my man's sister as a nurse. I would almost rather have his regard than any man in the squadron as it is worth something. There are a pair of them, MacDougal & MacLagan, known as 'the two Macs'. They are absolutely inseparable & report has it that if by any chance they were separated they would pine & die. They run my mules & very well they do it & are worth their weight in gold. They won't go inside & insist on bivouacking & are living out now & have never been inside since we came out. They both want to get a remount job now & become officers & I am trying to get it for them but it will be a very sad day for me if I do lose them. I should like you to see the sister.

Many thanks for the children's letters. It was good the lectures being appreciated so much.[93]

My love to you all.

19th December 1915 – No. 11 – Vaudricourt

Just a few lines before I go to bed. I have moved out of my fairly decent billet & now am in only a moderate one & the men worse off than they have ever been before, but still they have got a roof over their heads.

Today has been glorious and there have been more Hun flying than I ever saw before in one day. We saw a grand fight again today but I think that the Hun got away in the end. There were four of them over us this morning flying very high.

Our hostess is grousing like anything as she wants to lock up & I must go off to my billet.

My love to you.

---

[93] During his leave Robert had lectured on the war to the people of Cowfold.

20th December 1915 – No. 12 in answer to your 8 & 9 – Vaudricourt

I am so glad that you have at long last got my No. 2 and that you like it. It is difficult to write you decent letters now as we have got such poor billets. I have got a very comfortable room to sleep in but it is at the other end of the village & is rather too cold for sentiment – here in our mess we are equally cold and have five or six lads chattering & the gramophone going.

I am glad you liked my reason for Ben old dear, & we will certainly hope he won't have to stand proxy. The cow is doing really very fine work & I must congratulate her. I will try and remember 7 p.m. every Friday. I am so glad the Chugs like their money. The Xmas pudding and the cake both arrived today. Thanks.

My love & best wishes for a brighter New Year.

21st December 1915 – No. 13 – Vaudricourt

A blank day today like the day before yesterday but your two nice letters of yesterday are still sticking by me like a good fid of plum duff!

I have at last got my way & bought the trees for making horse cover & hope in a few days to have a good portion of the squadron completely covered over. I rode into Béthune today & bought some tools & hope to get a lot done tomorrow if it is fine but today it has been too wet to work but my axemen felled 30 trees before lunch so we have a good bit of stuff to start work with tomorrow.

We are starting a class of instruction for young Divisional Cavalry officers & Cecil Howard, 16th Lancers, & I are to run it here. Harry Rawlinson sent for me today & I met Cecil at lunch there. I am going to spend a night with him at Cavalry Corps H.Q. next week & so should see some old faces again. It really has been a most depressing day today, rain, rain & nothing but rain, simply teemed. I expect it is something to do with the increased amount of firing. I have got a strenuous day's work in front of me tomorrow so shall be off to bed dearie now.

Best love.

❧ ❧

24th December 1915 – No. 16 – Vaudricourt

I have been building all day & completed another stable today for another troop. That means cover for 70 horses. It is splendid getting the stuff & by next Saturday I hope to have the whole squadron under cover. They are just Dutch barns covered by tarpaulin sheets, each 30 ft by 30 & three sheets to a shed which makes the ground covered 85 feet x 28 with two rows of horses' heads inwards 18 on each side of the centre line of poles.

No. 16   Decr 24 1915

My dear old girl,

I have no news for you again to-day I fear as for one reason there has been no mail again & for another I have been building all day & completed another stable to day for another troop. That means cover for 70 horses. It is splendid getting the stuff & by next Saturday I hope to have the whole squadron under cover. They are just Dutch barns covered by tarpaulin sheets, each 30 ft by

30 & three sheets to a shed which makes the ground covered 85 feet x 28 with two rows of horses heads inwards 18 on each side of the centre line of poles.

It was a great days work getting the shed finished to-day & I was awfully pleased about it & I feared it would have to be left

How I wish I was going to spend tomorrow with you & the Chugs & have them running in, in the morning, with their things.

Best love my own old dear & all blessings on you & the Chugs.

Christmas Day 1915 – No. 17 answering your 13 – Vaudricourt

So far as I am concerned I have not had a particularly lively Xmas. First of all I wanted to go to church and didn't wake up in time which annoyed me muchly. Then it rained like Hades most of the day & the horses are absolutely up to their eyes in mud.

I gave the men a whole holiday from 9.30 today & at midday & evening stables the officers & Sergeants fed & watered the whole squadron & acted as 'stable guards' from 9.30 a.m. until 6 p.m. when the night guard mounted. We have, in consequence, had a pretty strenuous day I can tell you.

The men had a real good day, I think, in spite of all things and had lots to eat tho' we were disappointed over our geese which was a pity. They got as far as the station at Béthune but couldn't be got off the train. We made up with hams and they had two turkeys a Troop. We had a very nice plum pudding & old Mac got the thimble. Darling mine, somehow tonight I am in no mood for writing to you. I hardly dare think of your day at home & I can't write decently with other folk in the room. Perhaps I will be able to do a bit more when I go to bed. All being well I am going to Cecil Howard tomorrow & I might see lots of folk. Hope I shall.

26th December 1915 – No. 18 – at 4th Corps H.Q., Lillers

I motored over here today & am staying with Cecil Howard. I left Vaudricourt in a car he sent for me about 1.45 and got here just before 4 p.m. So far I have seen no one as we have been discussing schemes etc. for this class we are going to run on January 3rd.

I wish I could have been at the Xmas Tree. I certainly was thinking of you all yesterday dearie, in my weaker moments, I couldn't help it. Our longed-for Xmas at home & all bust by this damned war. I doubt very much if we shall even get the next but we will hope on all the same.

My love to you old darling & to the Chugs.

29th December 1915 – No. 21 – Vaudricourt

I have such a wealth of letters from you to answer that I hardly know where to begin.

You have no business to read anything in my letters that isn't actually written down – it's a dangerous practice & you might read into them something that wasn't intended so give it up, but bar rot dearie, it has somehow been a bit of a job settling down again & it was really far easier going before than it was this time. Your bird books proved themselves invaluable in that last half hour after lunch & I don't know how I should have got through it without them.

We don't seem to have lost any of our parcels, so far as I can see, in the train fire. The Chugs' pipe certainly arrived alright & I have smoked it ever since & a very nice one it is. Quite a brainwave that tape measure. Congratulations!!

Jacksons[94] have made up for their initial error by sending us three consignments of parcels one on top of another, two complete lots have arrived together today.

I think if I had stayed at home for Xmas I should never have come back at all. It all sounds so very jolly & I can see the whole show especially old Mairky blowing the surprise!! I thought over that stocking business and could see you putting the 'onge' [orange] in the toe & I am so glad that they still prove a joy.

There has been a lot of gunning here today. I don't know what about but the air has been bristling with shells a few miles off. Thank goodness they don't come here.

I have got all my horses comfortably in now thank goodness, the last troop going in this afternoon & as last Tuesday the trees were growing it's a pretty creditable performance tho' I says it who shouldn't!

My love to you my own darling.

[94] Of Piccadilly.

30th December 1915 – No. 22 in answer to 17, 18 & 19 – Vaudricourt

For the moment my class is off. The idea was that should the time ever arise when we make an advance a very great deal of work would be thrown on the Div. Mounted Troops. The work that they have been called to do up to date is so totally different that many of the younger boys know little or nothing of the general role of Mounted Troops under those circumstances. Every opportunity is being taken to train them theoretically when troops are in the line and practically when at rest. Should we succeed in breaking the Hun line the role of the Div. Mounted Troops will be a very important one, therefore the very highest training is necessary.

We were going to a town near here, in fact the place we detrained at originally,[95] where there is a good hotel where we could feed, we were all going into a large house where we could sleep & do the indoors work. Cecil was coming to stay there too & we were to have twelve pupils. Cecil is on the staff of the Cavalry Corps.

It's most amusing. Henry was over here while I was at the Cavalry Corps, throwing out feelers as to whether I would take him back again & today I get the enclosed from him. I am very glad, as I don't think I should have taken him back as he is senior to Mac & I am not going to have him make a convenience of the squadron, tho' I should have loved to have had him really, as I was so awfully fond of him.

I am glad you are letting Vio have old Bobbo as it is a good thing for him to have a jaunt or two away from home before he goes to school. I am afraid old girl the time will fly for you till Easter when he will have to make a longer visit. Little Ken will have a big burden on his shoulders when he has to do proxy for us both.

[95] Lillers.

31st December 1915 – No. 23 answering your 20 – Vaudricourt

I gathered we should be rich from what the Governor said & I only hope it won't be very long before we have a chance of spending it. It's difficult to think of a suitable gift as most of the current subscriptions are doing alright. I should like tho' to find some of the older funds that are feeling the pinch, especially one connected with the poorer-class children where one could do something perhaps. What could one do about endowing a bed in a children's hospital? Could you find out one or two like that as I feel we ought to do something of the sort.

Will you thank Woolven for his letter & tell him I hope to be able to answer it later on. Congratulate him from me on his success with the engine.

My love to you all,

Ever your Robert.

CHAPTER EIGHT

FIRST CASUALTIES FOR K.E.H.

January saw little change in the fortunes of the Allies. The stalemate on the Western Front continued, though a German offensive near Arras in the last week of the month made minor gains. Retaining supremacy in the air, German Zeppelins dropped nearly 400 bombs on the English Midlands, causing more civilian casualties, and their U-boats continued to destroy and disrupt British shipping. The Russians, however, were making some progress on the Eastern Front, notably in Armenia, whilst the Allies successfully completed a covert evacuation of Gallipoli under the noses of the Turkish enemy. In London on 5 January 1916, Parliament introduced the Conscription Bill to raise 2 million more men for the armed forces, as until this time the British army had been an entirely volunteer force.

On New Year's Day one sergeant and eight men from 'C' Squadron went into the line as divisional snipers, working mainly in the Double Crassier at Loos, the twin slag heaps close to the town, which provided an elevated vantage point for snipers. It was here that the squadron would suffer its first casualties.

1st January 1916 – No. 24 answering your 21 – Vaudricourt

My dear old girl,

It was bad luck that the one Xmas that we had so looked forward to should be bust up but it can't be helped. The men did appreciate their holiday very much, as they said so in their letters.

Can you get me 20 pairs of the half Wellington clogs. The ones we wear are no good as one goes over their tops at once. This would run to about £10 & I should like them as soon as possible. To revert to your No. 20, all the spare men in the squadron & two platoons of cyclists hand the nails!!

Ever your Robert.

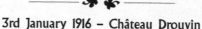

3rd January 1916 – Château Drouvin

It is no use having a wife unless one can use her in times of disappointment as well as in times of joy. As the time for the publication of the promised dispatch of 'Mentions' drew nearer the more certain I seemed to be that I should get my 'Mention'. While I was at home I hoped against hope that it would be published so that we could read it together. It didn't appear and I still hoped on & now it has come I haven't got it.[96]

I wanted it so much for your sake dearie, I didn't care for my own so much but I knew it would give you so much pleasure that lately it has become almost a mania. Now for the present my chance has gone. It may occur again but there is no opening at present so one will have to wait on in hope. I oughtn't to worry you with this dearie, but it damned near broke my heart this morning. I will write you again later.

3rd January 1916 – No. 26 answering 22 & 23 – Château Drouvin

In the first sort of flush of disappointment I am afraid I wrote you rather more than I ought but I had somehow made so sure about it. In the early days so many folk had said to me what a splendid work it was that I was doing for the Division. The General himself said to me that he would never forget what I had done for them & one day talking to a French General to whom he was explaining the school he said 'We are going to give him a medal for this'. However, there it is & it's no good grousing.

We moved today into our Château & are more comfortable than we have been since we came out I think, which is always something. I am so glad to hear that the Chugs did so well at their play & I do wish I could have seen them. Their essays were top-hole too. Lass dear as you say, we have two things to make us happy & the rest doesn't matter at all. I know in my own inner self that the old squadron is good through & through. I

---

[96] Robert was hoping for a Mention in Dispatches for his work at the Bomb School.

don't mind what they want of it, I have no misgivings at all that it will do alright & that is enough.

My love to you all.

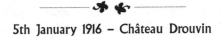

5th January 1916 – Château Drouvin

My darling old girl, don't set your hopes on anything resulting from my visit to Cecil & Co. I had a very pleasant time & they were all most awfully nice, but the impression that I came away with was that they were all professional soldiers & that for the mere amateur there was no room these times. One is looked upon even by 'K's' army rather with a quiet condescension these days, but nevertheless outside the Holy of Holies. I may be quite wrong but certainly that is my feeling. I don't much regret it – one can't expect once one has left to be remembered & I left to suit myself & would tomorrow if I could & the war was over.

I'm looking forward to another evening together I can tell you. Many thanks for the photo of the Chugs.

7th January 1916 – No. 30 answering your 27 – Château Drouvin

I got a lovely letter from you tonight on my return from the trenches. I have got 8 men & a sergeant up there as Divisional snipers & went up today with Syme[97] as a companion to see them. Things were very quiet today & bar a few light shells now & then there was nothing doing at all.

The class is on again & is only postponed for the present minute, & begins either the 16th or Feb 1st. With regard to the posts, your letter & old Bob's both arrived together so it seems that if you post at 8 a.m. the letter arrives the same time as those posted 6 p.m. the previous evening. You old rotter, of course I remember the first date in the book. Surely a certain evening in the garden at Staplefield!! 2*d* please.

---

[97] Lieutenant D. A. Syme.

It's getting very late now old girl & I have walked simply miles through very muddy trenches & so am for my downy couch.

Sunday 9th January 1916 – No. 32 answering your 29 & ? – Château Drouvin

I got two lovely letters as above today & was more than pleased with them. It is no good minimizing the fact that this has been the greatest blow I have ever had since I have been a soldier. I have certainly got over it now but I've had some rather bitter days this last week. Chaytor & old Harry[98] are absolutely furious about it which is something & it endorses one's own opinion & makes it not too egotistical. It is not as tho' I had failed them in anything.

If there is another Squadron with a better record in France outside the Regular Cavalry I'll take my hat off to it. We were the only unit to complete our horse standings during our rest & now other units are coming to see our stables because there is nothing like them in the country!! It's damned hard lines, & the squadron has dug well under heavy shell fire & the C.R.E. most grateful for the work done & most complimentary. It's practically the only unit in the Div. that can be put on work of that kind without super-vision from R.E. officers. There is on top of that, my inauguration & running of the Bomb School & the fact that I made the Battye bomb safe & I haven't heard of an accident since. I cannot now understand why I was left out & one can't ask!

How terrible about those women and children on the *Natal*.[99] I will try & find time to write to Mairky. Tell her I loved her letter especially the part about the 'Trakshunengen' for crossing 'ruf ground'. My love to you my own dear.

---

[98] General Rawlinson.
[99] HMS *Natal* was sunk in the Firth of Cromarty when munitions on the ship exploded, resulting in over 300 casualties – including a party of visiting schoolchildren.

10th January 1916 – No. 33 – Château Drouvin

I rode down to see the Cavalry today & was lucky enough to find old Vic out of the trenches & in the rest billets. I had a bit of a crack with him. I didn't think he looked well in fact rather bad but he had been up all night & it was probably only want of sleep. I was very glad to see him.[100]

I woke up with a beastly head this morning & have had it all day. I expect it was the unaccustomed warmth of the new eidy. I think a bottle of old Charles's tonic would be a good thing. I also want a bottle of hair wash & some toothbrushes.

My love to you dearie mine.

11th January 1916 – No. 34 answering 30 – Château Drouvin

I was very glad to get your letter & was hoping for two but only one turned up. Do you remember Shaw[101] the man who lunched with us at Sandy's after the London show? He was killed the day before yesterday. He was running our Maxim gun & was killed by shrapnel. I am afraid it will mean that I shall lose Syme, but I hope not as I hear they have got another lad trained as a machine gunner at home.

It is very bad luck that both our officer casualties should have proved fatal. However, such is war. The French papers say that in the letters of a number of men taken by the French at Hartsmannweilerkopf[102] the writers suggested to the recipients that they should kill their officers & come home!!

It is good news about Salonica & I am awfully glad they have got everyone

---

[100] His brother-in-law, Victor Hermon, who served with the Carabiniers, survived the war. He lost two of his three sons in the Second World War.

[101] Captain C. A. Shaw of the Machine Gun Section, 'A' Squadron, K.E.H., was badly wounded at Windy Corner and died the following morning.

[102] French Mountain troops had captured 1,300 Germans at Hartsmannweilerkopf in the Vosges Mountains in December.

off those damned Dardanelles. It really is one of the most wonderful feats that have ever been accomplished in war.

My love to you all my darlings.

12th January 1915 – No. 35 answering 31 & 32 – Château Drouvin

My dear wife,

I have already instructed you to the effect that you are not to read into my letters what is not down in actual words on the paper. I am perfectly well & as happy as circumstances will permit. I had a second go of whities last night with a trifle better result & am feeling much better for it tonight.

We will try and save all we can as then we can have a bit of a bust later on if things look settled & if they don't then we can probably tide over a bad time on the savings. I will think over the Dr Barnardo's Home Subscription or rather donation. What I feel about a big institution like that is that the particular child would be admitted just the same whether we paid for it or not & that if we could equip a bed at a child's hospital over & above their usual number then one would have done some definite good. We have got a lot of money & I am prepared to put down from £50 to £100 for a decent object like this & you could put what you like to it. If you could find out from Juckes if he knows any hospital that needs some of the latest plant for their operating theatre we could give it. Something to alleviate suffering. An X-ray plant or something of that sort. I should much rather do something like this & I should like it done anonymously.

It is rather an odd break from such a subject but my snipers got two Huns yesterday which has pleased them awfully.

We had a party of naval men from the fleet here the other day & they did awfully well. They were in our trenches when the Hun sprung a big mine & two of them manned a machine gun & had the time of their lives. Their officer said he couldn't go back without some Hun rifles, so in broad daylight he jumped over the parapet & collected 3, but the Boche made it so hot for him that he had to get into a shell hole & wait for two or three hours before he could get back again but he brought in his rifles alright. I hear one of the men is to get a D.C.M. out of it.

I don't think old Juckes' bill is too high if it includes both Ken's show & yours. Please note that the 'Chidley boos' are very expensive luxuries. The pen is fine old girl & I like it awfully now, since getting it I have used no other!!

My love to the Chugs.

13th January 1916 – No. 36 answering 33 – Château Drouvin

My darling old girl if you had been in the room watching me write the answer to that 2nd question you couldn't have described what took place more accurately!! It was on the tip of my pen to write 'a certain day when you nearly chucked away a damned good bargain'![103] And then I thought that it was so obvious that it couldn't be that & I plumped for the other!! I admit now I couldn't have told you the month to save my life, but I should have supposed it to be summer because you wouldn't have been at Inverloddon[104] & that is about as near as I could get without the book so far as dates are concerned, but both incidents I remember well!! I will admit that you have scored one this time because it exactly fits the whole dilemma!! I as near as anything put down the right day & it was a hope against hope that I had made a lucky shot!!

I am glad Ken liked his bottle, but you have done right well old dear, & this will give you a bit more freedom now.

Last night we had a magic lantern show which was quite amusing. One of the Padres came over with his lantern and we had Dickens' 'Scrooge' which was quite nice & very good slides.

Best love to you all.

---

[103] This seems to refer to a proposal of marriage which was not instantly accepted.
[104] A family home at Wargrave-on-Thames.

15th January 1916 – No. 38 answering 34 & 35 – Château Drouvin

Somehow tho' I have been keeping the 14th in my mind for days, when it did come I forgot all about its significance.[105] I was rather worried in the evening because my old man Macaulay was killed yesterday & being our first real casualty it put other things out of my mind. I am so awfully sorry about it; he was one of my best sergeants & was in charge of the snipers. He leaves a wife & a little girl, but I hear he had earned a pension of £1,000 a year so I hope they will not be too badly off. He was killed instantly by shrapnel.

Darling mine, I wish you were here & we could have had our day together, especially as today I have got one of my beastly colds, simply streaming!! I am going to bed now dearie & I will try and write you a decent letter tomorrow & answer these two I got tonight.

My love to you old dear.

16th January 1916 – No. 39 – Château Drouvin

I am so full of cold I simply can't write you tonight, but I hope I shall feel better tomorrow. I lost another man today, one of my snipers,[106] he was walking along a road & a shell must have fallen at his feet. He was carrying their daily report to the Brigade office when it happened. Old Steve has gone up to find out about it and hasn't got back yet.

I see Cecil Howard has got his brevet and my S.S.M. O'Donnell a Military Cross. I am too stuffy dearie & I must go & have a good hot stew for my feet & some aspirin & see if that will do any good.

---

[105] The date of their wedding anniversary.
[106] The second sniper killed was Private Murton. Another squadron sniper, Corporal Murray, had a miraculous escape in the same location: while he was taking aim at an enemy soldier, the rifle kicked violently in his hands. The German had fired first and incredibly the bullet travelled up the bore of the rifle, stopping six inches from the muzzle.

17th January 1916 – No. 40 – Château Drouvin

I am awfully angry that I forgot the 14th as I had been treasuring it up for days & how I forgot I don't know as I intended to write you a special letter to arrive on the day.

I've given up being fed up dearie mine and shall just go on & not worry now. I am rather worried tho' about 'A' Sqn as I hear many rumours of great unrest & almost mutiny. Their boss is most awfully unpopular, he treats the men like children & they naturally resent it.

Well done little Mairky not to fall off old Peg when she fell down. The Chugs could have some fine rides round here as there is quite a bit of park to this château. Chaytor took over the bomb school from me, then broke his leg falling off his horse & is now back as A.D.C. to '*Sir* Charles'.

No, Lillers is where the class is. We haven't quite settled how the classes are to run but each lasts a week and whether we shall have a gap between each or run straight on I do not know yet, anyhow while the class is on I shall be away from the squadron altogether & Mac will be running it.

It is funny how we have had all these casualties just lately. Sutton in 'A.' Sqn got badly hit in the leg a few days ago & will be 'hors de combat' for a long time & my two men were killed on two consecutive days.

My dear old girl, how dare you drop my bit of comfort,[107] I am so thankful that neither of you were hurt but as you say it must have frightened you a bit.

Lass dear, I am in no mood to adequately reply to your closing message, I can only endorse it. My head is too full of cold & I feel far too much like a boiled pudding to write half what I should like to. It's not been bad, has it?

---

[107] Their baby son.

18th January 1916 – No. 41 – Château Drouvin

I want you to send me a bottle of your patent tonic so that I can pick up as fast as possible. It would be too awful to get so run down that I had to come home. I don't think that really there is any chance, but I want to take every precaution, even to your beastly medicine.

I had a letter from old Nell & she sent us some biscuits & things which were very welcome. I sort of toddled as far as the stables today & bar that have done nothing much but sneeze & swear alternately. Thank the Chugs for their nice letters.

Best love my darling.

19th January 1916 – No. 42 answering 38 & 39 – Château Drouvin

I am much better today I am glad to say & taking quite a different view of life. Went out for a bit of a ride this morning and again after lunch. The Norton tonic rolled up today & I had my first dose after lunch but I think this is only a liver tickler & I want the other badly.

It has been a lovely day today, quite summer & it has made one feel quite different so perhaps you can read that feeling between the lines as you have read others!! A more satisfactory tone!!!

It was part of the conditions of the sailors coming to the trenches that they should go back and lecture to their ships but they said that they would never be believed & so had to have signed papers from the staff guaranteeing their statements. The object of their coming was to be able to let the Navy at large know the conditions of life of the Army as there was a feeling that the Navy was being harder treated than the Army & so this party came to see for themselves. They went into a part of the line where the communications trenches are 3 miles long & vary from one to three feet of mud & water in the bottom of them. They came in for a real big mine explosion followed by some of the heaviest shelling there has been for some time.

I am sending the Chugs some plain chocolate today. Keep the box. My love to you old dear.

21st January 1916 – No. 44 – Château Drouvin

Alas no letter today old dear but two tomorrow. I am now completely restored to health, just a sniffle but only residue that requires a handkerchief and my 'Church blow'.

Will you add the following names to my list of commissions & then let me know what the total is up to date.

Cpl M. G. Fielding	H. H. Kilby K.E.H.
O. L. Jacks	Cpl H. Whelan
L/Cpl W. W. Crowe	L/Sgt Dawson
Cpl W. F. Martinson	Cpl Morgan
J. A. FitzHerbert	W. C. Maclagan
W. T. MacDougall	

I am very busy now coaching my two young officers so that they may make a bit of a showing at the class when we begin. I think I shall get you to address my letters to the Town Major, LILLERS while I am there as being the best means of getting them as it is a good ten miles from here.

> *I think of you in joyous spring*
> *When hawthorn buds are blowing,*
> *And in the gorgeous summer time*
> *When roses red are glowing.*
> *In Autumn too I think of you*
> *But ah! in sweetest measure*
> *My thoughts are yours when Xmas speaks*
> *Of byegone hours of pleasure.*

That's very good for me!! I think it is high time I took up, perhaps better still, lay down the mightier weapon than the sword!!

Well, to bed my love.

With this Robert had enclosed a letter from the widow of Sergeant Macaulay in reply to his letter explaining the circumstances of her husband's death on the 14th. In it she says: 'I am thankful that he should not have to endure any more of the miseries of this hateful war if he was not to come through it.' And, generously, at such a time of grief, she asks for her husband's rubber boots to be given to someone else 'as I know they are much needed'.

22nd January 1916 – No. 45 answering 42 & 41 – Château Drouvin

I spent my morning with my two youngest officers & 4 sergeants giving them a little instruction of a technical nature & more or less practising for my class & am going to take them daily for a bit & try and work them up to a little higher standard.

I must say that to sit here & read articles like you refer to & that the Government is shilly-shallying over this compulsion business is really very hard indeed. Compulsion was to have come in on Nov. 30th & even now the bill isn't passed & they are making concessions right & left.

Sergeant Macaulay was the man from Rhodesia who Vic & Bernard both knew. He enlisted in the Regiment about Oct. 1914 & has always been in my squadron. His wife lives at Ascot with her father-in-law, Colonel Macaulay. I wish you could go & see her, perhaps she would come & stay with you, she has a nice little girl about Bet's age? and is quite young herself, I believe.

My snipers live in Maroc and they apparently had agreed that if they got killed they would bury one another just outside their billet & so they went up & carried him down there & buried him about 11 o'clock the same night in a little growing cemetery there, & the other man was buried there too, such a fine man he was too. The shells of both sides fly over them ceaselessly day & night.

Nothing I should like better than to build a pair of nice cottages at the gate, something like Arthur's only lower and if we could build them for £500 I wouldn't mind thinking it over. Ask old Fowler in a casual sort of way what a pair of decent cottages would cost? Good plain cottages with a fairly artistic outside. *Country Life* might produce you a good design & they have gone in a great deal for designs of good sound artistic cottages at remunerative prices. I would almost rather build two good cottages than spend £20 or £30 repairing that old one. We could get the Buckins in then if we wanted to.

My darling I fear it is going to be a very sad day for you when old Bobbo goes to school but little Ken will soon arrive at the interesting stage & he will have to be substitute for us both till this blasted war is over.

27th January 1916 – No. 50 answering 47 – Château Drouvin

I have been over to Lillers again today to make the final arrangements for the class which I am afraid are none too good as it is very hard to find room there, most of the billets being allotted.

I sent you Mrs Macaulay's letter without comment on purpose, just to see what you would think of it. Exactly the same thing occurred to me as I couldn't help thinking what a wonderful letter it was & what a brave woman she must be, but as you say she hadn't by then probably quite realized her loss.

Terribly short of news again dearie mine, I am afraid, & so far as I know likely to continue so unless the stimulus of the Kaiser's birthday stirs up the Boche to an effort.[108] Give my love to the little Chugs.

29th January 1916 – No. 52 answering 49 – Château Drouvin

There has been some very heavy shelling here these last few days, the old guns fairly pooping off & the old Hun has left his trenches in one or two places but has been very well hammered & made to go back to them for

---

[108] The 27th, the Kaiser's birthday, usually heralded an attack, and this year was no exception. German troops attacked the French south of the Somme; the British counterattacked the next day near Carnoy, the 'Liverpool Pals' succeeding in repulsing the enemy.

his trouble. This evening I have my sergeants' class for their bit of instruction and then dinner & letter.

I am afraid my little grey pony is going wrong in his feet. He has been rather dicky for some time now & I have been a bit anxious about him. I should be awfully sorry to have to lose him now as he is such a lovely ride but if he gets any worse I shall have to part with him. Your wretched old horse kicked Saxon on the knee just about Xmas & I am afraid he will have a permanently big knee. Your old rascal is very naughty & kicks other horses badly if he gets half a chance.

I hate the idea of leaving here, it is nearly as bad as starting out from home tho' I expect I shall like it alright as soon as I get the class started.

Every day I hate this damned war more & I wish to goodness it was over & we were once more leading the old home life but it would be a disaster of the first magnitude if it stopped now. We must fix it but I fear it will mean at least another winter before it is over. 'K' said three years & it looks very like it. I cannot see how it can end for a long time unless Germany has internal trouble & with all the population soldiers & under discipline, it seems unlikely that until utter exhaustion comes, the thing can end.

CHAPTER NINE

MARKING TIME FOR THE SQUADRON

February 1916 saw further progress by the Russians in Armenia but also witnessed the start of the Battle of Verdun in Lorraine on the 21st. The German Chief of Staff, Erich von Falkenhayn, knowing the importance of Verdun in the French psyche, had chosen the area for a major attack to divert French troops from the rest of the front. Verdun had been a key fortress since Roman times and was a symbol of resistance in the Franco-Prussian War of 1870–1. However, since the attack was delayed from the 12th to the 21st, the French Commander-in-Chief, Joffre, was able to act on intelligence and make defensive preparations.

Battle was waged along an 8-mile front with great ferocity, preceded by a heavy bombardment and the use of gas by both sides. Verdun proved to be the longest battle of the war, lasting ten months, until 18 December. Each side sustained enormous losses, but neither gained a strategic advantage. The Kaiser's hope that 'This war will end at Verdun' was not to come to fruition. Instead Verdun became a symbol of the utter futility of the war.

On the British Front, bad weather prevented major attacks but the Germans made small gains in the Ypres Salient. Meanwhile, the Anglo-French leadership prepared for a major offensive on the Somme later in the year. Robert attended a week's course at 4th Corps School for Divisional Mounted Troops at Lillers, taking Lieutenants D. A. Syme and H. M. Tulloch with him. Snow and ice in February made training very difficult for the squadron but in March training exercises recommenced.

Sunday 30th January 1916 – No. 53 – Lillers

I have arrived at Lillers and the class is now assembled & we meet all together for dinner at 7.30 p.m.

The class seems to be composed of a nice lot of lads tho' I don't expect that they know a great deal. What I am afraid of is that the weather is going to break as we had a very thick fog all day & it never lifted at all. Really you folk who live at home have absolutely no conception of the hardships that we poor soldiers have to undergo. Tonight I shouldn't have had anything to eat at all unless I had arranged with a potty little hotel to feed us and as it was, all I could get was oysters, soup, omelette, a very nice fricassee of turkey & purée de pommes de terre followed by dessert, cheese, butter & coffee, with red & white wine & now I have dragged my weary bones back to my wretched billet, with only a large feather bed, nice fireplace & every convenience & last but not least there is no electric light which I am accustomed to!! It's too hard!

My love to you all my darlings.

1st February 1916 – Lillers

My darling,

We had quite a nice day today & I have quite enjoyed it. On the way in tonight I called in on Russell & found Twopeny & Northcote[109] there, but so far I am glad to say there is no sign of Syme going but as soon as Cameron goes, who has the guns now, I expect he will have to go & I shall get the next [subaltern] from home. I am perfectly fit & well now & feel quite up to doing anything that is going once more. I sent the Chugs a postcard each & as Ken has you I thought I couldn't give him anything better so I didn't send him one. My love to you my own darling.

2nd February 1916 – No. 56 answering No. 53 – Lillers

I enclose your son's second letter & will send the other should it turn up. I can't help being amused tho' at his poor sorrowing mother sitting at home imagining her favourite son sitting in the middle of Vio's drawing room

---

[109] Major Russell was commanding 'A' Company K.E.H. Lieutenants Twopeny and Northcote were two of his officers.

crying his eyes out with homesickness!!![110] Ungrateful little beggars, chiddly boos, but never the less it is no doubt a blessing as it would mean that there would be a lot more sorrow in the world if it wasn't so & there is plenty as it is, more especially these times.

As you say, dearie mine, every day does bring the war nearer to its end but I am afraid the end is a long way off yet.

My love to you my darling.

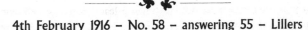

4th February 1916 – No. 58 – answering 55 – Lillers

I am really thankful that in the end I decided to come to this house & not stay at the hotel as it is the rendezvous of fellows going on leave & as the train starts about 2 a.m. they play the piano & sing until it's time to go to the station!! I am very quiet & homely here & it suits me very well indeed.

I had another of my sniper sergeants[111] hit the other day by a piece of shell on the side of the head & I am sorry to say that he has been evacuated, but I hope not to England or I shall not get him back tho' I hear he is not very bad, only they never keep wounded folk anywhere near the front – directly they are bandaged up off they go & in many cases are in an English hospital by the following evening. Funnily enough he was a great friend of Macaulay's & his wife's too. He only returned from leave & seeing Mrs Macaulay last Wed. week – went up into the line on Friday & was hit Monday. He is a most charming man & I should be awfully sorry if I lost him.

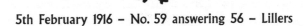

5th February 1916 – No. 59 answering 56 – Lillers

Well we finished today about 2 p.m. some twelve miles from here & Cecil went back to the Corps and we rode back here and tomorrow I go back to Drouvin.

---

[110] Their eldest son Bob was staying with his Aunt Vio in Cheshire to prepare him for boarding school.
[111] Sergeant Heath.

I had a few minutes at midday at Estrée-Blanche & wandered into the church just to see it & I was very much interested to see two kids, just about Betty's size come in & dip their fingers in the holy water & then go and say prayers. It seemed so odd these two kiddies all alone coming in like that. They seemed hugely amused at my being there & treated it as a great joke!

I am sorry to hear that Nurse is seedy & my poor little Mairky too. I should be inclined to risk Quick giving the kids the measles even if you let him take Bob alone but I wouldn't break into Bob's time if you could help it & after all there would be something in his getting Measles over in his own home tho' a bore for you!!

The grey pony carried me like a bird the last time I rode him so it may pass off. I think Harry had been giving him too many oats. My dear old girl, stimulated by your letter tonight I was strong enough to manage a second half-dozen oysters. They come up fresh from the sea every Friday!! so today they were fine.

My love to you my old darling.

6th February 1916 – No. 60 answering 57 – Château Drouvin

Today we had a circular confidential letter written by a senior officer who was taking a very active part in the evacuation of the Gallipoli peninsula, one of the most interesting letters I ever read & the way in which it was carried out was magnificent & reflects the very greatest credit on the staff. I wish I could have copied it & sent it to you or could tell you some more about it but I can't. There is no doubt that we can carry out a retirement with any nation in the world. We are so good that I believe if we were only to face our line the opposite way & retire before a flagged enemy we should have the Huns across the Rhine before you could say Jack Robinson!!

I have got a most extraordinary man in this squadron called Brennan, one of the finest types of Australian, about six foot three & weighing about fifteen stone. He went up to relieve some of my first party of snipers the other day. He has apparently had some family trouble lately & tho' he has lots of relations in New Zealand & is by the bye a New Zealander & not Australian he won't give in the names of any next of kin. Well, I think he is just a bit touched & have an idea that he wants to get shot but of course it is only an idea. Anyhow he had had a day's sniping and hadn't done much good in his own estimation so he crawled out along a gap one day this week till he was within 30 yards of the German line – then he stood bolt upright in broad daylight in full view of the Huns & waited. This so flabbergasted the Hun that two of them stood up too & looked at him & he drew his revolver quickly & shot one of them dead!! Not a bad effort these times tho' risky when one thinks of the number of snipers he had against him. Of course if he goes on like that he will be killed for a certainty but it was really rather a fine effort & a damned good shot.

I liked Mrs Macaulay's letter very much & it would be very nice if you could get her to come & stay with you later on.

I am so glad to hear that Ken is getting on so well & that he seems to have a fund of humour & enjoys life, & am more than glad to hear that La Vache still holds out its capital, keep it up!! He is nearly three months old now & I should love to see the little beggar again.

You know it is wonderful how out here you see the contrasts of life. There in Lillers you find war bringing prosperity to a little pub like that of such an immensity as to be beyond their wildest dreams in times of peace. Then, if they had half a dozen townsfolk in in the day it was quite an event & now they have an average forty or fifty officers in for dinner or drinks every evening and only 15 miles away I brought out of Loos a woman who kept an 'estaminet' three times the size who probably did ten times the business in normal times & she had what she could carry left of the whole of her worldly possessions & her 'estaminet' with its entire contents was a heap of bricks!

My very best love to you old darling & to the kids & please thank Meggie for her most touching postcard.

7th February 1916 – No. 61 – Château Drouvin

I went over to the Corps this morning but only to find all my friends flown. As I told you before my chief friend had gone elsewhere & now I find he has dragged off my other friend with him. Then I went down to the Div. & had a very pleasant half hour with G.S.O.1. Were we together

I could tell you a lot but not on paper, thank you. I am not going to take another Div. Cavalry Class for a bit as I am going to do some Training with the Squadron and cyclists in combination and I asked the Corps not to take me away just now as I wanted to be able to devote myself to my command.

Barber has turned up again tonight having been away from the Squadron since Dec. 20th & I am glad to say that his claim (i.e. having a very pretty sister) has not been strong enough to get him a staff appointment. It was so far as I know his only recommendation. However I am very glad to get him back again.

10th February 1916 – No. 64 answering 59, 60 & 61 – Château Drouvin

In such intervals as I can spare from mopping my eyes and blowing my nose I will try & answer your three lovely letters. I don't remember ever having streamed at eyes & nose as I have today & yesterday. I've got a damnable sore throat too. I have hardly done anything today but sit over the fire. I did go & wander round the stables for a few minutes this morning.

Sergt Heath comes back on Friday. He was hit by a bit of shell just in front of his ear & it was very lucky it didn't break his jaw. I went & saw him in hospital. It was the first time I had been into one of these hospitals. They are not very cheery shops, one poor bloke was terribly knocked about, never be very much good I am afraid. My love to you old darling.

Ever your red-eyed, sore-nosed Robert.

11th February 1916 – No. 65 answering 62 – Château Drouvin

I have just written the Governor a long letter. He wrote to me saying that Mimi had been to Eton & had seen the Head and evidently with the idea of breaking the news to me that he was to be left at Eton another term. I have never heard that Dick has ever once expressed himself as anxious to come out here. Damn it if he would run away from Eton & enlist it would be something but he hasn't got the guts. Now Mac's brother who was 17 last November has come all the way from Australia to do his bit & here is Dick six months older & has no idea above a ferret, tho' there's man's work to be done. I only pray that if we are at such a crisis when Bob is his age that he will see his duty a bit plainer.

I am much better today tho' of course my throat hasn't by any means gone yet.

Well dearie I'm for bed & a good soak for my toes.

13th February 1916 – No. 67 answering 64 – Château Drouvin

This morning I got a letter asking for recommendations for the 'G' side of the staff so I wrote a line to Burnett-Hitchcock asking him to get the G.O.C. to consider my name with any others as I couldn't very well recommend myself! I enclose you his answer. Of course if I was to get the offer of a job on the 'Q' side I should have to take it tho' it isn't the side I want, but there is no doubt that the 'G' side are wanted & I feel my bent lies on that side rather than in the 'jug & bottle' department. However, we shall see what we shall see, but do not set too much store by it as very likely another year will see me still plodding along with the same old squadron.

Old Winnie was lucky to have got out, but my dear old girl you wouldn't have been allowed to come so don't get any false ideas in your little pate please. I don't think your joke about Egypt is at all nice & to tell you the truth it took me a long time to see it & then it flashed on me all of a sudden. You see I forget these things so quickly & warnings & frights become things of the past!

My love to you my darling.

15th February 1916 – Hurionville

I am writing now where I wrote you my No. 4 I think, if I am not wrong.[112] Two months ago & yet it seems ages away now & almost as if it belonged to another life.

It has been the most awful day in a way, blowing a hurricane. When I was called at 5.30 it was blowing and raining fit to burst itself, but by 8.30 the rain had cleared & it was fine but 'strong hard' wind & now it is raining hard & blowing v. hard from N.W. Not at all the sort of a night I should care to be at sea. Very dark too.

My love to you all dearie mine & I simply long for you tonight my own dearie. Would to God this damned war was over & we were together to pursue the even tenor of our ways with the little Chugs once more.

18th February 1916 – No. 72 answering 66 Vol. II and 68 – Hurionville

I simply can't get rid of my cold somehow & tho' it doesn't in the least inconvenience me it is a damned nuisance. The medicine I got from the hospital is awful muck & tastes like beer & sulphur. I don't at all know what is in the box at S'hampton unless it is drawers & vests for the men sent by Stamfordham.[113]

Couldn't you manage to give Ken an extra bottle in the night now? I am so glad to hear that your Ma seems so well & I hope she will mend a lot under the balmy influence of Brook Hill. Grandpapa tells me that 'Bet' proved a very good companion to him in his walks!!

Sergt Heath is back again now I am glad to say alright. I am afraid tho' that one of my cyclist lads is dying. He got very badly hit in the thigh, too high for amputation & now gangrene has set in & he is a gonner I

---

[112] The squadron had moved back to rest billets at Hurionville where they had previously constructed brick standings for their horses.

[113] The King's Private Secretary and Chairman of the Committee of Administration to K.E.H.

fear – a boy called Carpenter. I have had four platoons of cyclists in the trenches this time and this boy got hit patrolling between the lines. Part of his prismatic compass got shot into his thighbone up high.

I am glad to hear that Ken takes after 'Pa'.

My love to you my old darling.

19th February 1916 – No. 73 answering your 69 – Hurionville

I found your letter waiting for me when I got back and it was as usual more than welcome. Darling mine, I am more than glad that you are going to do a bit of work on the land. The whole day today as I rode along I saw women working in the fields. Here you see women in charge of the farm carts, they drive them out to the beetroot 'piles', load the carts & bring in the beet. They plough & so do the boys. I saw a boy, certainly no more than 12 years old, ploughing in a field with no one to supervise & doing a full day's work too. Every man of military age here is with his regiment & in the villages there is absolutely no one except old men & women. By the look of the country you wouldn't know that times were not normal, and I am prepared to bet that there is as big a yield this year, seasons being equal, as there has been in the past.

The women's work is beyond all praise and when one thinks of the number of girls there are at home showing themselves in their best clothes on a Sunday & too proud to do a handstroke of work in the week from fear of 'lowering themselves' it fairly makes one's blood boil. They say 'Who looks after the children?' Well anything of 12 years, boy or girl, is working in the fields. The rest are at school. Three miles behind the trenches the daily schools are at work even tho' within the shelling area. The children are being looked after and the work is being done. If you want to, read them this at the meeting & tell them from me that far from minding, the men will respect the women all the more when they know they are turning to, to help to bring the show to an end.

Nothing will stop the war but the united efforts of man, woman & child each working, not in its own sphere only but also where its work can be most felt. If women are needed in the fields then it's their solemn duty to go & work there, whatever their inclination is & if they've got any guts they will do it. How can it hurt Ken for you to go & work? There are lots of nursing mothers working here.

I saw two girls spreading muck the other day here & doing it real well too & they couldn't either of them have been much more than 16 or 18. It's a pity they can't send out batches of women here, as they do labour members, to see what is going on & then they could go back & tell the folk at home.

My love to you old darling.

20th February 1916 – No. 74 answering your 70 – Hurionville

A damned Hun aeroplane had the lip to come & drop some bombs here last night. One fell close to my comfy billet of the course & dropped into a family bedroom & rather made a mess of the family but as usual served no useful military purpose & killed a poor man & his wife & child. It's a dirty trick this bomb-dropping unless confined to military centres tho' I suppose it is possible to call this place that!!

The marmalade is not quite right old dear I am sorry to say. Do you remember you had to put in an extra pint of water last year or something of the sort. Anyhow it isn't as good as it used to be by a long way. I am glad you recognize that one's womenfolk are out of place in war. I will come home & see you when I can but you can't come here I am afraid.

Goodnight my dear, dear love.

21st February 1916 – No. 75 answering 71 & Bob, Bet & Mairky – Hurionville

Your nice letter to cheer me on my return from a long field day today. I am mending alright I am glad to say.

I quite realize that the Chugs are luxuries and expensive but a leopard cannot change his spots & I have been brought up never to study expense & am by an extravagant sire & out of a still more extravagant dam!! Nothing

EWH pursuing his love of sailing, off the Isle of Wight, before the war.

Betty looking for her dog with Bob, Mary, Meg and their ponies.

EWH at Aldershot with King Edward's Horse in 1911.

Troopers of KEH cleaning kit at Aldershot, 1911.

Cartoons sent by EWH to Ethel from *La Vie Parisienne* entitled 'Them & Us', contrasting the coarse Germans with the sophisticated French!

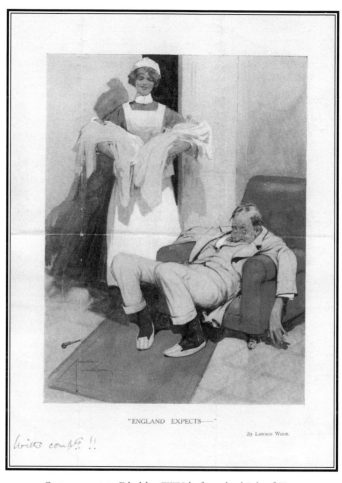

"ENGLAND EXPECTS——"

By LAWSON WOOD.

Cartoon sent to Ethel by EWH before the birth of Ken.

This photograph of Ethel riding side-saddle was sent to EWH in France.

EWH admiring one of the puppies while on home leave from France.

Ethel Hermon after the war with Betty, Bob, Mary, Meg and Ken on their ponies, taken in the drive at Brook Hill, circa 1920.

Mary Hermon's wedding to John McKergow, taken in the garden of Brook Hill, July 1929. Bob Hermon (*far right*) gave Mary away; best man Peter Haswell, Royal Scots Greys (*far left*); Meg Hermon (*seated, second left*); Una Hermon, Victor's daughter, is the child bridesmaid.

Brook Hill House taken in the 1950s.

The four-leaf clover sent to EWH by Ethel, 11 August 1916, and found in his breast pocket after he was killed.

(*Top left*) The bill from what would prove to be EWH and Ethel's final stay at the Berkeley Hotel, London. (*Top right*) The scroll sent to Ethel commemorating her husband's sacrifice in the war. (*Above*) The telegram from the War Office informing Ethel of her husband's death. (*Right*) Verses from Lt. Colonel John McCrae's 'In Flanders Fields', found in Ethel's Bible after her death.

less than two or three substitutes is any good now! Perhaps it would have been better had the squadron gone to Egypt after all.

I had a letter from Mimi today breaking the news to me that Dick is to remain at Eton until the end of the Summer half. What they can't see is that he is now 18, hasn't got a colour, & is doing no earthly good either to himself or anyone else where he is.

There has been tremendously heavy artillery fire today, the old Hun is getting very barbery these times. Barber's sister is still working I think & it has resulted in his being dragged off to the trenches for a further period of probationary training with the result that I have lost his services for six weeks already & am still to lose him for a further period of ten days. However such is the fortune of war. What is worrying me is that if he does go I shall get a captain from another squadron and old Mac won't get 2nd-in-command & he is so awfully good that I should hate to have someone else over him.

I hear that the wounded cyclist is just making headway & they think there may be a glimmer of hope but they can't move him yet even in the hospital barges on the canal, by which means all the very worst cases are taken down to the base.

I must go to bed now old dear, my very best love to you all.

22nd February 1916 – No. 76 answering 72 (correct!) – Hurionville

We have got really heavy snow today & the conditions are really beastly & it is snowing hard now. Poor old Steve is on a field day miles away with the infantry & I really don't know how they will get back again unless they walk & lead their horses.

I can't help being amused at old Barber as his sister's machinations have so far resulted is his being sent up to the trenches when there was the heaviest bombardment on that there has been since Loos, & that was yesterday when he went & today there is at least 3 inches of snow & it's still falling very hard.

My darling old girl you really mustn't get blued old dear because things will come right in the end, tho' it's a long way off I fear but it may end sooner than any of us expect.

Perhaps when the war is over old dear, things won't be so bad as we expect & perhaps they will be better than they were before, not so artificial & a little more sincerity in life & that will be no harm.

Good luck to you & keep smiling.

23rd February 1916 – No. 77 answering 73 – Hurionville

Hard frost last night & more snow today & freezing like Hades now. Couldn't do anything today but curse the weather. I did a bit of shooting with the cyclists this morning but got stopped by snow half way through.

If the Gaisford man was buried at Loos I don't think I shall bother about going to see his grave as I mightn't come back. If however he is buried anywhere else where one can go in reasonable safety I will, but Loos is far from being a haven of rest just now, & for that matter it never has been since I knew it. They tell me that it is now nothing more than a succession of footpaths between piles of bricks, & that there isn't a house left, hardly.

He isn't buried at the Château[114] if he was killed at Loos, unless his Division was opposite Festubert during the Loos fighting. If she knows where he was buried I will let you know if it is possible to visit his grave yet. Heaps of fellows of course were buried where it is still impossible to go in the day time, but if he was a Battalion commander I expect he will have been brought back & buried in a cemetery & may well be at Gorre.

24th February 1916 – No. 78 answering 74 – Hurionville

Poor old Bet, I'm sorry she has been naughty but it is the only thing to do, you must punish them occasionally. The great thing is not to niggle with punishment. It is far kinder in the end to do it well & seldom. I have

---

[114] The cemetery at Château Gorre near Beuvry is now one of the Commonwealth War Graves Commission sites. Like all their cemeteries, it is beautifully maintained.

got a gent waiting for me to apply the same principle tomorrow when he is sober enough to understand it.

I am so glad to hear that the little car is running so well & only sorry that I'm not there to drive her. My darling old girl I do expect old Bob to take quite a decent place in his school as I am sure he knows more than the ordinary boy of his age.

My love my own darling.

25th February 1916 – No. 79 answering 75 – Hurionville

Again nothing but snow to report, more snow & more frost. Couldn't get the horses out of their stables today at all, as the whole place is too slippery for words.

I want a new tin of camphor ice please & also some bromo.[115] We are getting no regular supply of the latter & should like it sent each week with the cakes please.

We are all wondering where the Boche attack is to come. I can't help thinking that all these little 'goes' all along the line are preludes to a real smashing blow somewhere on a very big scale. However I think that he will find us ready when he does make his effort & it will be pretty costly to him, which is just what one wants. The oftener he attacks the better because the attacker must be the heaviest loser & the more we can kill, the sooner the show will be over. The sooner the better once the object is accomplished. The old Russians seem to be doing very well at present.

I can see old Spoot so well putting on her most unnatural expression for the photo. We want the drawers & vests v. badly so send them off as soon as you can please. We have had a fall of snow but it is certainly *NO* warmer!!

Your numbers have been quite correct in spite of your diary going wrong. I feel you are thinking you're great!!

My love to you dearie.

---

[115] Camphor ice was a skin balm, and 'bromo' toilet paper.

27th February 1916 – No. 81 answering 76 & 77 – Hurionville

You say you got a lovely letter from me & I can't think who wrote it as I have written you such rotten letters lately old dear, that I have been quite ashamed of them.

I never heard such absolute bunkum as trying to make you give up the idea of working on the land. Why can't an English woman do what the French woman can? If it wasn't for what the woman is doing here the French nation would be in a baddish way for cereals this year I can tell you.

I hope to be able to have a bit of a field day tomorrow if it doesn't freeze tonight & make the roads impassable.

We are all rather interested in the Verdun attack but I can't help thinking that the Huns can never break through & that the French have them absolutely held in reality. So far they have only engaged very few of their reserves according to the papers & I think you will find that they will be a match for the Hun yet & the more he attacks the better. We can only end the war by killing them & the oftener they offer themselves as targets the quicker the war will be over. It is a very interesting problem whether this is their big offensive or only a feint & that they have something else in store elsewhere along the line. The next few days must show their hand.

Many thanks for doing the vests and drawers as the men want them badly.

28th February 1916 – No. 82 – Hurionville

I have apparently fallen foul of James.[116] Without thinking I recommended a capital fellow for the regiment & quite forgot to write & consult James before doing it. He takes the gravest exception to this & wrote to the W.O. & managed to get the thing cancelled, & the poor fellow has had to put up with a commission in the 9th Lancers!!!

[116] Major James, also known as Jimmy, was commanding the Reserve Squadron K.E.H. in Ireland and was senior to Major Hermon.

Also you know that Syme was wanted for the gun. Well the 1st Army wrote to me and asked if I had any objection to the transfer & I wrote & said that I had. Mac wrote & told me he was furious, some time ago, & I forgot to write & smooth him down so he wrote me a severe reprimand. As a matter of fact I didn't know at the time that Jimmy had made it a special point that Syme should go to the gun. Poor little Syme, when I showed him the final edict that he was to go, he broke down completely & wept!

During March the Battle of Verdun continued with more intense fighting and heavy casualties on both sides. General Pétain took command of the French Second Army at this time, personally taking control of the artillery. On 2 March the French repulsed an attack on Vaux where a young officer – Capitaine Charles de Gaulle, the future President of France – was taken prisoner. Escaping from a prison camp in the east of Germany, he almost reached the Swiss frontier, but was recaptured and remained in captivity until the Armistice.

Vaux changed hands thirteen times during the month. Reports in the British press detailing the casualty figures would have made alarming reading.

1st March 1916 – Hurionville

I got what you call a 'snippety' letter today but it gave me great pleasure so you need not have worried. Don't be depressed at the news. The French are doing fine & killing the Huns like anything & it is only by killing in very large quantities that the war can be brought to an end. If the Hun would attack like this every day of the week & all along the line it would finish the war in two months!

Many thanks for getting the parcels off; I hope they will arrive alright. I had a long letter from Sheppard a day or two ago enclosing his photo!

My love to you all.

2nd March 1916 – No. 85 – Hurionville

The old French seem to be holding their own alright at Verdun tho' I am not quite sure if the Hun hasn't got quite a good position out of it from which to make a further advance but the exhaustion, consequent on an attack of the magnitude, is so great these times that it may be very likely three months before he can make another effort.

They say they just flung over 700,000 shells in something over 4½ hours tho' this sounds a good bit & there must have been some elbowing in the air. Rather like the rush for a Cheshire gateway!![117] It is quite possible because if they had 200 batteries there, & they probably had quite that, it is only 12 shots per battery per minute. If you go on at this & concentrate it on a mile of front it is more than one shell per yard of front per minute or 300 shells on every yard of front in the 4½ hours. It just gives you some idea of what the moral effect must be. It is not to be wondered at that men lose their reason under it. The miracle is that anyone retains it.

I heard of a fine piece of work the other day. A shell took one of our airmen's legs off while he was flying over Don & he nevertheless brought his machine & his observer back to our side of the line and landed safely behind Les Brebis!! It must have been [an] anxious time for the observer knowing his pilot was so badly hit & might faint at any moment!!

I must to bed now old dear.

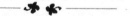

6th March 1916 – No. 89 answering 85 – Hurionville

Man proposes, God disposes & he chose to send about 4 inches of snow last night & so our little jaunt was off today but we are booked to start in the morning, but I am afraid that it is going to freeze like Hades tonight & the S.S.M. tells me that all the 'chickens' that roost every night in a tree outside his door have thought better of it tonight & have gone to bed in

[117] On the hunting field.

the fowl house so it looks rather as if the roads would be a sheet of ice tomorrow.

Did you ever see anything like Shep's photo? Buxton says 'You can see he 'ain't no real soldier or he wouldn't have a stick – looks a proper fop!!'

My love to you my darling.

7th March 1916 – No. 90 answering 86 – Marthes

It froze very hard last night & I started at 9 a.m. walking & leading the horses, but a mile from Hurionville it came on to snow & so I turned back & waited but it got no worse so at 11 a.m. I started again & we rode 9 miles against the snow & got here just after 1 p.m. I was so frightened at the early start that I should get here & find my wagons snowed up some miles away and no forage or rations for the men & horses, but all panned out alright. Weather conditions are beastly, the whole country is under melting snow & I very much doubt if we shall have our outing tomorrow.

Dearie mine, I really don't think it is worth while bothering about the Zeppelins.[118] If you are for it, you're for it & tho' it may be silly one rather feels it is rather 'infra dig' to go diving about in the cellar when so many in the village haven't got a cellar to go to. If you could extend the freedom of the cellar to the village it would be different, but really the chance of a Zeppelin hitting our house standing alone in an insignificant country village is so remote as to be almost negligible.

My love to you my darling. I have got a very nice billet, a fine double bed with white curtains over it, & feel quite like a bride!!

[118] On 1 March 1916 Zeppelins had raided Broadstairs and Margate, resulting in one death; however, as is often the case, the psychological distress caused by these random attacks on civilians was far greater than the actual damage caused.

11th March 1916 – No. 93 answering 89 – Bruay

Well I arrived at my new billets yesterday at midday. We marched about 20 miles through the snow & when we got here found that the staff had made no arrangements for billeting us at all, or rather what arrangements they had made were too futile for words. The result is that I have two troops with me here in this part of the town and Steve and Tulloch are two miles away right across the valley on the other side of the town.

This town is very like Wigan, nothing but miners' houses, mines, coal, mud & snow. My horses are worse than they have ever been before and the only saving thing is that I myself have most comfortable quarters. I have got a beast of a throat again, all this cold & slush lately has been simply beastly & my poor horses that were looking so lovely & well, I don't know how they will come out of this.

I am also annoyed with myself because I meant to give up my smoking all together during Lent at least & after the worry & bother of yesterday & today I had a cigarette after dinner each day & I am annoyed that I wasn't strong enough to resist the temptation!! But you will no doubt say 'Did you expect to be?!!!!!.'

However I will endeavour to turn over that eternal leaf, how often it has been turned—— it is almost threadbare now.

12th March 1916 – No. 94 answering 90 & 91 – Bruay

First and foremost let me tell you that I am feeling very much better today, it has been a lovely warm day in spite of a great deal of snow still lying about, but which under the warming influence of the sun is fast turning the streams into rivers.

I am sorry to hear about Miss Gaisford's brother & where he was killed. There are hundreds of them lying there now & never been buried at all or likely to be. It is impossible to get there, but I shouldn't tell her that as she no doubt expects the Hun buried them. Of course he may have been buried, but all round Hohenzollern our folk were driven back & between the lines it has been out of the question, first of all to find anyone special in the dark or to get them in anyhow. I believe that there are any amount there still, tho' I expect wind and weather have by now finished the job & there must not be much left.

There is an awful lot of influenza out here & I know several folk who are down with it.

Well done Ken, he really is doing fine. I should so love to see him as I feel I don't know my second son at all & if I met him in the street I shouldn't know him!!

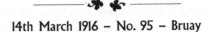

14th March 1916 – No. 95 – Bruay

Tomorrow I exchange the squalor & filth of a mining town for the even more filthy country village lately occupied by our gallant Allies. They tell me the lice left behind are as big as walnuts. In occupation of the said village I found Monkey Tilney and Wilfred Royds. Old Monkey Tilney was in great form and I lunched with him & had a rare old chat.

If as you say you have so darkened the house that no light shows outside I shouldn't bother even to put out the electric light. Zeppelins don't come all that way & risk £250,000 to drop a bomb on Cowfold! Just see that there is no skylight that shows upwards i.e. that in housemaid's closet & Jane etc!!

18th March 1916 – No. 96 answering 93, 94, 95 & 96 – Magnicourt en Comte

I am sending little Meggie a small birthday present of some French buttons worn by a soldier who gave his life for his country at Souchez.

Tonight after dinner an old French man came round to say his mare was slipping her foal & had we a vet, so I went round to see if I could be of any assistance. The whole show was really rather amusing as we were in a tiny little bit of a shed with the mare, a calf and four cows; all the neighbours had turned up to lend a hand, same like we, but when I got there I found that there was a man who thoroughly knew the job, so in reality the only help I was, was to get the mare properly twitched which either through drink or something, the bloke who was holding her head couldn't manage.

The whole operation was under command of the lady who owned the mare & who held the lamp, & what with the crowd & one thing and another, well! It was a case of the birth of a foal that had been dead some 8 or 9 days and a mal-presentation at that. However it ended alright & I hope the mare will be alright; I think she will tho'.

You will no doubt be amused but I have worked things and now have got Syme back with his whole command of machine guns as well, much to his delight!!

I am glad you are taking old Bob to Eton to get his clothes & I should certainly get him fitted out at the man's shop that the boys go to. I think even when I was there Tom Brown was rather relying on his pristine glory.[119]

My throat is bad again. That beastly snow & cold gave me a third cold & throat after having thrown off two others. However, I am mending now. I have reduced my smoking to one cigarette after meals!!

I am at the back of the front, out of harm's way, so far as my billet is concerned tho' during the time that the Division is in the front line, as now, one has to go up there occasionally & I am just going to start a bit of digging.

Love to you all.

20th March 1916 – No. 97 answering 97 & 98 & 99 – Magnicourt

I ought to have written this last night but had had a very long ride & walk up to Carency & when I came back I found it was 10.15, so I turned in. It was very interesting being under the Notre Dame de Lorette spur[120] and

---

[119] Bob, their elder son, was about to go to St Aubyn's preparatory school at Rottingdean as he was now eight years old.

[120] The Notre Dame de Lorette spur in the Artois region was the scene of heavy fighting in 1914 and 1915. The Germans had captured Notre Dame in October 1914 but in May 1915 the heights were regained by the French.

especially so seeing it from this western side. We have lately taken over this piece of country from the French & all where I was yesterday some of the heaviest fighting of the war had taken place. The villages are absolutely flat, Carency being a pile of bricks only, with no shape to houses even to show where they have been.

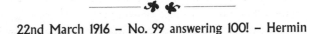

22nd March 1916 – No. 99 answering 100! – Hermin

We have fetched up in our new billet after a long & weary march of three miles! If you change the 'o' in my name (surname) to an 'i' you have the shop. It's not so bad but it might be better. We haven't got such a good mess tho' I have a fairly nice room, but my bedroom becomes the general sitting room because it has an open fireplace.

The Harrods cake[121] was alright for those who like shop cakes. I don't. My love my darling.

23rd March 1916 – No. 100 answering 101 – Hermin

This morning after a week of the most glorious weather it snowed! I rode down to Villers au Bois & then walked down past Carency to see the Cyclist platoons that I have down there doing trench maintenance. A most extraordinary state of affairs has existed here for some time in that tho' the artillery have been fighting & shelling the support and reserve lines, the infantry have had a sort of truce, & talked to one another all day & night. The Huns opposite are convinced that they are beat and that now they are fighting for terms. That is very good news, and last night we got a little Hun prisoner who said that it would be all over in six months, & that Germany couldn't last any longer.

I have had four platoons of Cyclists in the line for a week & four of them got knocked out with a shell I am sorry to say. However as one of the

---

[121] Sent by his mother.

wounded said 'These things are inevitable in war' & there you are. Then I rode on to Le Bois de [word crossed out], a big wood where I had some business and it is astonishing how like the woods at home it was, especially the Roman woods. Deep ravines, just the same & the same Hazel, young cut & everything. Green woodpeckers and all & it made it feel wonderfully like home I can tell you and I longed to be back with you once more.

Will you please order me another pair of heavy shooting shoes from Moykopf.

Will you also send us a good boxful of loud gramophone needles as we are nearly out of them.

My love to you all.

24th March 1916 – No. 101 answering 102 – Hermin

I awoke this morning to find four or five inches of snow on the ground and still falling fast. However this afternoon it cleared & the sun came out and it was really quite nice again. As far as I can see we are settled here for some time tho' of course one can't be certain. The Corps Commander came round and saw me tonight and asked me to dinner.

Talking of rats, they abound here in millions, & are so bold they won't bother to get out of the way!

27th March 1916 – No. 104 – Hermin

Unfortunately no letters today & I fear that they may have all got spoilt in the *Sussex* disaster.[122]

I am having great fun now with my shop. I have started a Field Force

---

[122] The *Sussex*, a cross-Channel passenger ferry, was torpedoed by a German submarine on 24 March, with the loss of around fifty lives. Earlier in 1916 Germany had instituted a policy of allowing armed merchant ships (but not passenger ships) to be torpedoed without warning, but in spite of this the *Sussex* had been attacked.

Canteen & it opened tonight for the first time from 6 to 7 p.m. and we took 150 francs in that time. I want you to send me if possible by post:

3 doz. bottles	'aspirin'
2 doz. bottles	Quinine tablets
2 doz. bottles	Enos Fruit Salts
2 doz. boxes	Beechams Pills
2 boxes	toothbrushes

You must let me know what is the price of the things or send the bill so that I can see their cost & make a small profit!!

I must confess that acting on your advice I went back to my pipe this afternoon, but it tastes so beastly that I don't know whether I shall stick to it or not.

My love to you all my dears.

28th March 1916 – No. 105 answering 106 – Hermin

I fear your 105 has gone in the *Sussex*. We got no mail yesterday and today I got the right mail for the day. I want you to get me several more things for my shop.

The enclosed matchbox covers:

1 doz. Nickel
2 doz. Black

I also want:

a gross of refills for 'Tommy's Cookers'[123]
a doz. Tommy's Cookers complete
1 doz. Burnishers
2 doz. Selvit Cloths

I want them as soon as possible please also 2 doz packets of playing cards.

---

[123] The 'Tommy' field cooker, a simple portable stove fuelled by solid alcohol. It was smokeless so as not to attract the attention of enemy snipers, but not particularly efficient.

Trade is very brisk & today we beat all records by taking 250 francs!! It is really wonderful how the men appreciate it. They have got B.E.F. canteens and one gets one's things from them & sets up on one's own. I put down 624 francs as capital to buy the stock & since 5 p.m. last night we have taken over the counter 370 francs!

I do so wish I could have been at home for my little Meggie's birthday.

I should love to see you on your milking stool,[124] how jolly awkward you will be to start with!! It has been an awfully blustery day today & cold too.

My love to you all my darlings.

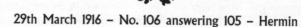

29th March 1916 – No. 106 answering 105 – Hermin

I am at present properly poggled as I have got to write to Queen Alexandra & thank her for some comforts for the men that she is sending. I'm not in the habit of sending 'billets doux' to Queens & I don't know how to begin & in the secretary's letter it says expressly that I am to write & thank her!

You won't get a letter from me at all tomorrow old girl as I shall be away most of the afternoon and night as I am going up to see Steve's digging party at work & as theirs are works of darkness I do not expect to be back until the early hours of Friday morning. Talking of Egypt it might amuse you to know that the Khedive gave a dinner party last week & no less than 96 British Generals sat down to it!!

Can you send me some of those cotton bandana handkerchiefs for my shop, say 5 doz. I think they run about 2d or 4d each. It still goes well. Over 200 francs again today!!

Love to you all.

---

[124] The family had acquired some goats at this time to ensure a supply of fresh milk.

31st March 1916 – No. 107 answering 107, 8 & 9 – Hermin

Oh! my dear old girl my Mac has been wounded,[125] thank God not badly but sufficiently for him to be evacuated. He is in the best of spirits and hopes not to be sent to England. He was in a trench with the infantry and got three shrapnel wounds in his left arm. I am terribly sad at losing him, but I was with him at the Field Ambulance before he was evacuated & he was walking about with me in the best of spirits.

The old Huns here know all about the losses at Verdun & I think it is making the rank & file think a bit, but what seems to worry them more than anything is the bits in the home letters on the food question. They shouted across the other night 'What do you want to go on digging for, you've won the war'!

My dear old girl, when I say *shoes* & heavy shooting shoes too, why you should imagine I want boots or even a new hat I don't know. Am I not in the habit of calling a spade a spade? I have got a pair on now and as they have neither 'soles nor uppers' I thought it time they were renewed. I have, as a matter of fact, tons of boots & really didn't want another pair but they may be handy later on.

It is awfully good of your Ma to give you so handsome a present, tho' I am sure you are wise not to have a motor bicycle. I am afraid old dear it wouldn't suit you and a puncture on a motor bicycle is the devil to mend. Will you thank old Mairky for the bullseyes & tell her that I have one in my mouth now and also Meg for her cake & candles which we had lit on the table for lunch today!!

Yesterday I had a very interesting day, starting by going to see old Mac. He was in a little bad bit of trench, there were thirty men in it & at the end of the day 14 had been hit. He was hit early on in the day & had to stop there till dark. I then went on to a demonstration of a German *Flammenwerfer*,[126] one of the liquid fire sprayers.

---

[125] 'Mac' was Lieutenant D. MacKinnon (later Captain) who was hit by shrapnel. The War Diary comments that he was 'a serious loss to the squadron'.
[126] The portable *Kleinflammenwerfer*, operated by one man, could spread a stream of fire 20 yards; the two-man *Grossflammenwerfer* could spread the flames much further. *Flammenwerfer* operatives quickly became marked men and if the fuel tank was detonated by rifle fire, the resulting explosion killed them instantly.

I can now quite understand fellows quitting when they first saw them.

It really is a most terrifying thing but fortunately its range is only about 25 yards at its best & the portable one doesn't last more than 2 minutes. I expected a long thin jet of flame, like from one side of a double acetylene burner, but actually it was a huge barrel of flame, probably 2 yards in diameter and 20 long. As we were within easy shelling range with a large crowd of men, tho' out of sight we had a large battle plane up to keep off the Huns & it was rather jolly having it circling about overhead. Then I walked down to what was once a village & quite a big one, but now is merely a heap of bricks. I had a very good dinner there & tho' there was a certain amount of shrapnel coming into the far end of the village, it soon stopped & was a most peaceful evening.

After dinner Steve picked me up and I went out to where he was digging. The whole ground is absolutely one vast shell crater. You can't find a complete crater anywhere, because somewhere its circumference is cut by another. There isn't a single inch that hasn't been blown up, & a building that has played a very prominent part in the fighting was a wonderful sight.

My love to you old dear.

Have just learnt that old Mac is to be evacuated to England tomorrow. He said he would come & see you some time, so he may ring you up. If he does, ask him to come & stay with you.

CHAPTER TEN

SPRING 1916

Throughout April, Verdun remained the chief area of conflict on the Western Front although British troops were also in action, with the heaviest fighting taking place in the Ypres Salient. In May, the French achieved successes at Douaumont, Mort Homme, and fought a bitter struggle for Hill 304. British troops were engaged in fighting around the Hohenzollern Redoubt and La Basseé, and on Vimy Ridge. German losses since the outbreak of the war were estimated to be more than 2½ million dead, with 80,000 casualties from Verdun alone. The French had lost nearer 90,000 in the battle so far, which had another eight months to run.

British generals, meanwhile, planned an offensive on the Somme for June and on 25 May the Military Service Act became law and married men were now to be conscripted. During this time Robert had a temporary staff job at Divisional Headquarters.

1st April 1916 – No. 110 answering 110 – Hermin

My darling old girl,

Another nice letter today old dear.

Started the day by taking stock in the shop. Then old 'Naughty Charlie'[127] came round or, in other words, our distinguished Divisional Commander & I had a crack with him – the rest of the day I have spent finishing off the new stable & the horses go in tomorrow.

I am glad to hear that my younger son is a merry lad & I should like to see him again very much, as I doubt if I should know him again now. Will you please write to Falmouth and get my sextant and parallel rulers

[127] General Sir Charles Barter, the divisional commander. In September 1916 Barter was dismissed at an hour's notice for the huge loss of life at High Wood. Although there was never an official inquiry, he was largely exonerated.

home so that you could send them out to me if I wanted them. I am only going to sail on land tho' this time.

I am heartbroken at losing old Mac but in a way it frees me a bit as now if I got the offer of a job of any sort I should take it. All my old officers have gone now bar old Steve. I am most awfully fond of old Steve, almost as much as I was of Mac, but Mac had qualities none of the others had or ever will have.

Now that he has gone home you will see him and he will tell you about us which will be something. It is a pity the photo was so bad but if you had only seen it being done you would have screamed with laughter, in the back yard of a measly dirty little 'estaminet' & the camera propped up on an old barrel & the most footling old Frenchman you ever saw taking it.

My love to you all my dears.

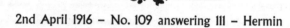

2nd April 1916 – No. 109 answering 111 – Hermin

I got a simply topping letter from you today & it has cheered me up a lot.

With regard to coming home old dear the case is this. At the present time there are 61 N.C.O.s & men in the squadron who have been out the whole time & have not yet had leave. I know that in most Corps the officers consider it a right to go home directly their three months is up quite regardless of the number of men who have had leave, but when we have had no special stress I feel that the men are just as much entitled to their turns as the officers and tho' reserving my right to come home at any time should circumstances demand it, I want to get the original men home if possible before one goes again.

Yesterday as I told you old Barter came over & he said that they felt that they were not getting full value out of me & how would I like a staff job! I of course jumped at it & so today I went over to Div. H.Q. to see Hitchcock on the subject. Webber is our G.S.O.2 and is likely very shortly to get preferment to G.S.O.1 & I have arranged to go & work in the office and understudy Webber, the idea being that I should step into his place as soon as he is promoted. Of course this depends on how I get on & if I satisfy Hitchcock & the G.O.C.

If I were to get this Staff appointment & I hope to do it, I should be able to wangle a bit of leave no doubt but it is all so very much 'if' at present that it hardly bears thinking about. Anyhow it starts tomorrow & I go as a learner & it is now up to me to keep my end up.

I should have liked to have seen you at your tea-party at Victoria but as you say there is something about the men that makes them stand out. If you only knew how cheerily the men go through it, & what they have to go through, you would wonder how human beings stuck it. The general conduct of the rank & file is beyond all praise, they are simply magnificent.

Now with regard to the hospital gift, of course I couldn't consent for a minute to have the brass tablet idea. What I want is to do some permanent good as opposed to just defraying a portion of their running expenses. I would pay the salary of an extra nurse if they liked for a year or, say, 2 years, if they actually did increase the staff accordingly. I wouldn't mind paying £200 altogether if it is necessary & would like you to go & see the block. I'm not very keen about naming a bed. I can't see that there is anything special in that & it merely means that you pay £300 to their running expenses. I want if possible to give something that they haven't got & would like. Otherwise one might just as well send the money to the 'Star & Garter Home'.[128] You might see what they want there, but I fancy that they have everything they want there and mismanagement as well!!!

I must to bed now dearie mine so as to be at my brightest & best tomorrow but you musn't think that the job is accomplished because it isn't & it's only making the tiniest of beginnings.

4th April 1916 – No. 111 answering 112 & 113 – Hermin

Yes, the shop is a D.M.T.[129] show, just ourselves & cyclists and such oddments as the Div. Laundry, which is here. Tell the Chugs we sell mostly tobacco & tinned fruits but there is a great rush on chocolate & that at present wins hands down. I had a letter from old Mac today & he tells me that

---

128 In 1916 Queen Mary had expressed concern for disabled servicemen returning from the battlefields and instructed the British Red Cross Society to find a suitable home for them. The society subsequently purchased the Star and Garter Hotel in Richmond as a residential home.
129 Divisional Mounted Troops.

his arm is worse than they thought at first as he has a nerve cut and it may result in another operation. He is awfully upset at getting sent home. I had a fine long letter from old Pongo tonight & he has just got back to duty again after measles himself & then his wife. Buckin has got a nasty cold again but seems to be mending.

My love to you all old dear.

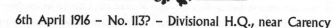

6th April 1916 – No. 113? – Divisional H.Q., near Carency

I have moved up here now & have a canvas hut in the garden. I expect I shall wake up nice & fresh tomorrow as it is pretty parky tonight. I don't know what length of time I shall spend here, but I am thoroughly happy & enjoying myself very much & I only hope that it will lead to my getting a job, preferably here, as Hitchcock is such a real good man that I should like to learn under him.

I am as you will have seen on the 'G' side of the office which is what I wanted. I thought it might interest you to see the enclosed diagram:

STAFF OF A DIVISION

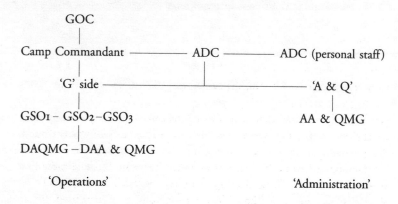

Goodnight old dear & hope to get your letter sent on in the morning.

7th April 1916 – No. 114 answering No. 115 – Divisional H.Q.

Lass dear, it is very hard to know quite how to answer your question as to what to tell old Bob. So far as I can remember on going to a small boys' school they haven't arrived at the age when sexual matters are talked about, it is later when he goes to Eton that you want to warn him most. Tell him to keep before him always the fact that 'Would Dad & Mum like to hear me say that or see me doing this' & he will find the answer himself.

Explain to him that this does not apply to ordinary naughtiness because one does not want him to grow up a prig but just that it is talking about nasty things & doing dirty actions. I think he is a bit small to be fully initiated yet & I do not think that there is any fear of him learning anything from young boys yet as they are not old enough to have any feelings that would prompt the thoughts.

I intended to talk to him myself when I was at home but the thought of leaving you all was so mixed with up the instruction that I couldn't make a start & didn't want to worry him by being too shaky of voice.

I sent home some £80 yesterday to my bank so when it comes time to weigh in with a cheque for that hospital just let me know & I will send it to you.

My love to you all my darlings.

8th April 1916 – No. 115 answering 116 – Divisional H.Q.

Just a few lines as it is late. I had a very pleasant day today starting with a walk over some high ground in fairly close proximity to the enemy. It was a wonderful sight because it was on a bit of ground where I doubt if the fighting at Verdun has been as intense. The ground looked more like a Gruier [Gruyère] cheese than anything else & the number of skulls & skeletons lying about told how intense the fighting must have been. It was a glorious morning & as I had my telescope, one was able to have a good look into the Hun territory.

It's awfully kind of old Vio & as soon as the cigarettes turn up I will distribute them & will write to her. Many thanks old girl, for doing the shopping but if the 'Tommy' refills haven't started cut them down by half. Will you send me a collapsible primus stove please, same like we had on the boat.

It is odd how nature adapts herself to circumstances & there is no doubt that now the rats out here are doing incalculable good in eating out of corners & crannies all sorts of beastliness & the hawks & weasels too are increasing tremendously & they in time will prove the antidote to the rat I have no doubt.

I shall be most anxious to hear how the lovely officer's wife gets on or is it an officer's lovely wife?

Best love my old dear.

10th April 1916 – No. 117 answering 116, 117a & 118 – Divisional H.Q.

Vio's cigarettes turned up alright & were most welcome. The matchbox covers, burnishers & in fact all *your* purchases have also turned up. I have just run over to the post office & found 117 waiting for me there & a real fine effort it was dearie mine. Isn't it bad luck dearie mine, losing old Mac & you have expressed exactly my feelings in the matter. He has been my companion mostly, tho' Steve shares my regard very closely with him but there was something particularly taking in old Mac & Henry. I would like you to tell him how much I miss him when you see him.

I am more than glad to hear Tommy has got a Military Cross. I wish I could see old Spoot's picture & am glad it's fairly good. I am sorry to hear she is falling off a bit but I shouldn't worry, she will soon pick up, I expect. Nothing picks up quicker than a dog.

11th April 1916 – No. 118 answering up to & including 118 – Divisional H.Q.

I must continue to answer the orgy of letters I seem to have collected. I am glad you liked my letter about the front. This morning I had to take a high dignitary of the 1st Army, the senior in old Cowie's profession, all round our front-line system of defence & had a most interesting morning as I hadn't been in the front line in this sector before & as one is only some 50 to 80 yards from their trenches, it was most exciting.

I had a splendid view of Souchez too from the far side from here and it really was a wonderful sight. The trees are so wonderful, just stumps, every bit of branch is smashed & it was a wooded village it looks simply wonderful. I should have loved to have had you there as things were comparatively pleasant & there was only very light stuff being thrown about by brother Boche. The rats simply swarm & are in millions. I should give old Spoot a worm pill, it will do her no harm & it doesn't matter her being a bit thin.

Undated, postmarked 11th April 1916 – No. 118a – Divisional H.Q.

I want you to send me a catalogue of Dixie's & Nyrette & Zamba's showing Prismatic Magnifying Periscopes. I also want you to send me a small 'automatic pistol' bore about .250 to .320 or even smaller. I want something I can just slip into my pocket when I go round the trenches as one has a terrible long walk to get there & an ordinary revolver is so heavy.

You must send the ammunition with it. I want the smallest possible weapon that has killing power as I don't care to go down absolutely unarmed, tho' there would probably be lots of rifles to pick up if there was trouble while one was there. I should try Holland & Holland for this, telephone them what I want & let them send it at once & direct to me at Div. H.Q.

14th April 1916 – No. 122 answering 121 & 122 – Divisional H.Q.

Today we have had snow, high wind, thunder & really heavy rain. After tea tonight I went out for a bit of a walk & watched the old Boche having a go for the next village, but he wasn't very successful. You were asking the other day if we were in front or behind the squadron, but we are in front a good bit. I live close to Carency and the Boche at present is holding the ridge this side of Givenchy about 3 to 4 miles away. Anyhow he can shoot over us tho' he hasn't done so for about three weeks but we expect he will have a go one of these days.

We got a bulge on him today alright as we sprung a camouflet[130] & blew in his gallery and as he was working away at the time only 8 feet away I am afraid that some of them got hurt. When one is mining, one side burrows away & the other side burrows out to meet him. There are two sorts of blows. You put in, in one case, a devil of a charge & blow up the whole surface which leaves a huge crater like they did at St Eloi or a camouflet as we did today which blows *through* into the enemy mine without disturbing the surface. Say the enemy is working 8 feet away we place our charge of so many thousand pounds of explosive & then tamp it in with earth for four or five times the amount of earth that there is between us & the Boche & then the explosion following the line of least resistance blows in the piece between us & the Boche & blows up his gallery & kills everyone in it.

15/4/16. Not an hour after I had written the above the old Boche replied to us in the same way tho' I hope, whatever success he may have had, ours was greater. It's a dirty game this mining.

Couldn't you send that lovely officer's wife to me to look after? I seem to like the idea of the 'beautiful eyes'!!

I wanted the primus chiefly so as to boil some water for washing, but it will do for all sorts of jobs. That lucky devil Webber is just off to spend four days with his wife & family in Paris & so I am going to be his locum altogether while he is away & shall do my best to turn it to account. You probably will therefore only get some very scrappy letters these next few days in consequence.

16th April 1916 – No. 123? – Divisional H.Q.

To my great joy, tho' no doubt very selfish in a war, Webber went off until Tuesday to Paris so I am left on my own as G.S.O.2 until he returns so I am having a bit of a chance which is something. Have kept my end up alright so far today.

The Tommy's cookers have arrived but so far no sign of Morrish's medicines tho' I have already acknowledged them, which was a mistake.

---

[130] An underground bomb or mine.

Will you thank kindly for the peppermints & toffee which arrived safe & sound.

After having spent large sums on one's family's education, this from Betty makes good reading 'Last Saturday I bought a *ceneary* & it sings *lovely* when we do lessons.' I don't expect I shall get time again to write you more tonight as I am going to kirk after tea as I couldn't go this morning.

Thank old Bet for her letter & with love to you all.

16th April 1916 (second letter of the day) – No. 124 answering 124

Very many thanks for bothering about the pistol. It is just what I wanted. The shoes are now on my feet & very comfortable. I am so glad dearie you are cheered up as I most certainly am. This job is what I have set my heart on and I shall be bitterly disappointed if I don't bring it off by hook or by crook. Anyhow they haven't defeated me yet.

I should love above all things to bring the car & drive you & old Bet & Bob round this front when the war stops. It would interest you beyond words & be a fine education for the children, tho' I was reading a forecast of the war the other day which began '*1946, the 32nd year of the Great War*'.

It is sad tho', one goes down into Ablain St Nazaire where there is only one house left & the poor church just rears up its broken tower & parts of its walls, still holding out above the surrounding desolation. It is really very sad, but Souchez, like the ruins of Jerusalem, hasn't one stone upon another.

Tell Dale that Macaulay didn't want to leave the squadron, until one day his conscience got the better of him & he applied for a commission & was flung out on account of his age. He was simply delighted when I told him & tho' I tried to get him something else, he wasn't having it.

The names you ask for are Sir Charles Munro who commanded in Potchefstroom before B. M. & Sir Henry Wilson. Do you know that Beecham (phonetic) and the 'Goose' will be living only a mile from me in a few days. Isn't it funny! I shall be so glad to see them both. The primus will do fine, many thanks.

My love, my darling.

18th April 1916 – No. 125 answering 123

Only a short letter again I am afraid as I have been awfully busy this morning & have walked miles & miles with Hitchcock this afternoon. I have got a budget of things for you to do for me:

(1) I want a mackintosh called a 'Hurricane Smock' – they say it is advertised in *Land & Water* & I want the cavalry pattern.

(2) I want, next time you are in town, two really nice thumbsticks as I want one myself & also I want to give Webber one.

(3) Will you tell Jacksons to send in their parcel a tin of curry powder once a fortnight & a tin of baking powder once a week please.

You will have to send the sticks by M.F.O. [Military Forwarding Organization] as they won't go by post. If they object to them not being 11 lbs, put a couple of bricks in the parcel. My dear old girl the whole place has gone mad over your cake, long flat raisin one & Hitchcock tells me to tell you he has been looking for one like that for years!!

19th April 1916 – No. 126 – Divisional H.Q.

I've had a very amusing day today with an officer & 13 O.R. from the Grand Fleet & have been taking them round showing them all I could. It really was quite fun & they were most thoroughly happy. I managed to get them to a point about 3000 yards from the Hun line where they could look straight at it & they loved our shells going over their heads & seeing them burst on the Hun line. They saw a good few come back too. They go up into the front line tomorrow for 48 hours & then have a day with the artillery before going home. I must be off now to dress for dinner.

21st April 1916 – No. 128 (if you have a 127?) answering 128 – Divisional H.Q.

I am simply delighted with the photos & the one of old Bob with the hat on is simply top-hole. Ken *has* grown & looks simply topping & does 'La Vache' the very greatest credit old dear. You are getting your hand in alright & the next half doz ought to be corkers!! I was so glad to hear all about old Mac.

Those fools at the squadron never sent the pie on & I found it all mouldy there today. Such a pity. I'm just off to an evening service as there is one in the barn & I can get there, as I have been out all day looking at ranges for musketry practice. I have no news I fear old dear, so must stop.

24th April 1916 – No. 131 answering 131 – Divisional H.Q.

You are quite right about those dispatches & your opinion is that of the whole army I think. I find that this Monro is not the Munro I thought he was.[131] This man was Commandant of Hythe where we spent an ever-memorable honeymoon or perhaps 'commenced' would be better, because I have no recollection of its ever having ended.

Today the morning was simply glorious with the most wonderful lights & the old Hun took full advantage of it to throw as much heavy stuff over our way as he could spare. I was out all morning with Webber watching the shooting & doing a bit of supervising [of] work going on on our line. You would have laughed if you had seen us both dodge behind a house once. We had driven in our car to where we get out & walk & had just got up a hill when the very unmistakable sound of a shell that is coming straight at you caught our ears but as a matter of fact it was two hundred yards short of us.

[131] General Sir Charles Monro had been given command of the First Army in France in January 1916 after executing the successful withdrawal of Allied troops from Gallipoli, and was confused by Major Hermon with the Charles Munro he had known in South Africa.

During the 2 hours we were out, the Hun put 109 others in the same place, each shell being 6 inches in *diameter*. It was awfully interesting watching the shooting as the Hun is perfectly wonderful with his guns. I don't know what the cost of a shell of this size but I shouldn't wonder if that wasn't close on a £1000 shoot. The results I will tell you in another number.

Leave opens again shortly, so Harry[132] back in a few days now. He is certainly looking forward to it. If you can I should very much like you to do something for him. If you could send him & his family to Brighton for the day to a Theatre or something. I have the most unbounded admiration for Harry. He has done splendidly. He is always ready to do anything he's asked & I have never heard one single word of 'grouse' pass his lips since he has been out here. Harry is the only one of us, I think, whose language hasn't depreciated! I have never heard him swear once, & old Buckin who used to prate to me how awful it was living with men who swore, instead of keeping up his high standard has simply let go, tho' to give him his due he has done me most awfully well & so far as my *personal* comfort is concerned I am quite all right. Harry is loved by everyone.

28th April 1916, 10 a.m. – No. 134 answering 134 & 135 – Divisional H.Q.

We have been having a pretty strenuous time these last few days as there has been a lot of unrest on our front. Mines & counter-mines galore to say nothing of gas & suchlike oddments, tho' the gas was a few miles off. Anyhow the advent of this lovely spring weather has made both sides feel very lively! By the bye I must have my thin jackets please. Send me the two best ones and also another cap with badge from Jacksons please.

Thank the Chugs for their nice letters and explain to Betsy that the word 'Exam' is spelt by all the best people 'igzam'.

At present I rejoin the squadron on May 7th & leave for my training area on early morning of 10th so letters to arrive on 7, 8 & 9 should be addressed to the squadron.

[132] Parsons.

The oaks are coming out here before the ashes I am glad to say, & I heard the Cuckoo three days ago and the nightingale last night for the first time. I simply love my photos old dear & they are stuck up over my dressing table – the two of Bob & one of Ken in the middle. Yours I have put away as it isn't at all like you. I like both old Bob's but especially the one in the hat as he looks such a nice manly little bloke.

I am glad you say Ken is a merry lad & he does look splendid. A real fine baby I think & I should love to see him again. I should have loved the Sunday walk old dear & I can picture it all so well & it seems really so close. I am glad you realize the enormity of your offence! You are forgiven now!!

The pistol arrived yesterday & is exactly what I wanted. I had some practice with it last night and made some very respectable shooting. The marmalade parcel rolled up alright yesterday.

My love to you my dears.

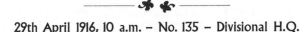

29th April 1916, 10 a.m. – No. 135 – Divisional H.Q.

Strenuosity still continues & old Beauchamp is having a very rotten time. I was over with them yesterday afternoon & they were all looking down their noses a bit. However tho' unpleasant it's not serious. I am glad to say we have just got a Hun aeroplane tho' I am afraid he fell just in the next Div. area & so we shall not get him in here. However it is a bit back on our bloke a few days ago.

We really had a most amusing evening last night as owing to 'strenuosity' we couldn't go to bed so we played bridge to nearly 1 a.m. & had the cheeriest evening I have had since I came here. I managed to make 8.50 Frs & as we play the old Governor's points of 5*d* per 100 it wasn't bad.

The pot of marmalade was very much appreciated again & everyone is on it like a pack of wolves!

30th April 1916, 10.30 a.m. – No. 136 answering 136 & 137 – Divisional H.Q.

The Hurricane Smock arrived safe & sound & I will give it a good trial & if I like it will get you to get me a new one. I am sitting in the office now and just sweating. The weather this last few days has been too glorious & far too good to use simply for killing folk. Last night Hitchcock & I stood out on the steps pondering this same question while the guns were going like anything.

Poor old Beauchamp is in a proper mess & was trying to mend it but I am afraid he failed badly & it was the old goose who had the job. He is in a terrible way as with all his trouble here he has got his good woman in the hands of the rebels in Dublin[133] & has heard nothing at all. It is terrible bad luck for him. Many thanks for seeing about the map case. Your letter to Morrish was really fine, how I wish I had a business head!!

Try & get Hatchards or a library to send you regularly a Magazine *Revue de Paris*, in it you will find an account of all the fighting which took place here & I believe it is to continue in other numbers. It is well worth reading tho' being in French it rather boils me.

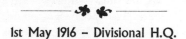

1st May 1916 – Divisional H.Q.

Strenuosity still reigns supreme. Last night at 7 p.m. the old Hun blew two mines on us & a Hades of a battle ensued for a couple of hours & then quietened down. You can hardly imagine what a 'boost' a show of that sort means. Everyone of both sides who has a gun lets it off as fast as it damned well can go & there is more stuff in the air than you could pick up in a lifetime. The Huns have been awfully busy lately all along the British Front & the ammunition they must have must be colossal when one thinks of what they must have expended at Verdun.

---

[133] The Easter Rising of Irish Nationalists.

2nd May 1916 – No. 138 answering 139 – Divisional H.Q.

Had a nice walk yesterday round some of the reserve line trenches with Webber & were much pleased to see the old Hun had wasted a good deal of his heavy ammunition lately.

They have just discovered that Trench Feet is a sort of infectious fever, and are convinced that it is carried by the lice the men collect in the trenches. The R.A.M.C.[134] orderlies get it in the hospitals tho' they never saw a trench in their lives!! I had a very interesting talk to our P.M.O.[135] the other day about it. They haven't actually discovered it yet, but that is the line of research at present.

It would be splendid if you could get old Mac down to Staplefield as I am sure he would like it better than London.

The weather here is glorious too & the nightingales in the trees at night round my hut are simply top-hole. All the woods here too are fine and the trees wonderfully well 'forested'. You see none of those poor scraggy trees one sees at home & every tree with lots of room. My love to you my darling.

3rd May 1916 – No. 139 answering 140 – Divisional H.Q.

My time here [at Divisional HQ] is now fast drawing to a close & I shall be awfully sorry when it does come to an end as I have had a really top-hole time & got on the best with the whole crowd & especially with the G.O.C. himself I think.

Townshend[136] I don't hear much good of & that letter you speak of I am told is a habit, in case things go wrong!! It's not Kut, it is the feeling in the East that is the trouble, especially Afghanistan. I see that both old Cowie & Ted Impey[137] have lost their boys quite lately. Here I get the

---

[134] Royal Army Medical Corps.
[135] Principal Medical Officer.
[136] General Sir Charles Townshend.
[137] Edward Impey, his housemaster at Eton.

current day's *Times* after dinner each night which is a real blessing. One hears something about the war now!

Two nights ago at 6.30 p.m. we asked for some air photos of our line, the flying fellow being here in the office at the time. At lunch the next day the prints were in my hand!! Not so bad?

My love to you old dear.

4th May 1916 – No. 140 answering 141 – Divisional H.Q.

Yesterday I had a rather wonderful sight of a modern battle. The old Hun had been very aggressive on this front for some time, blowing mines and generally making himself thoroughly unpleasant so we thought we would set about him & give him something to think about. I was up in a tree some 6000 yards behind our line but where I had a most wonderful view of the whole show with a telephone direct to the office, reporting progress. At 4.47 we 'upped' with two huge mines which was the signal for the show to begin. There was the most terrific bombardment you ever saw for an hour and one wondered how any man could live through it for a minute whereas our casualties were so small one could hardly realize it possible, I am glad to say. It was the most lovely summer evening you ever saw. The woods were simply perfect and the whole place seemed at peace & one could hardly realize that two huge armies were doing their damnedest to kill as many of each other as they conveniently could. Then it was a splendid sight to see the infantry rush into the craters when the artillery lifted & I am glad to say that the whole show was quite successful & I hope will give the old Boche [something] to think about for a bit.

This mine-fighting tho' is a most beastly business & I shall be thankful when it is all over, not that it really concerns me very much, but one hates it for the Infantry as it means a lot of intense fighting on both sides without any very great material gain to either except a little local advantage here & there. A mine throws, as a rule, a big lip of earth all round the edge of the crater itself and this has to be occupied by one or both sides & in most cases, one side sits on one side & the other on the other & hurls bombs at one another.

The chief advantage is that eventually if you can consolidate your side alright it gives you a high point between the lines from which you can get

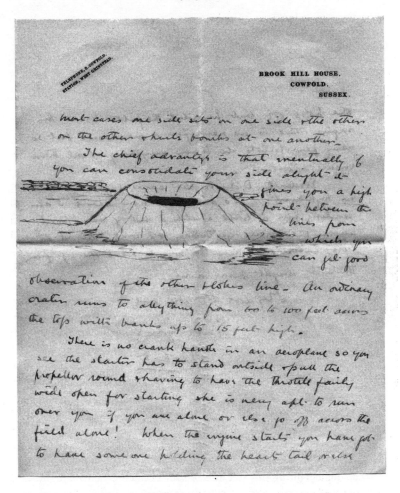

BROOK HILL HOUSE,
COWFOLD,
SUSSEX.

most cases one side sits on one side & the other on the other & hurls bombs at one another.

The chief advantage is that eventually if you can consolidate your side alright it gives you a high point between the lines from which you can get good

observation of the other blokes line — An ordinary crater runs to anything from 60 to 100 feet across the top with banks up to 15 feet high.

There is no crank handle in an aeroplane so you see the starter has to stand outside & pull the propeller round & having to have the throttle fairly wide open for starting she is very apt to run over you if you are alone or else go off across the field alone! When the engine starts you have got to have some one holding the beast tail or else

good observation of the other bloke's line. An ordinary crater runs to anything from 60 to 100 feet across the top with banks up to 15 feet high.

No more news now dearie. I am sending you a little sketch I did of our front during the battle yesterday & will post it to you later on when it won't have the significance that it might have now.

My love to you all.

5th May 1916 – No. 141 answering 142 – Divisional H.Q.

Yesterday I rode over to see the squadron & I must say I am not really very keen to rejoin now again as once having tasted better things it feels like a retrograde movement somehow. However we shall see. I haven't the remotest idea how I stand here. Everything has been more pleasant here since I have been here & no one could have been nicer or kinder. Did I tell you I hope to get Henry back again shortly? He wrote to me the other day & said he wanted to come back if I would take him & of course I jumped at it.

6th May 1916 – No. 142 answering 143 – Divisional H.Q.

There seems to be so much to tell you & I am just a trifle light-headed into the bargain that you will probably just be as muddled at the end as I am now. This morning the Corps rang up on the telephone and told me that the Cyclists & the Squadrons of the Division are to be lumped together & become Corps Troops instead of Divisional Troops. Our regiment will come together and become a Corps Troop Regt & similarly the Cyclists will become a Cyclist Battalion, Corps Troops. The whole will be under one command & will amount to a small mobile Brigade. Headquarters will come out from England & there you are. Now the problem is this. Who commands the lot? James & I in command of Regt. So far so bad! On the other hand I might become chief staff officer of the push with a decent Cavalry Colonel in command. That not bad. Then on my talking to Hitch-cock on the subject he said 'Well it won't affect you because you will get a staff job almost at once as the General has sent your name forward.' This is absolutely secret, first of all because H. had no business to mention it to me, & secondly because the staff job has not yet materialized, so keep it to yourself, but anyhow it means that I have justified myself here which is always something to be pleased with!

Of course, if I could get command of this mobile force it would be top-hole but then one is hardly senior enough perhaps, but I am really a very senior Major now as things go at present. Anyhow things seem to be more hopeful than they have ever been before & so I have no doubt you will be as bucked as I am at present!! It's too early days yet to know what will happen but just sit tight & hope on!

No more now old girl. I return to the squadron tomorrow, unless anything unforeseen turns up meanwhile.

7th May – No. 143a answering 144 – Hermin

I have been back some hours now. When I left [Divisional HQ], the papers about the forming of the Regiment had come in & I had a long talk with the G.O.C. on the subject of my advancement. At present the idea is that I am to get command of the Regt. This would suit me real well and would satisfy me for the present especially if I could get command of the Motor Machine Gun Battery and the cyclists too when we get all together. It would be a top-hole command & as the C.O. of the Cavalry Regiment is a Lieut. Col. they would have to make one at least a full Colonel or Brigadier if they run the lot together & they must do this in time as the one is the natural supplement of the other.

On the other hand, should James[138] come out I should, of course, go at once or as soon as I could get my job as G.S.O.2 & the G.O.C. will take me tomorrow as that, or help me in any way that lies in his power. Prospects are indeed bright now & I am happier than I have been since I have been out. The Corps Commander knows all about Jimmy & isn't for him in the least which is always good hearing & I very much doubt if the Pseudo[139] would let him come out if he wanted to.

I was very sorry at saying goodbye to the Div. today & they too are genuinely sorry, I think, at losing 'your splendid squadron' to use the G.O.C.'s words. Every soul said something genuinely nice to me about the squadron & meant it. I only hope the 1st Corps will think likewise.

---

[138] Major James, senior major in the regiment.
[139] A reference to Major James's 'mistress'.

9th May 1916 – No. 144 answering 145 – Hermin

Only time for a short note. Have had bad luck lately. Lost a sniper on Sunday morning & yesterday my S.Q.M.S. (Alderton) was killed by a fall from his horse. Address my letters 'C' Squadron King Edward's Horse, B.E.F. only for the present.

Fearfully busy getting ready to move tomorrow. Don't expect a letter for a few days.

Friday 12th May 1916 – No. 146 – Carly

We are now at a village called CARLY between Boulogne & Samer. I don't know if I told you that throughout the fight the gentleman in the foreground continued his ploughing and actually sowed his field while I was up in my tree!! He was in full view of the Boche too at the time!! A mile & a half away there was a most awful inferno of shells you ever saw.

The Squadron seemed quite pleased when I got back and we have certainly had a very pleasant time since. I am amused at what Harry told you & I know if I go my Sgts Mess will all be off like a knife, but we must see what is on the cards first. You ask just what we are doing here. Well there is a central house they call the 'Mounted Troops School' & Ing, (Bays) Parsons 19th Hrs [Hussars] & an Adjutant from the Bays runs it & the Cyclist Coy & Squadrons are billeted round and drill about every day doing a fortnight's ordinary squadron training supervised by these fellows. They say they are a bit shy at taking me on & want me to lecture to the school. I am not going to if I can help it. 'A' Squadron is here & they have also applied for 'B' Squadron to come & I hope it will.

I get command of the Regt until such time as the Hd Qrs can come out from England. The Division doesn't go back to rest at all now as we have only a Brigade in the front line, a Brigade in support and the third resting, so they relieve one another alternately. Our training here ends on May 29th & I expect we march back to CHOCQUES that day or rather start on our march as it will be a two days' march. Henry[140] is going to the Guards now I hear & has sent in his application. His whole family are in the Guards & so he is going to join them.

I am off to pay my respects to Dick Mullins now so adieu for the present.

14th May 1916 – No. 147 answering 149 – Carly

I got two nice letters from you yesterday and a really awfully nice one from old Bob in answer to mine. Yesterday it rained like the very devil all day & we did absolutely nothing at all.

Will you please send me:

1 large bottle Stephens ink (1 pint)
1 doz linen collars (Khaki from the man in Regent Street same as usual – either shape don't care)
6 glass cloths
2 Dusters
1 pr Sock Suspenders
3 Prs real good black bootlaces

I also want you to get me a stencil made by Harrods of our Regtl Badge so that I can stencil my wagons. Size of imprint to be about 8 inches high. You will have to give them a badge which you can get from Sandon. Better get the big cap badge (men's) so as to make it easier for them to copy. Must go to stables now old dear.

14th May 1916 – No. 147a answering 150 & 151 – Carly

I got your two letters about old Bobbo's school day after lunch today & I was so very sorry for you old dear, & that I wasn't there to help you through.

---

140 Feilding.

You seem to have had so much to go through by yourself but we will hope you have finished for a bit now.

I am so glad that the old boy was so brave & it was nice of him wanting dear little Mairky to help him through. What a funny little tea-party it must have been just those two in the car. I've loved your letters about the old boy so much dearie mine & it brings home so close & makes one long so for another glimpse of you all. I don't know when I shall get another go of leave & it is certainly no good thinking about it yet.

I wish I could be at the birthday party it sounds very nice. Lass dear, I feel I want you very badly tonight. We've got a nice little garden here & the river runs at the end of it and last night it was lovely, so still & jolly you would have loved it, dearie mine. You don't know how I have hated tearing up your two letters, old girl but they were so nice & so full of home that I felt somehow I daren't keep them – it brings it all too close once more.

16th May 1916 – No. 149 answering 153 – Carly

Tonight I have been wandering about in the garden with the river running so silently by & a lovely full moon & the gramophone going; miles away from war & not a sound to be heard – it makes it all very hard to realize. Whereas you seem to have the whole 'mental' part of the show, like the poor, always with you & the very great family gap too & I know it must be a gap. Dear old Bobbo I should miss him too most awfully & I feel he has been doing so much for you lately that it must be doubly hard, old dear.

With regard to old Bob's going to Eton, you want him to go so that if by any chance he failed to get in, he could have another shot. What I should do if I were you is to write to Todd & tell him that he will not be quite 13 & isn't it a bit young? Personally I wouldn't mind if he waited till the summer term 1920 but he ought not to be later than that.

17th May 1916 – No. 150 answering 154 & 155 – Carly

We drill at Hardelot,[141] a sort of little Worthing and Branksome Bournemouth combined, as for a mile or more from the coast one goes through pine woods and sandhills & it is really an awfully jolly place with flat sands stretching out a very long way.

Coming home we passed a very nice little house & garden with the folk having tea in the verandah & it seemed so funny after one has just come from the destruction of Souchez & Carency, seeing women in decent clothes and looking very nice, all round an afternoon tea table!!! And today one could just hear guns. The first time I have heard them since I got here.

You talk about the guns & they do get on one's nerves a bit tho' of course I haven't seen a hundredth part of what the infantry do, but one does notice fellows flinch when one is walking about, especially when one is in front of one's own guns as somehow one seems to notice them as much, or even more, than the Hun shells unless the latter are in very close proximity to one. Unless the old Hun is shooting directly at you one doesn't mind his shells. His shooting is so very accurate & so persistent that if his shells are landing a couple of hundred yards away, you can stand & watch them without them worrying you at all & it is extraordinary how the gunners and infantry treat them unless they happen to be the selected target. They take no more notice of them than you would of a fly & not half as much as I do of a wasp!!

Beyond telling me he had seen Ken, I don't think Harry told me any home news at all! We aren't going to Chocques at all now & so I suppose we shall go back to the same Corps that we left & I hope we shall. How long we are likely to be there I don't know but should say till the end of the War!!! The whole regiment will be together from now onwards.

My love my old darling.

---

[141] Hardelot-Plage, just south of Boulogne.

20th May 1916 – No. 153 – Carly

We spent the morning going round a most wonderfully well run Veterinary Hospital & saw some very interesting cases & then met my squadron on the beach just before lunch time. We rode our horses into the sea & then let them have a real good roll in the sand & then we all, *including your husband*, had a most lovely bathe. I sent the squadron home at 3 p.m. and we lay about on the beach in the sun for a bit & then rode to a most ripping sort of tea-garden place, where an old house & really lovely garden had been turned into a café. It was really top-hole, especially as there were several most lovely ladies in all their best clothes, which added considerably to the interest of the afternoon!!

It is really very pleasant seeing a decently dressed woman once more!! I must say this life down here is very nice for a short time but I shall be glad to be back again, as it is altogether too 'embusqué'. I don't know how these Cavalry folk stick it. With us one does get a job of work or two connected with the war, but down here it is too awful.

21st May 1916 – No. 154 answering 159 – Carly

The heat today has been too awful – all afternoon we have been lying about in the garden. I am so glad that old Mac is coming to you. Today Syme went off to England & has gone to Bisley for some job with armoured cars. I told him he was to ring you up tonight as he was with me at 11.15 a.m. today. My darling, how near & yet so far! I am sure old Mac would love to see him & I told him he was to go down & see you & Mac.

You may not take to him at first but he is one of the nicest-natured boys you ever met & the friendship between him and the old Baron was too amusing.

I walked two miles this morning to hear the poorest parson I have ever heard in my life. Thank goodness I didn't take any men – I think they would probably have mobbed him. Lass dear, it's been glorious here this afternoon & I have longed to have you here. I looked hard across the sea yesterday dearie mine but I couldn't see you, and to think that that wretched little 'Slimy'[142] is probably in London now!

My love to you all my darlings.

23rd May 1916 – No. 156 answering 158 & 160 – Carly

I expect old Mac will pick up alright when he gets with you as he had no one he knew in London & he must have been bored to death. You can take him out in the car because that will brighten him up & if you can get him fit & well again you will be doing a very great service to the nation, as if I get the Regiment I want him for my Adjutant.

I can quite believe that you miss old Bobbo's presence & the house must be very funny without him but you will appreciate him all the more in the holidays.

For goodness sake don't grow like old Miriam. The effect might be disastrous!!

My love my darlings.

24th May 1916 – No. 157 answering 161 & 162 – Carly

I'm a trifle sad tonight tho' no doubt I shall soon get over it. We had a long day today with the regular troops & I must say I have never been so bitterly disappointed in my life. To start with we formed up in column of route with the 19th leading, one of whose squadrons was advanced guard. Before it had gone a mile it was completely lost, & so the Brigadier sent out the two remaining squadrons of the 19th Hussars to take the place of the erring one. These in their turn also became completely lost in the next two miles & the whole regiment never was heard of again! I believe however it was eventually able to find its way back to its billets before dark.

Then the P.B.Y.[143] in the person of your husband's distinguished corps

[142] Lieutenant Syme.
[143] Poor Bloody Yeomanry.

had to take up the onerous duties of Advance Guard & oddly enough were able, with the aid of a map, actually to keep to the road chosen by the Brigade Commander & to carry out his wishes. Our Brigade Commander (Regular) & a Brigadier General, so disposed his force that at the decisive moment he was unable to put his hand on a single soul to throw into the fight with the exception of his own horse holder & a staff captain, who looked as if he drank. Fortunately the opposing brigadier had made as great a mess as ours, and as neither seemed anxious to settle it with their fists the day came to an inglorious end.[144]

Our brigade commander's task[145] today was to pursue some broken infantry retiring from an action fought last night. Infantry march 2½ miles per hour. Our commander in his original striking force had the 19th Hussars, 1 Battery R.H.A.,[146] 2 squadrons K.E.H. & a cyclist company. At no time was he opposed by more than half a squadron of the 'Bays'. At the end of three hours he had made six miles good & the infantry he was pursuing had gained a mile & a half on him since the start.

If they had both left the same rendezvous at the same time we should have had to have trotted for 15 minutes at the end of three hours to catch them up. However, I'm only a yeoman & therefore not in a position to criticize a professional soldier as because he is a regular soldier he must know everything there is to know about soldiering & our poor little P.B.Y. must learn, mark, read and inwardly digest & by gad he does & ponders these things in his heart. However there are other fields & pastures new, [where] perhaps he may venture.

It's getting late now dearie & so I shall go to bed & leave your dear letters to be answered tomorrow. I had a lovely letter from old Bob enclosing his marks which I send you herewith in case he hadn't a copy for you.

My love to you all my darlings.

---

[144] The Regimental History sums up this exercise with the comment: 'It can only be said that from the point of view of instruction the period with the 1st Cavalry Division was a waste of time; as a holiday it was a pleasant break from line warfare.'
[145] A training exercise.
[146] Royal Horse Artillery.

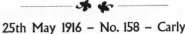

25th May 1916 – No. 158 – Carly

I am afraid that I wrote you a rotten letter last night but I felt like it then tho' now I am completely recovered tho' I have the prospect before me of starting off at midnight for a long night march.

It is rather a blow old Jimmy[147] coming out but perhaps the Pseudo will go sick again & he will have to go home.

I can't help thinking that if Jimmy has come out that it will free me from organizing the Regiment & if that is the case I don't see why I shouldn't have a bit of leave. If I can get it I shall try & come one day in the week June 11th to 17th so as if possible to be home to go to old Bob's sports. I was very glad to see old Bob was in third place in his class, perhaps when he settles down he will improve it. Anyhow we shall see; his Pa wasn't much use at book-learning!!

28th May 1916 – No. 160 answering 163, 164, 165 & 166

I seem to have a perfect budget of your letters to answer tonight.

I have just had a letter from MacDonald asking for news as they have only heard rumours so your tale of Jimmy coming to France is not correct so far, I am glad to say!! While there is life there's hope!!

Tell Juckes that he must fix up old Mac as soon as he possibly can as I want him back very badly indeed. Poor little Ken, I know exactly the glass smashing action, I've seen it before. I would love to see him old girl & perhaps I shall before long but I can see by Mac's letter today that I shall be very lucky if I get home when I said & personally I fear it is off for the present but we shall see.

Yesterday I looked across the Channel & saw the coast of home so close that it made one think a bit, especially as there was the dearest little kid playing on the sand where I was sitting who was the dead spit of my Meg. Absolutely in character & everything! I'm so glad you like old Mac, I

---

[147] Major James.

absolutely love the boy & he is real gold through & through. I think old Mac has a very exaggerated notion of one's capabilities – perhaps that's why I like him so much. I am sure from what you tell me old Mac is making real progress & I am very glad he is. Keep it up & get him fit for me as soon as you can.

29th May 1916 – No. 161 answering 167 – Carly

Well we are off at 8 a.m. tomorrow on our return journey & tho' we have had a very pleasant time down here a very great deal of it might have been much more profitably employed. We have been lucky in a way as we had a good fellow, one Parsons in the 19th Hussars, as our instructor & he was a thoroughly sound fellow, but the instruction given by the rest of the crowd, if it can be called instruction, was beneath contempt.[148]

You wonder when this war will end, well you needn't fuss yourself about it ending for another 15 months at the very earliest I am afraid old dear. If it does it's so much to the good, but you must make up your dear old mind to that, I am afraid. It is not a bright prospect and it is eating into some of the best years of our lives but it can't be helped. There is no doubt that the armies of both sides are now so equal that it will be very difficult for either side to do much against the other for some time. However if the folk at home will really back the army & not go on strike & holidays & generally play the ass, it will help a lot.

My love to you old dear.

Ever your Robert.

---

[148] The comment in the Regimental History says 'some of it highly instructive, some intensely comic'.

CHAPTER ELEVEN

REASSEMBLY OF THE REGIMENT

On 1 June 1916 the British and German navies engaged in the only set-piece naval battle of the First World War, the Battle of Jutland. Tremendous losses of ships and men were suffered, though neither side could claim outright victory. The experience, however, deterred Germany from any further naval battles and thereafter the enemy preferred to use the hit-and-run tactic of the U-boat instead. The death of Lord Kitchener on 5 June was seen by the Allies as another blow, but on the Eastern Front General Brusilov occupied Czernowitz, taking thousands of Austrian prisoners, giving the Allies some solace.

June 1916 also saw the continuation of the Battle of Verdun. In spite of losing Fort Vaux, the French maintained their grip on Verdun itself. At the end of the month, on the 25th, the preliminary bombardment, which would herald the major Franco-British offensive, the Battle of the Somme, began. The barrage was so intense that it was heard on Hampstead Heath.

With the reassembly of squadrons 'A', 'B' and 'C' in late May, Robert was given temporary command of King Edward's Horse. However, the regiment was still denied an active role and Robert began to experience considerable frustration at being ordered to take part in seemingly pointless cavalry exercises, while men were fighting and dying on the Somme.

31st May 1916 – No. 162 answering 168 & 169 – Valhoun

My darling,

Well here I am, with my regiment collected around me & I only hope I shall remain in command. We marched in here half way between Pernes & St Pol, today at 11.30 a.m., 'A' & 'C' squadrons, and found 'B' already here, as it had been for some days.

You ask what I want & I should prefer to remain in command of the Regt to going on the staff. I have made Steve acting adjutant & explained to him that he is merely keeping the seat warm for 'Mac' provided you can repair him in time. I will give you two months to do it in. If he is passed fit by July 31st he can have the job so long as it lies in my power to do it, but of course I couldn't answer for what Jimmy does if he comes out.

We had a very good march back here. I had a bad night last night, as two dogs made such an awful din under my window. At length I got up and by a fine flow of language drove them from the yard. In half an hour they were back & at it worse than ever. I was determined to stop them & had no other weapon than a half full & very large china 'Jane' [149] & as they passed under my window I let the lot go. It fell on a stone pavement right between them & burst like a shell. I don't know where those dogs are now, but they left the yard at a terrific speed & never uttered again for the rest of the night! The worst of it was, I shook so with laughter that I was nearly sick & sleep out of the question, but the effect was splendid & it only cost me 2 francs!! Tell Betsy she must be mistaken, as Dad has no naughty words 'on him'.

The Division is out of the line now & H.Q. quite close by so I hope to see them very shortly again. I wish I was at home to talk over things with you old dear, but I am at present out to command the Regiment & it will be a bitter blow if I don't get it. If I don't get it, I shall have a shot at a staff job. It will probably be at least a month before anything is settled.

My love to you old dear,

Ever your Robert.

3rd June 1916 – No. 165 answering 172 – Valhoun

Well I went over to see the Corps today & there the official application was made out for me to get command of the Regiment and I suppose will be signed by Sir Henry tomorrow and sent on. The only thing was that I had to be loyal to old James & as I had his letter telling me to apply to the Corps for him and H.Q. to come out, I insisted that his letter should be pinned to my application so that the Corps Commander could decide between us as to which he wanted. I shall know in a day or two what has

---

[149] Chamberpot.

been done & will of course let you know at once. I lunched with the Corps Commander & rode some of the way home with him as he was going to an inspection.

I heard about the Naval battle there. Perhaps it will help the nation to realize that there is a war on and that if they mean winning they have got to take it seriously. I have just been looking through the weekly illustrated papers. Makes one think a bit when you are close behind the Vimy Ridge, tho' a long way back & personally quite safe, nevertheless I have been talking today to fellows who were there & it wasn't all jam while it lasted.

Such a nice lad I knew well is missing & I fear done for tho' he may have been taken prisoner. He was with me the last time I was in the front line & in the very part the Huns took from us. Tell Mac they came across with their right on Tanchot, took Gobron & Erzatz and stretched away about 1000 yards further south. They had a hundred batteries concentrated on this piece by way of preparation and simply flattened everything. Tell him we now hold the 3rd line on the ridge & are still east of Zouane valley. Tell him that they put a lot of shells into the place I lived at after he was hit & so it had to be evacuated!!!

I called in & saw the old Div. on my way back & they were wonderfully cheery & pleased to see one & I have had a very pleasant day altogether. We are a very long way back I am sorry to say tho' perhaps it is as well. It would take me 2¼ or 2½ hours to ride comfortably to my old Div. H.Q. You say I am probably back again in sound of the guns & I just am, but that is all.

The Corps didn't take very kindly to my suggestion that I should keep the Adj. open for Mac, as once he is in England he is off the strength of the Regt out here & one is not allowed to ask for folk by name from England. I haven't given up hope so far & you can tell him he can rely on my doing my best. What is so annoying is that if it hadn't been for me sending him off on that job I should have him now which, tho' quite unavoidable, is very bad luck.

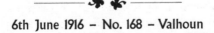

6th June 1916 – No. 168 – Valhoun

Many thanks for the gooseberries! We had some at Carly but these were most acceptable but they weren't quite cooked enough in the tart we had tonight & having a large helping I am feeling symptoms of a painful & sleepless night!!

I am very optimistic tonight. I feel that these attacks of the Hun[150] are the attacks of desperation & I believe he is on his last legs. It may not be that we shall have him beat until next year, but I am sure that he's out for something desperate. If he fails everywhere as I am sure he will, even tho' he drives us back as much as a mile or two in places, I believe he will bust up. However, mere speculation is not worth much.

I shall want my typewriter out & will let you know later how to send it. Perhaps you had better pack it at once and send it by M.F.O. See that it is properly screwed down to its board and if it is at present loose from the board, take out the screws from its rubber feet and you will find in a pigeonhole in my desk longer screws to go through the board which hold it down. Don't take off the rubber, just change the screws. Please also send me four packets of good typewriting paper from Harrods and a packet of carbon papers foolscap size.

My love to you all my dears.

7th June 1916 – No. 169 answering 175 – Valhoun

Today I assumed the rank of Lieut. Colonel! (Temporary Rank). Nearly all ranks are Temporary out here now. What it means is, that while I actually command the Regt they give one the Rank & pay. Now that the Regt is vacant by Sandy[151] having gone, I want to know if they are going to pass me over James, or not. If they do, I get the substantive rank almost at once and that is for good. I'm going to have a good try for it. As it is, if we fight, I believe I command a Cyclist Battalion & a battery of machine guns too. I believe I get this command administratively too, almost at once.

What a real tragedy K of K's death[152] is – it is almost unbelievable. However even the best have substitutes somewhere. One of the compen-

---

[150] At Ypres.
[151] Lt Colonel Sandeman.
[152] Kitchener of Khartoum: he was killed whilst on a diplomatic mission to Russia when, on 5 June, HMS *Hampshire* struck a mine laid by a U-boat and sank west of the Orkney Islands, with the loss of more than six hundred lives.

sations of life. My dear old girl, there's no more chance of the war being over in a year than of my being selected to fill K's place.

I didn't know Ralph Juckes had got the Military Cross. Do tell him how very pleased I am. I am sure it's wrong to have a piece of shell in so mobile a part as a man's arm & I long to hear that Mac has had it out. I am so glad to hear he is so much better in himself & I long to have him back again.

My love to you my darling.

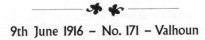

9th June 1916 – No. 171 – Valhoun

Today has been a slack one rather as the men have been to the baths and as usual handed in good shirts and drawn out lousy ones! It's scandalous that they can't get things done better than they do. I should have thought it would have been possible to set up steam laundries & have the things well done. However, ours is not really a very brainy or business-like army & one must gloss over its shortcomings.

The Remount man came & took off eleven horses that I wanted to dispose of & was glad to see the last of. Otherwise the day has been without incident. The rain seems to have gone for the present & good riddance to it too.

11th June 1916 – No. 173 answering 179 – Valhoun

Tell old Mac that I in no way despair of his getting the Adjutantcy as I have sent his name in, in writing & so far they haven't sent it back & that is some days ago. If I have to appoint Steve he says he will certainly resign when Mac comes, but I shall probably want a staff officer for the whole show & Mac should get that if the other were to fail.

Russell & I rode over & had tea with the Div. today & passed the time of day with them. They all seemed very cheery & well. I am inspecting all the squadrons this week just to see how they compare & it then gives one a better idea of how one stands.

Mimi sent me a couple of photos of old Bobbo with his rabbit! Please thank old Bet for the tobacco pouch which was very welcome as I bust little Mairky's Xmas present & my old one was full of holes. My love to you all my darlings.

12th June 1916 – No. 174 answering 180 & 181 – Valhoun

First & foremost I am more than relieved to hear that old Mac's operation has gone so well & I only hope that now he will go right ahead & get well quickly. He amused me very much referring to his efforts at thanks by saying that 'you could squash even better than I could'. The cake turned up alright & in good condition. White House pack theirs so badly they are always broken when they fetch up.

I don't know how any sane person can say the war will be over in a month – it is absolute rot, because they hold us everywhere, on every front & so far show no signs of weakening anywhere. If it ended in a month it would be a disaster of the first magnitude, an inconclusive peace with the power of Germany uncrushed. The one thing that we are fighting for is at least to stop a recurrence of such a thing in our or our children's lifetimes & that is certainly not done yet. God forbid that it should end in a month! Much as I want to be home again & shut of wars.

The Army Commander inspects us this week.

My love to you my own old dear.

13th June 1916 – No. 175 answering 178 & 182 – Valhoun

We had our field day today, in the most awful downpour of rain you ever saw. Really the last ten days have been worse than we have had since Christmas and it still shows no sign of clearing. How on earth we shall turn out tomorrow goodness only knows!

My dear old girl, it will be a blow if I don't get the Regt after all but life is full of little disappointments. I am delighted to hear so good a report of old Mac again. Tell Mac that I consider him quite unfit to be Adj. even of a fire brigade. He has no right to 'twit' his C.O. and when he comes out he will have to pay for it as I have sent his name in on paper & now Jimmy will strafe him well & serve him right!!

My love to you my darling, & let us hope for the best.

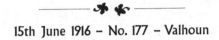

15th June 1916 – No. 177 – Valhoun

I have had to pay for getting two lovely letters from you yesterday, by going without today. However I am still bearing up in spite of the fact that I have just started Barber off to home sweet home. He is going to ring you up and is also going to try and motor over and see you, which I hope he will manage.

One of the officers of another squadron told me tonight that there isn't an officer or man who isn't desperately keen that I should have the Regiment which pleased me very much. I do want it so badly that I shall be fearfully disappointed if I don't get it but after Stamfordham's letter it is going to take me all my time to pull through.

Ever, my lassie, your Robert.

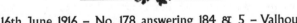

16th June 1916 – No. 178 answering 184 & 5 – Valhoun

I'm a little light-headed tonight so excuse this if it wanders all over the shop. Today the whole of the Corps Mounted Troops have been placed under my command and tomorrow the rest of them arrive in the next village. Bell[153] is acting as sort of Staff Captain for the present & I believe should do the job well as I have a very high opinion of his qualities.

These folk only march in tomorrow and I have got to have a Field Day on Monday with the lot, for the benefit of the Corps Commander, & what is worse it has got to start with a lecture by E.W.H. on the method of

---

[153] W. H. D. Bell, Cheviot Bell's brother.

handling the Corps Mounted Troops also before the Corps Commander who is himself a lecturer of the very first quality!!

I must answer your letter tomorrow dearie. I started at 9 a.m. by inspecting 'B' Sqn, got back to the office at 12 & was there until 1.15, passed 5 young officers out in the mechanism of the Hotchkiss Gun 2–2.30, at 2.30 motored to 1st Army Training area, got back at 7 was in the office until 7.45 p.m. Had dinner, returned to the office at 8.45 and left it 10.30 p.m. all for 25/-.

My love darling mine.

17th June 1916 – No. 179 answering 184, 185 & 186 – Valhoun

I see I got my 'Mention' at last, tho' I must say it has given me really very little pleasure. Had it been in the last Dispatches it would have given me very great pleasure because I knew I had done work that well deserved a 'Mention' but coming so late, it isn't quite the same. However one must be thankful for small mercies and if it has given you any pleasure, my darling, I am amply repaid.

I have been most fearfully busy today old dear, what with one thing and another. My command having suddenly leapt from 400 to a 1000 officers & men to say nothing of the beastly horses, motor cars & what not, keeps one fairly occupied.

Many thanks for doing all my shopping. The paper hasn't arrived yet but I expect it will tomorrow. While I am on the question of papers will you write & tell the *Times* & D.M. [*Daily Mail*] to change the address of my papers to K.E.H., IV Corps Cavalry 'B.E.F.'.

18th June 1916 – No. 180 – Valhoun

Only a short letter tonight as I am about to have my monthly bath. Things seem to be straightening themselves out alright now & after two very heavy days I think we have fairly broken the back of the heavy work.

I have been fairly sweating up my lecture for tomorrow as I feel that the day will decide my fate as I can't help thinking that the Corps Commander is coming with the idea of seeing what he thinks of one, prior to writing in his views as to who is to command. I'm going to have a damned good try to put up a decent show.

My love my darling.

19th June 1916 – Valhoun

I didn't get a letter from you last night but funnily enough I said to Steve 'I'm sure that it is in connection with the command of the Regiment that the Corps Commander wants to hear me give a lecture and also see me run the whole force.' We started with a lecture at 8.30 a.m. for 45 minutes & then we started on the field day.

He was in his car and spent the whole day with us, insisting on a conference and my making my remarks on the general conduct of the day before he said what he had got to say. The only criticism he made was that my 'scheme' didn't give quite as much information as it ought to. On the actual work & handling of the troops he made no comment at all. He was awfully pleased with the men themselves & very pleased with the answers he got from some of the N.C.O.s. He was most pleasant the whole time & we parted most amicably about 3.15 p.m.

I shall do nothing foolish old dear so you need not worry. I have heard of C.O.s being 'dégommé'. In one afternoon 'Goffy' sent home 1 Div., 2 Brigade and 5 Commanding Officers. Not a bad day's work?!!

I've simply loved your two letters tonight & I long for the time when we can meet once more, but when that will be, I don't know. They say absence makes the heart grow fonder, but dearie it grows wondrous fond these times.

I can't help thinking that your riding party cum cycle! must have been fine. Tell old Mac if he would put Mary on her pony, Betty on her bicycle & you in the car he could get some excellent practice in handling the Corps Mounted Troops! I think a photo of you three with Mac on Betsy's pony at the head, would make a fine picture of the Cowfold Corps M.T.!

My love to you my darling.

Robert now heard that Major James, his senior on the Army List, had been appointed to command the regiment and he was to become second-in-command.

21st June 1916 – No. 183 answering 189 & 190 – Valhoun

It is no good denying that I am disappointed at not getting the Regiment, because I am very, but at the same time it isn't anything like the crushing blow it might have been.

After all James is senior to me & it is perfectly normal in that way, but I have heard enough to know that if it was put to the vote in the Regiment there would be no doubt who got it then. The Regiment in itself is nothing to me, but the regard of the men is everything.

However we shall see how he gets on, but now he has won it's up to me to play up to him & for the sake of the men to do all I can to keep him in the right way & I have every intention of playing the game by him, as you know. I am not going to turn out of my nice house tho', unless he actually turns me out & I don't suppose he can be such a cad as that, tho' he has got a lot of hair in his heels. Anyhow I ought to get my leave now as I expect he will be only too glad to get shut of me.

Later

I don't believe I'm beat yet. If Jimmy does get the Regt, he is *not out here yet* & until he actually takes over I don't resign my temporary rank. I have got a letter tonight the meaning of which is not quite clear but for the moment it has turned despair into hope!!

26th June 1916 – No. 188 answering 194 – Valhoun

'C'est tout, c'est fini!' At lunchtime today I got a telephone message to say that our new C.O. was at St Pol station so I got a couple of my horses, your old horse and my pony & with an orderly I rode in to meet him & he arrived in camp, not riding upon an ass, but upon your old horse. There was no clamouring crowd to meet him and his entry was unmarked in any way.

He's here now & we have got to make the best of it. Lass dear, your letters have been a great help these days & I don't know what I should have done without them. I must admit that the Corps Commander's action has taken me completely by surprise & has been the exact opposite of what he led me to expect. The whole time that he was writing for Jimmy he was leading me to suppose that he was doing what he could for me. In all probability he was not conscious of it, but when I heard what were the facts of the case I must say I was absolutely dumb-founded. However it saved him the unpleasantness of telling me direct that he wanted to do old Jimmy a turn, but I rather like straight dealing, it seems fairer really.

Poor dear little Chugs I am so sorry for their sakes & it does look so as tho' one had been dégomméd for incompetency, but I don't think I have as no one so far has found a single fault either with me or the squadron since I came out. Certainly they have never mentioned it & if there had been anything wrong I am sure that these times they wouldn't hesitate. On the contrary the one cry has been 'I'd rather have six of your men than 20 others'. I've only had the Cyclists and M.M.G. [Motor Machine Gun] a little over a week & I hear from Steve that while Bell was over there this afternoon they were wild about it. They say they had never been so happy before, & were congratulating themselves & now it's all bust!

I'm not going to do anything just yet old dear, I must see Jimmy well on the way before I feel I can go elsewhere and it's much easier to say one will go than it is to get a job. I wish I was at home tonight as I should love to be able to talk to you, old dear. As you say, Jimmy steps into an absolutely going concern. We could march out tomorrow, the whole Corps Mounted Troops organized and ready where they are wanted.

Well dearie, I must make a fresh start now. Hope I shall find an outlet for my energy in some decent direction. At present I command Buxton and Harry but I hope to get the Regimental Transport later on.

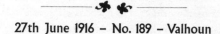

27th June 1916 – No. 189 – Valhoun

I'm in no mood for writing now dearie & so I shall stop for a bit and try later on. James got back from his lunch party whither he proceeded on your old horse!! I forgot to tell you yesterday that in climbing up on him at the station he burst his new breeches to glory!! I was having a talk with him when he got back & he said to me 'Did the Corps Commander give you to understand that you would get the Regiment?' & I said he did not in actual words, but from inference I certainly did expect to & he replied 'I rather gathered that from what he said at lunch!!' I must say I am absolutely beat over the whole thing. I can no more fathom it than fly. When Jimmy arrived at the base he was held up there on the 1st Army letter I wrote to you about. He wired the Corps Commander & he wired for him to come on. It's all so contradictory and so obscure that one cannot see daylight through it at all.

Darling mine, I am just daring to hope that I might get some leave after all & as they go now I shall try to leave here on July 13th & be home for your birthday. It's a possibility that is worth considering. Don't set too much store by it old dear & then you won't be disappointed, but I should love to come if I only can. We have had a lot more wet these last few days, there has been great artillery activity somehow lately and I expect that has made the weather bad.

My love to you dearie mine.

The enclosed was rescued from the Canteen for me where it was put up with the men's notices. These sort of things help one a lot now & Brake came to me today as representing the Rank & File of the *whole Regt* to express their great regret at recent changes. It was really awfully nice of them & I was most touched.

28th June 1916 – No. 190 answering 195 & 196 – Valhoun

I rode round with the C.O. today & he had the impertinence to talk to me about his wife & baby. I suppose he referred to his damned mistress & his blasted illegitimate brat.

My love to you my darling.

Since writing the above, all leave has been cancelled old dear so when we shall meet again goodness knows, but let us hope in the none too distant future.

O n 1 July the Battle of the Somme began with a massive infantry assault after an intense barrage, which nevertheless failed to break the defences. Ten mines were exploded under German defences and the assault began along a 25-mile front, but yet again, attacking British soldiers were mown down by concentrated machine-gun fire. Hidden in armoured emplacements, these guns had been protected from the barrage and reaped a deadly harvest. On the first day of battle alone, more than 45,000 British troops were lost, killed and wounded: the highest total for one day in the entire war. The intensity of the assault forced the Germans to move troops from Verdun to the Somme, which had been one of the aims of the Allies, and although fighting continued around Verdun until October, it ended any real hope of a German victory there. Fighting on the Somme would continue for another five months, until 18 November.

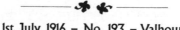

1st July 1916 – No. 193 – Valhoun

This morning I went in a car to see the French Mission with an interpreter & went in to see the Corps on the way. There I met old Rogey who was terribly grieved over the turn of the tide & the old man is still going to make an effort tho' what fruit it will bear it is hard to see. Personally I have no hope myself of anything being done yet. We are all very pleased to hear that they have made a good start down south & I hope it will be maintained.

I am hoping for some more news tonight as we have only heard that an attack has taken place.

2nd July 1916 – No. 194 answering 199 & 200 – Valhoun

I've had a somewhat slack day today, have done absolutely nothing nor is there a job of any sort to be found for one. I simply can't stand this life of idleness much longer. I would rather enlist in a Pioneer Battalion than go on doing nothing. I can use a shovel & could do quite good work either mending roads or filling sandbags but I shall go off my head soon if this goes on much longer & I see no prospect of it not lasting till the end of the war.

I am going to write to old C.B.[154] tonight & get him to put my name on his staff list if I can. He said he would & it only wasn't sent in before because I wanted to get the Regiment if I could. I shall take anything I can get now, so long as it gives me a job of work to do where I can maintain myself with self-respect.

My love my old dear.

3rd July 1916 – No. 195 answering 201 – Valhoun

Things really haven't been at all bad considering & there hasn't been, so far, the slightest unpleasantness between the C.O. & E.W.H. It's no good trying to pick quarrels & I have done my best to see that there should be no grounds for complaint whatsoever & things have gone alright.

It's only the awful dull days with nothing at all to do that worries me. The absolute lack of any work that you can call your own. I have just taken over the canteen but that's hardly a job, certainly not what I came out to do.

Thank old Bet & Mairky for their nice letters received yesterday. At a farm in the village here they have got some topping little terriers, I'd simply love to bring one home.

My love to you all my darlings.

---

[154] General (Sir) Charles Barter.

❧ ❦

4th July 1916 – No. 196 – Valhoun

I am at present wrestling with an awful problem & don't in the least know what to do.

C.B. has offered me the command of a Battalion in his Division. I am to go & do a fortnight in the trenches first just to get in touch with the work a bit and then, if I am a success, I am to get a Battalion. It's not exactly what I wanted but it's a start and has decided possibilities, as if one does well one ought to be able to get a brigade within reasonable time & one isn't at a dead end. It's an interesting job as most of the Battalions can be greatly improved & there is unlimited scope for work and possibilities of getting on. I think, my dear old girl, I must accept it, the only worry that I have is that I must say our field day[155] today did break down in my opinion terribly and I feel so that if an advance came I should be useful here, but this second-in-command game is no good to me I should cut my throat before long, it's too awfully dull for words.

Somehow I can see you turning up your nose at this but these infantry are splendid fellows and it's an honour to command them if I can live up to it. I know that there's none of the élan & the dash of the mounted soldier, but for real hard slogging on & conscientious work the infantryman has us beat stiff & I would just like to show them that if the Cavalryman hasn't done the work in the past he's none the less willing and able.

Anyhow I have till Saturday to think it over but I have almost made up my mind now, so you will have to look on your husband as a poor footslogger very shortly!! Damned funny war this, one seems to turn one's hands to all sorts of jobs & for me, this one almost makes me laugh!!! Old Mac will be amused I'll bet.

My love to you my darling.

---

[155] Under the command of the new CO.

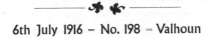

5th July – No. 197 answering 202 – Valhoun

I got your 'outburst' today and it was very welcome indeed & has caused me the very greatest amusement & pleasure. I can see your indignation old girl & I must say that I have felt something of it myself.

I know quite well that the officers that I take over won't be, in all probability, quite the same socially but on the other hand I know they are real good fighting fellows and have done as well as any Division in the country.

My only fear is that the folk here will think I have left them in the cart, & just put my own personal inclination above that of the Regiment but as you say I'm not a good 2nd-in-command as I cannot stick the awful lack of all responsibility & having no job of my own.

6th July 1916 – No. 198 – Valhoun

Well dearie mine, I wrote to C.B. today and told him I would come on appro when he liked. Whether for better or for worse remains to be seen.

If you tell old Mac that I shall be in the Div. front on the left of where he was hit looking towards the Hun he will show you where I shall be on the map – between where he was once concerned with some cylinders and where he was hit.

I must say that the idea of going is not appealing to me very much at present but I do want a job of work and after all one will be doing something to keep the show going, which is more than I am doing at present. My day's work today consisted of going for a ride on your old horse this morning and sitting on a log from 11 a.m. to 1 p.m. twiddling my thumbs, then lunch then reading a book on my bed from 2 p.m. till I feel asleep, woke up at 5 & had tea & am now writing to you. I'm paid £1 a day for that! Well, it really isn't good enough. I shall probably be horribly frightened in the trenches but I expect it will wear off alright after a day or two.

I think the flies are the worst part of the trenches in the summer & they are generally very bad, but it's not at all a bad part of line that the Div. is in at present and there haven't been a great lot of attacks there in the past so the ground isn't as foul as some about here.

I haven't broken the news to Buckin yet & am wondering very much if he will prefer to remain in the ranks here. I shall be very interested to see. Oh! you never told me if you paid his wife's debts for her. Let me know this will you.

7th July 1916 – No. 199 answering 203 & 203? [sic] – Valhoun

Last night the young gents set about me & begged me for everyone's sake not to go & I simply couldn't refuse. I have promised that I will stay on until Oct. 1st & then if nothing has happened I am at liberty to fend for myself. They have no faith in things as they are and they say that I can keep things going much more smoothly than they otherwise would. As it is, Jimmy has done nothing off his own bat, he drags me into everything & gets me to vet it before it goes out of the office.

Those watch protectors have gone like wild fire and I want other £1 worth please. This time I want one size larger & leave out the small size sent before. That will be 5 of each size please. Also I want another 3 doz. assorted toothbrushes and some more handkerchiefs.

You say you would give worlds to have a look at me now, well it's 9.50 p.m. & I am in my very comfortable sitting room, with my bedroom & Steve's opening off it, the windows all open & a nice warm night outside! You needn't worry about me in the least for I am nearly as comfortable as I should be at home & no one tidies my writing table.

I'm awfully glad for Mac's sake that he has been passed for light duty but I expect you will be awfully lonely as he is such a companionable old thing. I've always heard that Mac's brother was huge, I'm glad you thought he was a nice lad. When do old Bobbo's holidays begin dearie? I suppose about Aug 1st or 2nd. Well old dear, I must to bed now.

8th July 1916 – No. 200 answering 205 – Valhoun

I have had a very nice day today with the C.O. We started in a car & ran down to Carency and then we got on our feet & walked through the village, which was a bit of an eye-opener for even his 'war worn' eyes I think. We went on through Ablain St Nazaire and up on to Lorette where we had our lunch & looked down into the suburbs of Lens. For the first time since I have been out here I saw some real live & untrammelled Huns. I saw seven of the blighters running about in the streets. It sounds very odd having been out all this time that one has never seen the bloke one's fighting, but I haven't, except as a dejected prisoner.

I see the poor old Sussex Regt fairly took it in the neck. The casualty list shows 26 of them tonight – 2 killed 13 wounded & 11 missing. That makes a big hole in a Battalion. However on the whole things seem to go well tho' slowly & I am told that the Hun casualties have been appalling. Still he is a wonderful nation and if he would play the game, should be the admiration of the world.

I return you old Bobbo's letter, what a nice one it is, so awfully neat and tidy. I am so awfully glad he is still doing so well at school and is still top of his form.

I am glad to hear you have got the hay but my poor lawn!! Don't worry about me old girl, I am hoping leave will be reopened shortly & then perhaps we can have another pleasant week together once more. We really had a glorious morning this morning as it was a lovely day, very hot but still a nice breeze when one sat still.

In addition there was absolutely nothing doing in the way of shelling at all, and absolute peace & quiet reigned. I think I only saw two shells drop about 500 yards away all the time. We had lunch right on the end of the spur near where the chapel once stood, but now it is no more & the ground is so churned up that you can't find the place now, hardly. The whole spur was one mass of the most lovely poppies & cornflowers & looked simply lovely. There's plenty to fertilize them up there, bones & remnants of French & Germans absolutely cover the ground.

Well, goodnight old dear.

9th July 1916 – No. 201 answering 206 – Valhoun

I had a nice sleepy little letter from you today which somehow seems to bring you so close, dearie mine. I can see it being written so well, and all the room seems just as it might be here; it makes me long to be home again. I'd give anything in the world old dear, to see you & the dear little Chugs again. I expect my little Meggie has grown quite big & old Bet must be quite the young lady now. Fat little Pook too, give them all my love & a kiss for my unknown son!! I certainly couldn't pick him out of a bunch. I hope he realizes the gravity of his position & is fulfilling his role in a fit manner.

I am writing to the old Gov. tonight & as the Battalion is for the moment off. I shall tell him of the offer as it will help the old man over his disappointment that the other debacle caused him.

The stencil came today old dear & I think it will do fine as it isn't so big as to be very easily read. If the names show up too much I shall have to paint them out.

I had a nice letter from Mac today & he amused me most awfully by saying: 'I am trying to chuck smoking: I only started yesterday & it is a bit of a wrench. I feel that those wretched cigarettes do me a lot of harm & I shall never get in the way of smoking a pipe only, so I am going to have a cigar a day after tea & nothing else!' I think I see your finger in this pie old dear.

I nearly killed the C.O. yesterday by walking him off his legs. He kept on saying 'I think we'll just wait a minute while I mop my hat out'! I must say it really was very hot walking along the trenches & they were very wet and slippery which made it bad going too. I went to our church in the school today & we had quite a nice little service.

My love to you my old darling.

10th July 1916 – No. 202 – Valhoun

I am afraid prospects of leave are not very bright old dear & I fear once more you will have to possess your dear old soul in patience, but as Steve says 'I don't want leave, what I want is to go home & stay there'!

We are all very pleased with the news at present, we go slowly but we do keep on going & it looks very much as tho' the old Hun was going to have everyone at him shortly & I don't believe he can stand that for long. He is losing men on every front & we must have a great deal more of him killed before it can be a really satisfactory termination. It's fine that the French have got to Péronne & I only hope that they will get it in the next few days. It is a bit of a bridgehead & will therefore be difficult to take I expect. Anyhow at present wherever there is fighting going on the Central Powers are going back & we are advancing which is all in the right direction at last.

I wish we could have a go soon, it is very wearying work sitting here waiting & waiting. If the end of Sept. comes and we haven't had a go I shall most certainly go to Infantry, I can't spend another year & take so small a part as I have done this last nine months, it isn't fair.

However we must see what the next two months will bring & I wish it would bring the open fighting once more, unless it does it will mean an absolute war of exhaustion which is very trying & most boring. We must hope for the best tho' & perhaps the end may come one of these days fairly suddenly. I wish to goodness it would buck up. There's nothing of any interest to tell you old dear I am afraid & as I did not get your letter today have none of the proper sort of inspiration.

My love to you my darling.

12th July 1916 – No. 203 answering 207 – Valhoun

Very many happy returns of your birthday tho' may the next find us all spending it together, which I believe it will.

Things seem to be going really well on all fronts & I have just heard of the capture of Péronne and a large Russian Victory too & if really true it is magnificent. How I wish we could have a go, you don't know how I long to lead these magnificent men of ours at the Hun. Perhaps it will come in a few weeks now or even sooner. I really believe that soon now the Hun will have to retrace his steps towards home.

Jimmy came over here and is now down where the boost is so he went right into it. Our man, until I took him that day and made him go, had never seen the front-line trenches anywhere except in the illustrated papers. He had no more idea than the man in the moon of what the modern trench system meant. The depth it extends back or anything to do with it and how he intends to lead us through it I don't know. However all things are supposed to be for the best and there may be some great blessing in it, but it's difficult to see yet.

I am glad to see in the *Times* today that a Hun officer seemed to think that some of our new devices were rather hot stuff, they seem to have surprised them a bit.

I am awfully glad we have been so successful with their observation balloons as they are damnable things tho' I can't help thinking that they don't really see as much with them as we give them credit for. It's beastly having them looking right down on one as one always thinks that they see you even if they don't.

We have just had an awfully nice Med. Officer posted to us which is a great thing as they are very like the curate's egg these times.

12th July – No. 204 – Château at Bomy

I'm certainly not going to allow you to have any more wounded heroes to look after, it seems to have affected your brain a little. Please therefore give the enclosed to Betty and Mairky for a birthday present.

I am at present in the most glorious château at a place called Bomy, & have got a most lovely room which I am sharing with Steve. It reminds me very much of our room at the Kellys' only I think it is bigger, a glorious big bed, but very lonely by oneself. We have got some nice ground to train on here.

By the bye, will you stop the cocoa please as we are very much overstocked. The jam too might be halved, i.e. double the intervals please. The bacon I want to continue as usual. I think Barber is writing you about what he wants done as we started the H.Q. Mess today, we weren't able to have it before as we couldn't find a suitable place to have it in. Will you thank the Chugs for their two very nice letters please. I enclose you old Bobbo's effort & also one from Mac.

The old baroness who lives here tells me that she has got badgers here in her woods & by the number of stuffed foxes they have in the hall I can quite believe it.

My love to you my darling.

13th July 1916 – No. 205 answering 208–211 – Château at Bomy

My darling, I love your grouses & it makes me feel that even tho' I am so far away I can still share some things with you, which is everything. Really dearie, things aren't at all bad & you need not worry as there has been absolutely nothing at all that you could take the slightest exception to in Jimmy's behaviour since he joined us. The lads said, when they begged me to stay, that I could keep him in the straight and narrow way and he certainly has been most amenable & has adopted every suggestion I have made so it all works well. Of course I haven't got a day's work but I have now taken the Hotchkiss guns under my wing & amuse myself with them so it gives me something to fill the mornings with. You pay me a compliment about carrying on but I've seen too many 2nd-in-commands working against their C.O.s & I told him that I would support him in every way & so far as I can, I think I can conscientiously say that I am.

Lass dear, you mustn't worry too much about the trenches, they are very much safer really than you would suppose. For every shell that falls in them there are hundreds fall harmlessly outside & it is only when there is a really heavy strafe on they get a bit unpleasant. However they have got to be occupied by someone & I have had or shall have had 18 months out of them so it's only fair that I should have a go now. It was certainly nice getting the offer of the Battalion & I shall certainly go when my promise is up.

I did want to hear what you thought old dear & have loved every word of your lovely letters today, & I envy you your splendid calm courage old dear. You are quite right, I couldn't say no or I could never have asked for anything again, but I wrote and explained the whole situation to C.B. & I know he will understand.

What a jolly day you must have had on the shore at Rottingdean. I feel I would go as far as having a bathe to share it with you? I am so glad to hear the old boy looked fit & well. He told me he made 46 runs the other day & 20 something another. I'm all for a present to old Mac from us both with 'Brook Hill 1916' on it. Yes, I have got the shirts and they are top-hole. Wasn't Chev's a nice letter? As you say it is awfully nice how all these boys seem to care for one & all the other squadron lads are the same & these cyclists too seem alright.

Will you find me the simplest, child's 1st [French] grammar book & send it me please, & if you can get a small flat dictionary I should like it as I want to learn to talk this lingo & I seem to have had a bit of a chance to learn lately. I also want a really good pair of wire cutters in a leather case to carry on the saddle, real good ones. Price no object. Can you send us from time to time some mint (roast lamb mint) not peppermint!!!

Goodnight old dear.

14th July 1916 – No. 206 – Château at Bomy

After the avalanche of letters I had yesterday I have had to go without today. It has been a glorious day today & we are all very bucked at the good news from the Somme & are hoping great hopes in consequence. I hope old Chev has come to no harm, tho' I am a little fearful that they were thrown in too soon.

My love to you dearie, sorry this is such a rotten letter.

The 'good news from the Somme' included the British capture of Mametz Wood on the 12th, and large numbers of German howitzers and munitions on the 13th. On the 14th the British took Longueval, Bazentin-le-Petit, and Trônes Wood, marking the end of the first phase of the Battle of the Somme.

15th July 1916 – No. 207 answering 212 & 214 – Château at Bomy

You say the master told you some news, well it's quite correct. At the same time you needn't be at all downhearted over it. Things do go very well & what to my mind is a great point, the counter-attacks of the Hun are now nearly all beaten off & if he does succeed in gaining a point he is very soon outed again.

I think now you may say we are beginning to see the beginning of the end. It will probably be another year before the end actually comes and there will still be some very heavy fighting probably heavier than there ever has been up to date, but I really think that we have him set now. I certainly don't think you are doomed to disappointment, but don't be misled into believing that there is going to be a procession to Berlin because there isn't unless it's from the East. If we could get them back to the line of the Meuse that is as much as you can possibly expect & would be splendid, but they aren't going back even so far without some real proper scrapping & they are at present by no means short of men. Where they get them from goodness only knows but the fact remains that they have got them & that they fight in the trenches almost as well as ever they did.

I haven't heard from C.B. because I haven't had a chance but I put things in my letter in a way that I don't think he could take exception to. Of course, if the old man was to go sick or anything between now & then, well I should be boiled!!

Cakes & marmalade have turned up alright. Can you get Jacksons to put in his parcel a good bottle of acid drops! Good for the summer months & the C.O. wants them & I am Mess President!

Please thank Bob & Mairky for their nice letters. Hope the new cock will be a success 'because we are going to eat poor Sam on Saturday'!! Heartless little wretches.

17th July 1916 – No. 209 answering 216 – Château at Bomy

It is very odd but only yesterday I was wondering who was in the cottage now & was thinking of offering it to Buxton. I have always known that they were living beyond their means, but having had a fellow feeling, have never said anything because if they like to do it that is their affair.

What I should like to offer her is to let her live there rates & taxes free instead of paying her debts and for you to continue to pay her what you have done in the past. The rent is nothing to me, everything to her & I should like her to go in as soon as possible, & by this means she should be able to pay off her debts by Xmas, but it is to enable her to pay them off and to live free of debt afterwards that I am doing it. She should be easily able to do this as she should save 6/6 a week.

I can remember that evening at Potchefstroom, & also writing the exact time on the wall on the right-hand side of the mantelpiece. What a long time it is ago & yet one can see it so very clearly.

Dear little Chugs I am so glad that they enjoyed their party, they are lucky to have so little knowledge of what is going on, tho' I look forward to the time when I can bring them out here & show them what war means in a country as it might be useful to them in after life. I should like them to see Lorette, Ablain & Souchy, Carency and the country round Loos. They would never forget it & perhaps later on when questions of conscription or suchlike things cropped up it might be very useful for them to have seen it.

I am very anxious to know what the Government will allow you as a quarter's consumption of petrol. I see you are all going to be put on an allowance.

Tonight I went for a walk up in the wood to see my badger sett again and it is in very active occupation and by the length of the small white hairs about there must be several pits there, probably four.

18th July 1916 – No. 210 – Château at Bomy

I was very pleased to see by the Intelligence Summary that the old Boche has been taking it in the neck. A captured messenger had on him a message giving the strength of his *Battalion* – 3 off: 2 N.C.O.s & 19 men!! We had nothing like that. There were a lot of messages captured, & the Hun wasn't liking things a bit.

I had a happy morning with my guns & am going to have some shooting with them tomorrow. We've had marvellous weather lately, awfully overcast, just the same sort of days as our ever-memorable sail from Brixham to Weymouth. Well old dear I am quite dried up. Many thanks for the toothbrushes, you didn't say what they cost. Perhaps you will have done so in your letter. Will you send me a tin of toothpaste please.

20th July 1916 – No. 212 – answering 217 & 218 – Château at Bomy

We had quite a decent field day today & I enjoyed it as I had a command once more. Our mutual friend H.W.[156] inspects us on Saturday & then sets us a scheme. We are in the 'training area' at present, doing just what we should do were we at camp in times of piping peace.

The army rents a piece of ground about five miles square where we are allowed to ride over the crops & go anywhere, & then they have claims officers who go round and pay for the damage done. The worst of it is that the whole ground is under crops & you have to ride through standing wheat & when bread is so dear it seems a sin. As a matter of fact one can't bring yourself to do it & really there is very little damage done at all.

I think old Mairky's little pencil effort simply sweet, & old Bet's 'pres' too. I am simply starving for a sight of the Chugs. I had a postcard from old Bob telling me he is still top of his form which is splendid. I am most awfully pleased that the old lad is doing so very well.

I must change for dinner now & will add a bit when I come to bed.

[156] General Sir Henry Wilson.

I've just had the most amusing evening's bridge I ever had in my life. The last three hands I and my partner lost 200 in the 1st, 200 in the second and 800 in the third!!!! and I lost one franc on the evening.

You asked about our hosts. Well, they asked us in to tea the other night. We had tea & cake – they all put the cake into their tea & eat it like porridge!! As soon as this was over a bottle of champagne was opened, glasses handed round & the health of the 'Armée Britannique' drunk. There were at least a doz. folk there & everyone had to start by clinking glasses with everyone else. This entails 132 clinks!! Then we drank, then James, in the midst of a red-hot Royalist household, proposed 'Republic Française'!!!! This produced a capital effect tho' it is doubtful if the one desired. The old man turned his glass upside down & the situation looked desperate till we all began to laugh & then things came round again but the whole show was too funny for words.

The Baroness is really quite a nice old girl & I talk to her a bit but as she only speaks French & I only speak lingua Franca-Britannica it's a bit odd but we manage somehow, but she is seen at her best discussing the flush tank of the Jane with Buckin.

My love to you my darling.

23rd July 1916 – No. 215 answering 220 – Château at Bomy

I have a sort of feeling that you cannot have got one of my letters, because I wrote and asked you for a second lot of those watch guards omitting the smallest size. At the same time I wrote to old Grandma at Merrow, Balcombe & you say she has never received it.

In the official report we get of operations it said that 'the Cavalry had been ordered forward', & in view of Chev's letter I expected that he would have gone. However, so far as I know he didn't. We get the wildest of rumours that you can possibly imagine and really know nothing. We depend principally on the newspapers received from home & when special fighting is going on we get a wire about the same time as the papers get it in England.

Tell old Bet she may buy her goat if she is very keen about it & she seems to want it badly.

Yesterday we had our inspection & field day under a scheme set by the Corps Commander. I personally had nothing whatsoever to do & was merely a spectator. The whole show went real well & the Corps Commander was thoroughly pleased & heartily congratulated Jimmy on his fine Regiment.

I can't make up my mind whether I am regretting have stayed on or not. At present I rather think I am, & I wish now that I hadn't listened to the lads, but it was very hard not to. Anyhow it seems that I have thrown away three months for nothing but it is too late to grumble.

Many thanks for the wire cutters which turned up alright today & are fine & just the sort that are the best for the job out here.

My love to you my darling, it's on evenings like this, when one isn't feeling just quite quite, that one seems to long for home once more, almost so badly one feels one can't bear it much longer. However, joy cometh in the morning & there you are!!

24th July 1916 – No. 215 answering 221 & 222 –
Château at Bomy

Will you write for one of the enclosed please for me, as I am not quite sure that my present tin hat is quite as thick as the Government one. Size of head 6 ¾ – and have it sent out direct.

Last night we had a bit of a concert here, which wasn't bad but not as good as I hoped. Nearly all these villages have a room with a stage & as this village has a very good one, we took advantage of it.

You would have laughed if you could have seen me paying the Baroness this morning for the use of our part of the Château!! It seemed too funny paying her direct. It will be lunch time in a few minutes and then the mail at about 2 p.m. I simply live for the mail these days & count the hours till the next one comes. I am hoping for two letters today as I got none yesterday but they are read so quickly & there is then a whole 24 hours to wait for the next.

I am so glad to think that Miss Cooper[157] has gone. Your new one sounds alright, quite makes me want to come home! You seem to think I have no

---

[157] The governess.

memory. Anyhow I don't address your letters to Falmouth or any other place that takes my fancy!!? Many thanks for the handkys which arrived safe & sound.

My love to you old darling. Please thank dear little Mairky for her very kind thought & her present of cake, we are going to have it for tea tonight.

♣ ♣

26th July 1916 – No. 217 answering 223 – Ohlain

I have forsaken my château for a tent now & I am not sure that I don't like it much better. It's healthier. We are doing a bit of digging now & this afternoon I am going to ride round with the doctor & see the parties. I am now in a very small village which we will call 'O' some 6000 yards N.W. by W. from where I was with 'Rogey' in April.

On the way home I met a pal who is a Brigadier. He was horrified to find that I wasn't a Brigadier too & couldn't make out why I hadn't a D.S.O. Very nice of him. Anyhow he at once offered me a Battalion in his brigade if I would take it. Now I am fairly up a gumtree. His Brigade is a New Army one & his Div. Commander is in a very much better position than C.B. They have each offered me a Battalion & I personally would far rather have this than the former one. I don't know what on earth to do.

The lads now realize that I am fairly boiled if I stay here. Jimmy acquitted himself alright on the field day & they know that he will hold his own alright now & they see my point of view & are willing for me to go. I am going to dine with the Brigadier tomorrow & shall discuss it with him & I shouldn't be at all surprised if I became an infantry C.O. one of these days very shortly. It's rather odd getting the offer like this of two Battalions one after the other; shows someone still thinks your poor husband is still worth something.

As you say the fighting on the Somme has been absolutely desperate. I have seen a few folk who took part and it certainly was pretty stiff. At the present minute there is a ceaseless thunder of guns going on there & as we took Pogieres yesterday I expect it is a Hun counter-attack going on. Anyhow it is a pretty good strafe tho' it appears to have died down for the minute, now it's starting off again.

There is no doubt we are jolly near through the Hun there. I wish to goodness we could bust him for good there & make him go back. It seems so small a bit that has been done when one looks at it on a map of the whole line. However if we can only kill enough of them in their counter-attacks it will help. The great thing is that we do continue to advance. Slowly, but still each day we gain a good piece.

27th July 1916 – No. 218 answering 225 – Ohlain

I don't think I've ever known such a fuggy day as it is today. Last night one simply lay in bed & sweated & today it is just the same. I see that most stringent regulations are being brought in about the amount of news that is being sent home so my letters will be even duller than usual. It is really awfully wise because there is no doubt that folk are very foolish in what they write and more so in what they talk about in restaurants etc. The date & place of this last offensive was common talk in London long before we knew in the Regt here & it is hard enough these times to conceal movements of troops without all the babbling that goes on.

I've just broken it again to Jimmy that I am probably going & he tells me he has heard that most of his young officers at home are going to the Flying Corps which is worrying him like the devil. He says it's perfectly ridiculous that when officers get a bit dissatisfied that they can just go and do what they like. This was intended for me!! tho' toned down by saying that I ought to get something better than a Battalion.

I got a letter from little Mac today thanking for the watch & he seems very pleased with it. I am so glad to hear little Ken is doing his 'bit' for his country & that he is really fulfilling his mission. What on earth have you been putting on your writing paper, it simply stinks. Do you think Gladys[158] put her kit down on your writing pad or anything because it simply stinks of bath salts or some such muck!!

The battle seems to be catching us; above the continual murmur of the Somme battle they are having a rare old artillery duel up between La Bassée & Loos which one can hear very plainly. Just been for a good long walk to get a little exercise; sounds funny in the midst of the world's greatest war but is none the less true.

I've just read your letter again. I'm convinced that Gladys has put some of her stinks down on it. I simply can't do with it any longer & am going to burn it!!

28th July 1916 – No. 219 answering 224 & 226 – Ohlain

Well, taking the bull by the horns today I advanced on the Corps, & was met with 'Well, there's no further word about your Battalion, it's been back once & we expect to hear any day now!!' Well, so far as I can gather old C.B. has never got either my telephone message or my letter saying I wanted to wait until Oct. 1st & his application has gone forward & I am likely to get the job any day now.

Anyhow it's Kismet & if it rolls up I shall pack up and take it on. In some ways I should have preferred the Battalion I was offered these last few days, but these are not times for picking & choosing & if the thing comes through alright, I shall take the first that comes along & do my best with it.

I believe I am as good as the average C.O. but I haven't really been put to any test of that sort yet & that is the only thing that is going to prove it. Anyhow there are thousands of other ordinary mortals doing splendid

---

[158] Gladys was a second cousin.

work every day & perhaps one will be alright. Apparently this man, whose place I am to take, is very ill & had to resign first, or something. However, as I say, I shall take the first that comes now as I can't go on doing nothing any longer.

Besides which I want to go & do my share where there's something doing. One cannot go on sitting in peace & comfort at a nice safe distance behind the line any longer & still keep one's self-respect. Come what may I'm going to have a go now if I possibly can. I can't stick another 'embusqué' winter such as last.

Poor old thing, I can see you so well looking 'greasy' after your wrestle with the car, but they do run much better on petrol!! It is very seldom indeed that it is magneto trouble that is wrong with a car, always start in your diagnosis from the petrol end & see that the carburettor is full & then work down the wires to the magneto last, & before tackling that undo the wire from the end of the magneto that leads to the switch & start like that. You can always stop the car by putting a screwdriver on to the terminal (which you have disconnected) & putting the end against any portion of the engine.

There is a lot of flying going on today the last three or four having been quite impossible so they are buzzing about like bees today. There's a fine article in *The Times* of 27/7/16 page 7 columns 1 & bit of 2. Absolutely true & fine!

29th July 1916 – No. 220 – Ohlain

Just a very short note this evening because I am going up to have a look at the Hun & have a picnic dinner on the hillside & then on to see the digging party at work. As per usual I have done nothing at all today & we got no mails again so there is no excitement of any sort to stir me to a special effort.

I've heard nothing further about my Battalion yet. The Corps Commander came round today & I wandered about the lines with him but he said nothing.

My love to you dearie.

❧ ❦

30th July 1916 – No. 221 answering 227 – Ohlain

We had a most pleasant evening for our walk. We went out to the end of a hill about 1000 yards behind our own front line & sat in the grass where we could overlook the whole show & watch the transition stage from day to night conditions. We reached our position about 8.30 p.m. just as the light began to fail & saw the old Hun put some very heavy *minenwerfer*[159] over as a sort of 'kiss good night' & then very shortly afterwards our guns had a proper hate on his line & for an hour & a half he got the most concentrated essence on a portion of his trenches as would make him think a bit. We stayed on until twilight merged into darkness and the Verey lights began to go up.

It is really a wonderful sight, because it's all quite silent except for the guns & an odd rifle or two & it seems impossible to believe that two great armies face one another across a small strip of field, in many places not a hundred yards wide, & that you never see a soul move. As we came away about 11 p.m. you could see the whole line stretching right away on both sides by the Verey lights & star shells & in the distance away to the south the glare of the gun flashes on the Somme, which lit up the whole sky just as one sees the lights of a big seaside town from the sea. It all brought back so clearly our day on the end of Portland Bill, and I was talking about it all to the doctor as we walked home again.

This latest Russian news is splendid & I expect they will be very soon at Lemberg & Przemysl again now. I think William, emperor of all the damned Germans, will soon be having a very funny feeling in his tummy. All his legions appear to be tumbling home & I hope he will find them shortly crowding up the streets of Berlin.

A damned calf has been in my tent & I suppose seeing the attractiveness of my bed & scarlet eidy, proceeded to lie down on it with disastrous results to the bedstead, but having my air bed I don't mind & can get the bedstead mended here very easily as there is a workshop at the farm. Best of love old dear.

---

[159] *Minenwerfer* ('mine launcher'): these were German short-range mortars.

31st July 1916 – No. 222 answering 228 & 229 – Ohlain

Two nice letters today old dear, most cheering. The heat today has been too awful for words, thank goodness tho' I had nothing more strenuous to do than walk over and get my meals & even that was almost too much trouble. I am going to be inoculated again tonight as it is a year since I was done. As you say old dear, just fancy it being two years since one lived at home permanently. It must be at least another and possibly two before one does again.

Buxton tells me he is quite prepared to come with me to the infantry. I must say that I rather doubted whether he would, as lately I think he has been in a stupid mood. I am afraid ordinary soldiering has done him no good.

I've loved your letters old dear & like the 'grouses' too.

2nd August 1916 – No. 223 answering 230 & 231 – Ohlain

I am feeling alright again today I am glad to say. Yesterday afternoon and evening I was very small bones indeed, but by going to bed without any dinner and a liberal indulgence in aspirin I am beginning to hold my head up once more.

In your mail 229 you say that life on the whole has been pretty kind & there is no doubt you are right old dear & that we have every reason to be thankful. If it goes as well in the future as it has in the past we can be still more thankful. I wish I had been holding the hand of your dream old dear, only dreams don't come true, especially nice ones like that & I see no chance of it for some time.

My love to you old dear.

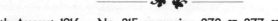

3rd August 1916 – No. 224 – Ohlain

A most boring day & I was rendered thoroughly homesick as I spent the afternoon sitting in a motor car in the road & there were two kids playing there whose back views were so like Mairky & Migwig that I couldn't help watching them. I fear my dear little Wig will have grown so terribly big by the next time I see her & that I shall have missed so much of her dear little life. This is a damnable war tho' no doubt very good & chastening for one!!

Love to the Chugs & welcome home to my old Bobbo.

4th August 1916 – No. 215 answering 232 & 233 & 233! [*sic*] – Ohlain

I wish darling mine you could have heard all the folk who have been to one lately to say how sorry they are that I'm going, the men have been so awfully nice & their regard is worth so much more to me than that of one's seniors. I'd far rather have it than the praise of all the generals in the army.

Not five minutes ago a man told me that practically the whole Regiment would march out with me if they could. It really is awfully good of them and it is the greatest comfort to know that they feel like it. Especially when one realizes that they come from all parts of the world & are generally supposed to be very adverse to the rule of anyone who isn't a colonial like themselves. Anyhow there it is and Jimmy may take the Regiment, but that he cannot take.

5th August 1916 – No. 226 answering 234 – Ohlain

You are right in your guess of where I am but I want you to keep names of formations & places entirely to yourself. We have had a special appeal not to send home any information at all & so for the future I shall send you, if possible, even less than I have up to date. Folk at home will talk at restaurants, in the train & at all kinds of places and there isn't the slightest doubt that we hardly do anything out here that it isn't at once known across the line. You would be doing good work to stop anyone you hear chatting about things.

I was rather amused today by one of the staff saying, when I proposed a certain Battalion, that H.W. would want to keep me in the corps if he could!! Jimmy has had to issue an edict that he won't recommend anyone for a commission who isn't an N.C.O. & I hear every Sergeant in 'C' put in for a commission last night!!

You needn't worry yourself old dear this time as I had fully decided & done the necessary without consulting you so you need not think that it was your persuading that has, or is, going to make me an infantryman tho' I am delighted to get your letter & your views as I have a very high opinion of your views of right & wrong & am glad that you think I can take this other Battalion if I get the chance.

My love to you my darling.

7th August 1916 – No. 228 answering 235 & 236 – Ohlain

I have just got your two most lovely letters old dear & your bit of poetry[160] which is simply champion. I saw it in a paper only a few days ago & liked it very much indeed & to the best of my belief cut it out but don't know what I have done with it. Anyhow it has now a very much-enhanced value, but it wants a good deal of living up to in practice.

I don't know whether Mrs Buxton has written to Buckin or not but he hasn't said a word of any sort to me on the subject.[161] Never broached the subject at all. Similarly I have said nothing to him. It's rather amusing. I don't mind what arrangements you come to old dear, I just want to feel that she is fairly comfortable & not having too great a struggle to keep her head above water. Anything you fix up between you will suit me alright.

---

[160] Rudyard Kipling's 'If'.
[161] Mrs Buxton had been offered a gardener's cottage in the grounds of Brook Hill.

As you will have already gathered I want this Battalion most of all (27th Battalion Northumberland Fusiliers). I went & walked round its transport etc. last night with Trevor.[162] They tell me that they have got some top-hole reliable company commanders still left. The Brigade I was talking to you of was the 1st 100,000 – Ian Hay's lot.

I expect one will be alright really, as you say. Everyone has got to make a start and after all everyone does so well that there's no reason why one shouldn't do the same. It's just the feeling that men who have been through it and stuck out Delville Wood for five days[163] must be better than one is oneself who hasn't seen it. However we will go & see. Your verses are lovely darling mine & I'm simply delighted with them & will make some attempt to live up to them tho' the standard is very high indeed. Dearie mine, au revoir.

9th August 1916 – No. 230 answering 237 – Ohlain

Well old Mac rolled up today alright & I was very glad indeed to see him.

I hear this morning that the application for me to go to the 27th Batt. N.F. went in two days ago so now perhaps it won't be long before I take up my new duties. I shall be thankful to have a job of work to do. [Here he has crossed out two words.] I know that will make you curious!! Well I was going to tell you where I was likely to go to but these times it is not allowed and so you will have to possess your soul in patience but from what I have told you, you will be able to make a fair guess.

I am very glad that Mrs Buckin agrees to Buckin coming with me. I too, am very glad that he is coming, as I should certainly miss him awfully. I should like to see you & the Chugs on your bikes going to Angmering. Old Bet & her goat amuses me. I hope she likes it. I'm all for them having a small kid.

My love to you all.

---

[162] Brigadier-General H. E. Trevor, Brigade Commander, 103 Brigade.
[163] The struggle for control of Delville Wood, largely by South African troops, began on 15 July and lasted for five days, with intense hand-to-hand fighting. It was one of the bloodiest actions of the war. The wood was finally taken by the Allies in August.

12th August 1916 – No. 233 answering 240 – Ohlain

Well I'm off in the morning and until further orders you must address me just 27th Batt. Northumberland Fusiliers, B.E.F. It's odd how 13 seems to mark so many crises in my life but it's the 13th tomorrow and all my bits of good luck seem connected with 13 & I think it's quite a good auspice. I am not going in the trenches for some time, so you needn't worry your dear old head for a bit.

You see I got the erring 240 alright today & it saved me a blank day as 241 was before his time. It's dinner time now so I must stop & I will write you more when I come to bed.

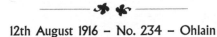

12th August 1916 – No. 234 – Ohlain

I feel I must write you a few lines on this my last night with the old Regt. One is going off and one doesn't know quite where it will eventually lead; let us hope to an early peace & happiness once more.

I am afraid that mine is not the only rather unhappy heart tonight as lots of the folk I am afraid are feeling my going, but I believe in the end I am doing the right thing & I only hope it may turn out to be right. Anyhow, I have lots of work ahead & very interesting work too, as it will mean starting from the very beginning, reorganizing the Battalion & training all the drafts. It is just what I want & I only hope I shall be able to do it. Anyhow I shall do what I can. There is no doubt in my own mind that folk like myself who have had previous soldiering knowledge are badly wanted to help in these Battalions.

My position is that in 30 days from the date of the last C.O. having gone sick I become Lt Col. If he comes out again, then I become 2nd-in-command. He is, they say, almost certain to get a brigade at once, directly he returns, if he does return. They tell me he was a right down good one, so I have got a lot to live up to, I am afraid!!

My love to you my darling,

Ever your Robert.

CHAPTER TWELVE

CO, 27TH BN, NORTHUMBERLAND FUSILIERS, THE TYNESIDE IRISH

Fighting on the Somme remained intense during August and September 1916. Like Verdun, neither side could achieve a decisive victory, yet the human sacrifice continued unabated. When conceiving the plan with Sir Douglas Haig, General Joffre had intended the battle to drain Germany of her reserves, diverting troops from Verdun, but in reality the armies of both adversaries lost huge numbers of men with the Allies gaining but a few miles of territory and sustaining even greater losses.

Transferring to the infantry, Robert, now a lieutenant colonel, was given command of 27th Battalion, Northumberland Fusiliers. He hoped this new role would, at last, enable him to play a fully active role in the war, and to help bring that war to an end.

13th August 1916 – No. 235 answering 242 & ?? 143!! – Gouy-Servins

My darling,

Well here I am. The old life left behind and a new one begun. I enclose you the old Squadron's last message to me. Keep it, darling mine, for it means much to me & I have had a very sad day indeed today. One fellow simply begged & implored me to take him with me, with the tears simply streaming down his face & it was all rather awful.

Dearie mine, the men are sending you a present. They say that King's Regulations say they mustn't give me one, but that there is nothing to prevent them sending it to you. It will probably be a bit of plate of some sort but I knew you would love to have it.

I've just had a long talk with Buckin & he is most grateful & very nice about things. He's got a ten-mile march before him on Tuesday so I think it is a good thing that he knows now. I was very glad to hear of Ralph.[164] I hope his wound is bad enough to keep him out of the war till it's over & not to permanently affect him. The war has fairly shown us how we depend on other countries hasn't it?

I have made up my mind that if ever I come to another war I shall be an officer's servant. There's that beast Buckin talking away to a damned nice girl in the kitchen & I get no show at all!! It's most unfair & it's always the case. I'm sure if his wife knew how jolly well he got on with the local ladies & the time he spends in their society she would be horribly jealous.

The old man[165] was very nice really when I went & said that he 'hoped sincerely that he would very shortly have to touch his hat to me'. I really think he means it too as he has what he is pleased to call 'a very high opinion' of one.

My army was originally Tyneside Irish but are now made up with Yorkshiremen but all north country lads & a fine lot. They fought like the devil I believe from all accounts and are top-hole fellows. I'm very pleased with the few officers I have seen so far. Fine fellows, N. country & rough but look to me the absolute right sort. Tuesday I shall see them all & will let you know more then but as you say it will be difficult to tell you much in future but you shall hear what I think permissible.

Fellows get to hear, & it's impossible not to know by putting two & two together, when operations are about to take place & then perhaps weeks before write & tell their friends who, loving to show their superior and first-hand knowledge, go & blurt it all out in a railway carriage before a lot of strangers who well may be enemy agents. There is no doubt if they closed the Ritz & Carlton too, it would do no harm. There is a lot heard by the next table to you.

Do you know, old dear, in spite of all I'm happier tonight than I have been for a very long time & I look forward to the future with the greatest pleasure. Many thanks for seeing about the helmet lining. Will you ring up Hawkes and tell them my new address as they are fixing up another helmet for me. If you add 33 to my Corps you will get my Division, similarly by adding the result of multiplying this magic figure by two and adding it to your first sum you will get my brigade!!!

[164] Ralph Juckes.
[165] Lt Colonel James.

I read a fine article on the landing of the force in British East Africa & the Huns kept on stirring up the wild bees with strings tied to their nests & it was most unpleasant!

I would like you to have the cottage thoroughly whitewashed & re-papered.[166] I will defray the expenses but I particularly want it thoroughly cleaned & papered.

14th August 1916 – Gouy-Servins

The Battalion comes out of the trenches tonight and we do a spell in the reserve area for a bit which is nice & gives me an opportunity to get the show running and enables one to get to know one's officers etc.

I expect I shall have my work cut out for a bit, as there seems a lot to do but it is just what I want and if one can get the show running and in real good order it will be a great thing. I had no letters today so have no inspiration & am consequently off to bed.

My love to you dearie mine.

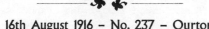

16th August 1916 – No. 237 – Ourton

I fear I didn't write you yesterday but I was marching in the evening and old Buckin & all my kit got left behind so I had just to tumble into bed as I was. We started about 5.15 & marched along well until the last two miles when things began to go to bits, but fortunately not until the Brigadier had seen us go past!! However the men had only just come out of the trenches and their feet get soft there & they were tired.

We've had a good rest today & start work tomorrow. I was complaining that I had not enough work a short time ago but there's enough work here to make your hair curl.

So far as I can tell I have got a very good lot of young officers, I doubt

---

[166] For the Buxton family.

if there are more than one or two 'gents' & I am not quite sure if there are as many but they are all keen so far as I can see at present. One has got to look at it from the point of view of a 'means to an end' and hope for better things as time goes on. I haven't had a letter from you for what seems years but I hope that I shall very soon get one. I've been moving about & so goodness knows where they have got to but when I do get them I shall have a real beano!

You would have laughed if you could have seen me marching my Battalion through the village where the Regiment is billeted. There were very few officers about but all the men rolled out & it was really most amusing. I had quite got over my 'upset' feeling at going, but I think a good many of them would have liked to have pulled me back.

I've got a jolly good Quartermaster I'm glad to say & the Adjutant, tho' not a great man at smartening up the Regt, is a top-hole clerk, with short-hand & types like fun & is really very good indeed in the office. Two or three of the subalterns are really nice boys tho' some are moderate, one of which stammers so badly he can't speak at all. I don't know how he could ever have been passed. So far as I can see there isn't much chance of my C.O. returning so I hope once I get my Lt Colonelcy I shall keep it now.

I can't think of anything more to tell you just at present old dear, & as it's getting late I shall stop & will try & write you a better letter tomorrow tho' I've got to fit 24 hours work into about 16 these days.

Love to the Chugs.

17th August 1916 – No. 238 answering 145 & 245 ??? – Ourton

I got two more lovely letters today old dear & was delighted with them and more especially with your fourleaf [clover] which is lovely old dear & more appropriate than you thought, because the Battalion, and in fact the whole brigade, wear a shamrock patch on each sleeve.

My Battalion wears a black one & each Battalion has a different colour. Really dearie, yours is awfully nice & I simply love it & so very nicely got up! Nothing could have been more suitable.

18th August 1916 – No. 239 answering 146 & 147 – Ourton

As you see I have got the paper and it is top-hole. I am simply fearfully busy, you wouldn't realize the amount of work there is to be done – it is keeping me going hard from early morn to dewy eve but I am liking it very much and am, as I have told you, thoroughly happy. I am off to a conference of C.O.s tomorrow with the Div. Commander where I expect there will be a great deal of talk & damned little done. However I will tell you if I am mistaken tomorrow.

Poor little Wig I am so sorry to hear that she has been stung. I have been bitten to bits by mosquitoes these last few nights but got my curtain rigged last night. I had two capital letters from old Bet. Please thank her for them.

I am so glad to hear that Ralph[167] is safely home & I hope he will go on alright now. Mac commands 'B' Squadron, Furse has 'C' and Russell 'A'. Dick[168] becomes 2nd-in-command & runs the HQ Mess same as I did.

We had a very good cook but a man with a fearful temper & I hear that Dick has begun to upset him already. He wanted most tactful handling & there's not much tact left in these parts now! I did get the mackintosh alright old dear & I want you to send me one for Harry.[169] He's done me so well I should like to give him a good present. It should be a size larger than the last one you sent me.

About the petrol & paraffin. If it works all right it is worth trying but paraffin doesn't burn clean & there is a sooty deposit & it would mean she sooted up quicker perhaps & you might experience difficulty in starting [the car] but you can do no harm at all by trying it and certainly the taxi-cabs all use it.

Darling mine it is 11.15 & I must stop. Many thanks for the *Yachting Monthlies*. When I shall find time to read them goodness knows.

My love to you my darling.

---

[167] Ralph Juckes.
[168] Major M. F. Dick.
[169] Parsons.

20th August 1916 – No. 240 answering 148 – Ourton

I have been very pleased with the improvement made by the Battalion, even in this short time & I expect in a week or so that things will have assumed an entirely different aspect, anyhow I hope that they will.

We are busy trying to start a band but I am very keen about it as it is a godsend on the march. I think we shall be successful all right as I have found a corporal who is a Band instructor by profession. Apparently the Irish like the pipes as well as the Scotch. Anyhow we have some & they seem to blow all day practising!!

I hear also that once one becomes a C.O. you don't count on the Battalion leave roster & so haven't got to take turns with anyone. However I have far too much to do at present to give the idea of leave a thought but as soon as I can, I will come. I'm awfully glad, old dear that you have got your house and your sea trip properly fixed up & I only hope that you will have decent weather when the time comes. Keep the salt & water on Teeny, it's the only cure. I admit at once it's yours!!! It's an awful nuisance if the pups are going to be spiteful with errand boys, you will have to hide them.

I expect if 'Pa' has got any money to give away I shall be very glad of it here. Especially for the band, as really it is the very best kind of charity to give these fellows everything that you can to make their life more endurable. The infantry soldier suffers everything out here, and the effect of a little music on the march, a tune or two in his rest billets cheers him up & brings him along as none of the usual 'comforts' would. There's absolutely nothing like it. The men start singing to it at once and it makes them as jolly as anything even under the most adverse circumstances.

Well darling mine, fare thee well for the present.

My love to all the dear little Chugs.

21st August 1916 – No. 241 answering 249 & 250 – Ourton

The Adjutant told me this morning that the Battalion was better already than he had ever known it before! Rather a compliment in five days but it was said quite spontaneously and not at all intended as a compliment. Anyhow there begins to show some sign of organization & tho' things are still very far from being what I want you can simply see them growing every day & I see no reason why the Battalion shouldn't maintain its name as the best in the brigade. Anyhow I mean it to if I can manage it by hook or crook.

As you say it was far away harder to say goodbye to the men than the officers, tho' I was very loath to part from old Steve but he had been alienated for so long by being Jimmy's satellite that it really made it easier. I saw so little of him really the last month. Many thanks for 'financial details'. You will probably have £100 or so in hand at Xmas which will be something.

I'm much too busy old dear to be any sort of 'sick' & have settled down very much better than I dared hope. It is odd how these boys look on one as quite old & not 40!!! I am glad you like the men's letters, they are all very nice & they really did care I think. Harry tells me that they are very down on their luck now. He used to go over for the letters & they all wanted to come back with him, so he says.

You will be able to put Lieut. Col. when you get this as I am due for it on Wednesday and shall get it this week. Harry & the horses are with me, tho' I had to leave the pony behind. My commando talk a foreign language all right & you can hardly understand some of the men but there are so few originals left now. My Adjutant & Q.M. both are very north country and some of the other officers combine a strong Irish brogue with broad Newcastle so it's a bit weird.

My dear old girl, mathematics isn't my strong point, & apparently it isn't yours. Anyhow you have not got your sum correct. Try again. Starting from the bottom the answer should be 27: 103: 37: 4: 1.[170]

There is not a pre-war officer in the Regt. Well dearie mine, adieu.

---

[170] 27th Battalion, 103rd Brigade, 37th Division, 4th Corps, 1st Army.

On the same day Buxton wrote to his wife:

> *Father[171] has got plenty of work now smartening up this lot. They like him altho' they think he is rather 'mustard' at present. He makes them turn out clean and properly dressed and there is certainly a great difference in them already. The officers are all very young and fresh out – most of the others were knocked out in the 'Big Push'.*

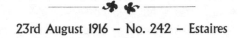

23rd August 1916 – No. 242 – Estaires

I went out & had a very nice evening with a fellow called Temple (old Rifle Bde) who was 2nd-in-command of this Battalion & now commands the 25th Battalion, on Monday evening. What he doesn't know of this Trench Warfare business isn't worth knowing as he went into the first trench that was ever made and has been in them ever since. It's a great help having a fellow like that near one and also one who is as keen as mustard in the whole thing & a really first-class man. He did awfully well on the 1st July and with 80 men of this Battalion took a German strong point and captured 450 of them!! So far as I can see he has got nothing out of it.

Talking of the Battalion Commanders one of my confrères is a great big 'hail-fellow-well-met' sort of a bloke. He wears a diamond ring on the first finger & another huge one on his little finger & I asked my adjutant who & what he was in civil life & he told me 'A commercial traveller' & very well known in the North. Sounds so awfully odd after the old soldiering life, but these fellows are doing grand work, and after all they can't be bettered these times & to tell you the truth I don't believe that some of them could have been equalled in earlier days.

It's a wonderful country I'm in now & from the train[172] one could see nothing but cornfields as far as the eye could reach. Here all the corn is cut & in the stook & it is a most wonderful harvest. You never saw anything like it and if they get it in all right, it ought to make up to the folk for

---

[171] 'Father' refers to Colonel Hermon.

[172] The battalion marched to Calonne Ricquart and entrained to La Gorgue then marched to Estaires.

many things that they have had to suffer through the war. No doubt Germany is equally reaping the benefit & damned lucky she is. The country here is absolutely as flat as the palm of your hand, perhaps a 'looking glass' would be a better simile. I never saw anything like it.

The direction I've gone in is toward Leonardslee & about as far as Gatwick & Horley.

Give my love to the Chugs.

24th August 1916 – No. 243 answering 254 – Estaires

252 & 253 seem to be wandering somewhere but will no doubt return from their wanderings tomorrow.

I am glad to hear that Ken is the admiration of all beholders. Wasn't it odd dearie mine, about that clover and its genuine appropriateness? I was awfully glad to get it. I laughed over your sum too, as I told you. I merely changed regiments in the same Corps to start with, which was our old friends & you were quite right in that. I got the Battalion because he didn't want me to leave the Corps. There is no doubt old dear about the 'right' of the case & I am very glad & happy to be where I am & the more I do, the more convinced I am that one has done the right thing.

Give my love to the Chugs & I hope old Bobbo doesn't burn his fingers on the engine. Thank him & Meg too for their nice letters.

25th August 1916 – No. 244 answering 252 & 253 – Estaires

The two wanderers turned up today alright & I was more than pleased to get them.

I'm awfully glad to hear that old Bobbo is mechanically minded, keep him up to it as I should love him to be keen on those kind of things and he would be such a help to father in handing tools later on. I should love to see little Mairky on her tiny 'bike'. Dear little fat Pook. Give her my love.

Get old Brown to come over & see the pony. It can easily have worms without there being any outside evidence. He is the best man you could ask. Perhaps its teeth want seeing to? You want to give it half a pint of linseed oil with 2 tablespoons full of turpentine in it & drench the pony well & if he doesn't scour, give it him again in four or five days.

No, I don't walk on my feet, the C.O., Adjutant, Senior Major & all Coy Commanders ride. I certainly did walk the other day, because I sent the horses by road.

You mustn't worry about me old girl as I am as right as rain now, lots to do & not a minute to brood! I'm only sorry that I expect for the next week or so you will get very sketchy letters as I am going into the line for a spell.

Sunday 27th August 1916 – No. 245 – on message pad – Laviéville

Just a few lines to assure you of my 'bon santé'. I am in quite a nice little village[173] & have just been out for a Sunday walk or rather 'sit down' (not what you mean) & read the paper. I couldn't help being amused in a way as coming in I passed a funeral party at the grave with the Parson and among the audience which consisted of a dozen soldiers from the Field Ambulance, I saw Buxton taking a most lively interest. That was his bit of Sunday amusement. C'est drôle!

I've very little to tell you old dear, tho' we've had a fairly strenuous week. Will you thank Mimi for her long letter & tell her that I will try and answer it shortly.

My love to you old dear & to the Chugs too & my dear old Spootie.

[173] The battalion marched to Merville, entrained to Longeau and marched to Allonville.

29th August 1916 – No. 246 answering 255, 256 & 257 – Albert

I've had three lovely letters from you these last few days & have thoroughly enjoyed them. Try 'Pukka' for Pucker!![174]

I am afraid I cannot answer many of your questions re locale. It's rather difficult to write you a decent letter now as there is such a devil of a lot of gunning going on, tho' I'm not actually in it, the concussion & row is pretty bad.

I think your jumble sale was top-hole & you collected a fine sum.

Fortunately I have got a tent but the men are bivouacked, I am sorry to say & just about the very biggest thunderstorm you ever saw is beginning. They've got a little cover I am glad to say, but nothing to buck about.

I long to see the 'Scrap o' Comfort' – he must be topping now. He'll nearly be able to walk I expect, when I do get a chance to see him. It's all very well but surely it is you that is to blame over the 'Tribe'. I didn't make them, merely offered a suggestion which you seem to have taken up!! I shall want the files (British made only please).

Yes, things gradually go on in the Battalion I think, & only today the 2nd-in-command came & said that he thought it would make my work easier if I was to know that all the officers were absolutely satisfied & ready to back one to the last drop of blood. I thought it awfully nice & was very pleased as I have had to follow a man whom they all worshipped.

My 2nd-in-command is Bibby D.S.O., Adj. O'Hanlon, Coy Commanders MacCormack, Morrough, Aitcheson, Neeves. Bibby & MacCormack are captains. Transport Officer, Hobbs, Q.M., Treanor.

I had a very interesting day yesterday looking over the line & will tell you more about it later on. I saw Tollemache had been hit, I hope he isn't bad.

---

[174] He often teased his wife about her spelling.

30th August 1916 – No. 247 answering 258 – third-line trenches, Contalmaison

Just got a top-hole letter from you all about your day in town [London]. I am so glad to hear such a good report about old Bobbo's eyes. Poor little Mairky – she will look an odd little scrap with her glasses. Astigmatism I think, you will find present in 999 cases out of 1000 but they can correct it, I believe. I can see old Mairky sticking to her opinion with the oculist. You seem to have had a great day in town altogether. Tell old Bob I should just love to come & play with his engine & I am sure it is just exactly what I should like. You will always find in those small engines that you get a little oil blowing out through the pistons. I'm not sure I couldn't find old Mac a company if he was to come out after all, if you write to him tell him so, but tell him he won't find things quite like K.E.H.

It is very kind indeed of old Addie to take so much interest & it all helps out here knowing what folk are thinking. Take today for instance. All night last night it thundered and rained an absolute deluge after four or five days of heavy showers. The men had a few odd bits of tin to cover them and that was all. Today we moved up into the trenches tho' not into front line, but somewhere near it; since 8 a.m. it has rained without ceasing & the poor men are up to their knees in mud & water & wet through. I've been round their trenches this afternoon & in spite of my mac and high boots am pretty wet I can tell you. However we are all very merry & bright & I haven't seen Buckin so happy since he's been out here.

We're in an awfully interesting bit of line and I have a top-hole dugout. Nice entrance hall and kitchen combined, then down two steps into dining & living room, out of this down more steps you come to my room on the right, then to the left is my Adjutant, 2nd-in-command, signalling officer, machine gun officer & Dr, then a long passage where the signal office is. It's simply fine & really very kind indeed of the old Boche to have made it for us. It was lit by electric light!! And the globe still hangs over my bed & the whole 'sett'[175] is wired, but I am afraid that the dynamo that used to serve the country around is slightly out of commission in the place where the neighbouring village used to be. It's the outside that's the bother, there

---

[175] He is comparing it to a badger sett.

is liquid slush which must be five or six inches deep & the roads are terrible sloppy. The only relief is tho' that a few prisoners have just gone by who look the picture of abject misery. I've had a splendid afternoon walking round & really quite enjoyed myself. If it wasn't for the thought of the wretched condition of the men I wouldn't mind, but they're simply wonderful & it doesn't seem to worry them in the least.

Can you find me a really good acetylene lamp that one can have on the dinner table. It must fit into a box not too big for easy handling & must have $^1/_2$ doz spare 'Roni' burners. No shade or glass. Just the naked light. It doesn't blow out & one can get carbide, but living the life of the old 'Brock' one wants artificial light. The flysprayer too hasn't turned up yet & is badly needed. Post just off.

31st August 1916 – No. 248 answering 259 – third-line trenches, Contalmaison

Another nice letter today. Really it's wonderful how one gets one's letters, even up here. They all turn up alright with the rations every day. Thank goodness we have had a glorious day today & this country dries up as quickly as it becomes mud.

There's been a lot of flying by both sides today, tho' the Hun doesn't venture very much on our side of the line, & I don't wonder. Our aeroplanes seem to go about in squadrons of about eight or nine & as soon as the Hun appears they go bald headed at him. At one time this afternoon there were 23 of our aeroplanes we could see out at once just over our little pitch. Old Buckin has found a splendid game & spends all his time looking for corpses not properly buried & gets to work with a spade & covers them up & makes crosses for them. It's become quite a hobby with him. I had two blokes killed yesterday I am sorry to say, but funnily enough they were both of a company that I have attached from another Battalion.

I had a walk up towards the front line today but owing to the wet & the folk working in the trenches I didn't get very far & contented myself with having a chat with the officer commanding the front-line Battalion. Today it's been really lovely & I have most thoroughly appreciated it. It's a great relief after the awful wet time we have had.

British troops helping with the threshing near Franvillers, September 1916. EWH was billeted in Franvillers at this time, after having had his first experience of the trenches on the Somme.

British soldiers in billets, Vermelle 1916. EWH wrote to Ethel that Vermelle was 'the most perfect example of a ruined village you can see. Everything is destroyed and not a bird or a cat or sign of life of any kind.'

Souchez, at the foot of Hill 119, late 1916. EWH described the village as being 'like the ruins of Jerusalem, it hasn't one stone upon another'.

The ruins of the
cathedral at Albert,
September 1916;
EWH was billeted
there during this time.

Fixing scaling ladders
in trenches on the day
before the Battle of
Arras, 8 April 1917.

Scene on the road beside the Scarpe at Blangy at Arras, a few days after
EWH's death on the first day of the fighting, April 1917.

A British tank passing through Arras on its way into action, April 1917.
EWH wrote to Ethel about the new weapon: 'it's the very first thing in
which we have gone one better than the Bosche.'

Battle of Arras:
the cavalry resting
beside the St.
Pol-Arras Road,
April 1917.

Artillery moving
up through Arras.

A 9.2 inch howitzer
in action at Arras.

Battle of Arras: the scene on newly won ground near the Feuchy crossroads
with 18 pounders in action and a tank in the background, April 1917.

Battle of Arras: an 18-pounder quick-firing field-gun moving up into position.

Battle of Arras: an advanced dressing station during the battle, showing horse ambulances and German prisoners of war being used as stretcher-bearers.

A temporary cross marks EWH's grave at Roclincourt cemetery, 1917. Shortly afterwards 'Buckin' planted primroses and box shrubs round the grave.

(*Above right*) Marble headstone at Roclincourt CWGC cemetery, 2008.

Roclincourt cemetery in 2008.

Lieutenant Colonel Edward William ('Robert') Hermon D.S.O.

I was sitting outside my 'sett' tonight & really it's as like our old place at Ashington as anything. There's the heap of scratched-out earth and the 'pipe' behind on the slope of a hill & looking over the valley 500 yds off is what is left of the village. There are a couple of trees lying across our 'earth' & it's as like as anything. One sits outside in the sun & it's lovely & if things become unpleasant one just pops in like a rabbit!! It's a weird life.

Best love to you all, old dear.

1st September 1916 – No. 249 answering 260 – support trenches, Contalmaison

Well, we are getting on fine & as I walked back this morning to lunch in my new burrow[176] I couldn't help feeling that I was happier in mind & general well-being than I have been since I came to this country. I'm really taking my part now and after all that is what one is out for. Certainly at times it is very far from pleasant. I left my original 'sett' early this morning to be met on the way by those damned gas shells. There is no doubt that they are beastly, they make one's eyes water like anything. However our masks are 'quite all right' as the Chugs would say, but still it's unpleasant. My new home is a fine safe one – one goes down twenty-one steps into a fine room in the chalk. The room is a good bit larger than the small night nursery & certainly as high, 12 feet wide by about 30 feet long, with an entrance at both ends.

The roof carried on T-section iron girders. Again we have to thank the Hun for his industry. While I remember, will you send me the best pair of motor goggles you can find. They must fit absolutely tight to the face & have no ventilation whatsoever as this beastly gas affects the eyes only and a good pair of goggles are essential & tho' we have some very good ones indeed I believe one could get more comfortable ones from a good motor shop like Dunhill's.

Many thanks for the mackintosh which is fine. I am going to give Buckin

---

[176] The 27th Battalion moved from the third line of defence trenches to the support trenches.

the other one, & Harry will have to do with S.A.H.'s[177] tho' one the same size as my first one sent by the kids to Harry would be a very nice present & one he richly deserves. You would laugh to see old Buckin in his pantry, servants' hall, kitchen, scullery, larder, linen cupboard combination that he has upstairs in the road. Just a little bit of a sandbag house with a tin roof cut into the bank!! He was laughing about it this morning and wondering what old Woolven would think about it.

The 'Leonard's Lee' was the direction. North. The Gatwick was Armentières or rather just between Merville and Estaires. I am so glad to hear that Dick is really off at last.[178] High time too. I have several officers and damned good ones too, not much older.

My love to you my darling.

3rd September 1916, 3.15 p.m. – note – front-line trenches, Contalmaison

All well.
Robert.

O n this day the battalion relieved the 24th Battalion in the front-line trenches from Lean Alley to Munster Alley, east of Contalmaison. At noon they assisted the advance of the division on their right, who were operating against High Wood. Smoke bombs were released, drawing heavy artillery fire onto the front-line trenches. The casualties recorded were one officer and seven other ranks killed; forty wounded, two of whom later died of their wounds.

---

[177] His father's.
[178] Dick Hermon was about to go to Sandhurst and was later commissioned into the Coldstream Guards.

——— ❦ ❦ ———

5th September 1916, 1.30 a.m. – on message pad – front-line trenches, Contalmaison

Well old dear, I got two lovely letters from you today & they were more than welcome. I've had a pretty strenuous time these last few days tho' frightfully interesting. I was round my front line today & tho' exciting it was a wonderful sight as one has a goodish look at the Boche from there. I'm pretty tired just at present but hope to get a good sleep today later on. I haven't had my clothes off for five or six days. You needn't worry about the hour as I have to be awake.

My Battalion is in the line so I thought that I couldn't be better employed. I'm on watch at present but hope to get an hour's sleep about 3 a.m.

The pictures you talk about were taken here and I have seen the crater & I think the men you saw 'go over the top' were my own Battn tho' I can't be sure! Rather odd if it was. Poor little Mairky. Hope her knee is better. One of my best young officers got a piece of shrapnel just above the knee today. Awful bad luck.

You needn't worry about the trenches, it's all right I had heaps of opportunity of testing it today. My love old dear.

——— ❦ ❦ ———

6th September 1916 – No. 251 answering 264 – reserve billets, Contalmaison

Still right end up & going along all right. Having a very strenuous time just at present but our brave allies are taking tea with them in consequence so that's a comfort. The flies are almost our worst nuisance & they really are the limit. You never saw anything like them and Africa is a perfect fool to it.

Yes, I've got my rank all right. I'm very glad to hear you have the car running again. Never mind about the clothes old dear. I wish I could tell you more, old dear but I can't at present. Hope to be able to shortly. Yes I meant Alec Godley.

Bye bye old darling. I am very fit & well & thoroughly happy now.

------ ❧ ❧ ------

7th September 1916 – No. 252 – note –
front-line trenches, Contalmaison

Dear old girl.

Dans le premier ligne. All well. Post just off.

No letters yesterday or today.

Ever your Robert.

Signed by 'Lt. Colonel Hermon', the War Diary for the 7th records: 'hostile air reconnaissance very prominent between 7.30 and 8.30 a.m., as many as 12 German aeroplanes visible at one period'. On the 9th the Battalion assisted the Canadian Corps who achieved their objective on the east of High Wood, then, helping with the consolidation of these gains, dug a 200-yard trench across no man's land.

------ ❧ ❧ ------

10th September 1916, 2.45 a.m. – No. 253 answering 265, 267
& 268 – Contalmaison

Having a few moments, and through stress of circumstances not being able to go to sleep as I am busy battle fighting, tho' perhaps you might not think it, I thought I would guard against dropping off by writing to you.

I got two letters from you today right in the middle of a quite nice little minor battle. We opened the ball by catching two Prussians who had come out to scout & found themselves caught by our barrage & couldn't get back. One had an Iron Cross and the other spoke English. They were both young & fine big strapping fellows. I hear there is another up the line who is very badly wounded. They say he is very old & has a bald head!

The Div. on our left went over & took the Hun front line & we had to join up with them across no man's land which we successfully did and still hold it, having beaten off one counter-attack. I hope he won't attack at dawn as I am busy getting my Battalion out of the line & during a relief there are twice as many men in the trenches as are wanted & if one is attacked it makes the casualties so much heavier. Martinspuich.

I have just had a real good cup of Mr Ayrton's coffee & tho' not the best coffee, it seemed like it. The men want a bit of a rest as they have been 72 hours in a bad bit of line, & they have worked very hard indeed today & done magnificently. However, they say everything comes to him who waits and we've waited for a bit of a rest for some time now, so perhaps it will come.

Eighteen months ago batteries in many cases were on a daily rate of 6 shots per battery per diem. Today we must have used, in my hearing, hundreds of thousands of all sizes. The din is too awful you can't get away from it day or night. However there is something in it as the Hun doesn't like it at all. One of our prisoners told me he had had 30 casualties in his Company yesterday.

Now that he hasn't got quite so many deep dugouts as he used to have he pays a little more attention to our shelling & I see in his papers he is complaining that it isn't fair. Rather amusing. As you say I wish I could tell you more but there's too much knowledge on your side of the Channel.

If the car is difficult to start, try pressing the points of the plugs as close together as you can so that they will only let a piece of thick writing paper through. I can hardly believe 27 miles to the gallon. If it's true I'll take my hat off to you. I think you will find that 20 to 22 is all you can expect from an engine of that size.

Buy me a good knife, two blades & a corkscrew as I have lost my old Boche one much to my sorrow, as it was the best I ever had. I am awfully glad to hear that you think school has done so much for old Bobbo, I wish I could have spent his holidays with him.

It's beastly sitting here & hearing the Boche 'crumps' falling on the communication trench & knowing your folk are coming out of it, and it's especially trying for the wounded coming out. I fear there will be a biggish bill in the morning.

Oh! for the old *Gannet* [179] this lovely night, & what wouldn't I give for that comfy bunk. I am really quite comfy tho' even here, but not very safe as my dugout isn't more than rainproof!!! My dear, you would be damned glad to live underground & stop there if you saw some of these old crumps a bustin of. It's the very nicest place I know & the deeper down one gets the more pleasant it becomes!

[179] His father's boat.

Lass dear while you were calculating where I was, I was having free train rides to say nothing of motor rides and all sorts, so you can't know where I am or how I got there for the ramifications have been many. I am going to send you a pretty medal for your gallantry in surviving life at sea. Well done old dear, how I should have loved to have seen it but I am glad I didn't as I should have had to get wet & I loathe bathing.

2.30 p.m. Post off so will continue this later on.

11th September 1916, 11 a.m. – No. 254 on message pad – subsidiary line, Contalmaison

I'm back in my 2nd dugout just now, not the 'Badger earth' one but the next. We have done 72 consecutive hours in the front line and badly need a rest as it has been rough to say the least of it. We had been in 48 hours & were then told we had to remain another 24 when we were all pretty beat.

Well the folk on our left had taken a fancy to a big slice of the Hun line and at 4.45 in the afternoon, over they went in grand style & got in without a single casualty. It fairly scared the Hun, not only did the front line cave in but the 2nd & 3rd lines left their trenches & hared off. Then of course the fun began & there was a good deal of heavy shelling. However my folk managed to dig a trench 200 yards long, right across no man's land and join up with the right of the attack & consolidate the whole thing. As I had little or nothing to do with it I don't mind saying that it was a really fine show, well carried out & highly successful.

My left Company did splendidly & in spite of very heavy fire they dug right out in the open till they had got down a good 4 feet & got cover. A young boy who is attached to me & belongs to another Battalion of the same name was splendid, he just walked about on top all the time encouraging the men and taking about as much notice of the 5.9's the old Boche was throwing about as if they had been tennis balls.

There's no doubt that his fine example was a great help & I hope the lad will get his just reward. He was about the same age as Dick, a quiet lad, & most unassuming.

We had a very nice wire indeed from the Division on the left thanking us for our help & all that we had done for them. They took about 60 prisoners of the 211 Res. Regiment. Fine, big, upstanding Prussians. The two we captured were very indignant at being taken & said they had every intention of returning to their own lines at night. However they are in the bag now.

Apparently the Huns are told that if they are taken prisoner or surrender they won't be reinstated in their businesses when the war is over, so these two kept on protesting that they didn't surrender & meant going back as soon as they could if it hadn't been for our barrage cutting them off.

There's not much to tell you old dear. Temple who commands one of the other Battalions is such a nice fellow, was in the 60th. He lives at Puttenham on the Hog's Back & I think they would be just our sorts. He came into my bit of shelter about 4 a.m. yesterday & we had a real old buck about hounds and hunting & what not. We've got a great many mutual friends & he said it was a treat to have someone to talk to who talked the King's English!! You would have been amused if you had seen us, sitting in a bit of a hole dug in the side of the trench with a few boards over it & a few sandbags just enough to keep out shrapnel & for a couple of hours we forgot the damned war & simply screamed with laughter at times. I am awfully glad to have him, as I haven't a soul who ever saw a hound or heard a horn other than a motor horn!!

My love to you & the dear little Chugs.

Saturday 12th September 1916 – No. 255 answering 266, 269, 271 – billet at Albert

I've had a perfect orgy of letters & it has been grand. You ask me to let you know what my feelings have been. Well, I'm not going to say that I liked being shelled at all & the man who says he does is a damned liar.

Anyhow it didn't have a very adverse effect, I'm glad to say. During our bit of a fight the other day I was never calmer or had a better grip of things than through the afternoon & the whole of the night during which it was going on. I had the whole show to run as my 2nd-in-command collapsed in the evening with a nervous breakdown & I had to put him to bed where he was till morning. Poor bloke he wasn't very fit, & he was one of two who came through the 1st July[180] & it wasn't to be wondered at.

---

[180] Delville Wood.

If you could have seen what I have seen, not I'm glad to say in my own sector, but quite handy, you would wonder how men could come through it without losing their reason; it's the most awful thing you ever saw. The attacks on High Wood, for concentrated Hell absolutely take the biscuit. I was only 2000 yards away so had a very good view. During my time here I've seen a good bit – far more than I have since I have been out & somehow through it all I've enjoyed myself & been happier than I have been before.

Bibby said to me 'Well you ought to get a D.S.O. out of this' – well I only say this so that you may know that I wasn't so frightened that I couldn't carry on. Of course the D.S.O. is all rot, because I had so very little to do, all that was done was done by a subaltern who commanded my left company. I hope he will get a Military Cross out of it. He most richly deserves it as well as the other boy who I wrote you about.

My adjutant was very funny. He can't understand how a Cavalry fellow could come to infantry & run infantry in the trenches without any previous training & go right up into the forefront at the Somme & come out having co-operated with a successful attack & carried out the consolidation & linking up of the position won. It's fairly beat him. I think tho' they were all pleased that things went well, anyhow the General came round & congratulated us very warmly & we had the nice wire from our neighbours too.

I must say the first day I was in the trenches I was absolutely miserable. From my Head Quarters I could see the front line & see the heavy shells fairly pounding it & knew I could do nothing to stop it & that my men were having an awful time & that I was only a few hundred yards behind & yet was in comparative safety & couldn't go to them. After all, in the Cavalry it is one's privilege to go first & here one goes last & it's awful seeing them being pounded to death & knowing that they have just got to stick it & that they don't even fire back. There's nothing to fire at, both sides are down in their trenches & unless one or other attacks you've simply got to sit there & stick the artillery pounding away. As a matter of fact you would be surprised if you knew how few the casualties there were considering the amount and weight of shells that are hurled about. As a matter of fact, my casualties on this first day were heavier than the second time we were in the front & had rather more to do.

I can't tell you what my casualties have been as one isn't allowed to go into numbers, I was in the front line 48 hours & then 72 hours and if you add all at Brook Hill who bear our name & take off two that will give you the rough proportion. Old Mac wrote to me & said he would willingly come to me as a platoon officer.

I think from the probable date my 'interesting' day was my first day down here when I went with my runner to reconnoitre the place I was to go in the line. I walked up from Albert over all the ground over which the original push was made, saw a tremendous lot of the most absorbing interest. Really I can't describe it all, it's so vast, there's so much science in it, so much imagination that it's almost bewildering. The guns impress you most. I see the German papers say it is no longer fair we have such a preponderance of guns!! They don't mention their advantages at the start. They complain bitterly too of our gas shells!! Well, who started gas!!?

Our doctor went home today & I asked him to ring you up & tell you I was alright & happy. I never read such rot as there is in the papers about the war films. Why shouldn't the folk at home know that the men do suffer, suffer beyond endurance. They ought to know it. I saw a man of mine with genuine 'shell shock'. He was deaf & dumb and tho' 500 yds away & held by two men he was shaking so you could see his arms going continually. Why shouldn't folk know what the men in the ranks are suffering. Damn it, they'd think a bit more if they did.

I'm afraid old Mac isn't mending as he should. He ought to go & have a good opinion from someone or do something to get himself better. I'm out of the continuous banging of the guns, thank goodness, for a bit & it's a great relief as the concussion of one's own guns is almost as bad as the Boche shells tho' not so dangerous.

It's all very well to say 'take care of yourself' but you can't when you see how absolutely callous all the men around you are, about the shelling. Unless you saw the way they behave you would never believe it. My runners were coming back to me with messages all through the nights & going through heavy shelling just as one would go for a walk in the rain & not making any fuss about it at all. Just treating it as an ordinary parade. They are so fine.

Thank old Bet & Mairky for their letters.

13th September 1916 – No. 256 – on message pad – Laviéville

Back resting for some days which is a relief tho' my bedroom is only an old bit of a hovel, almost as good as the hovel at home but it has been used as a threshing room & has a good clean & hard floor. Last night I slept on a spring mattress in a deserted house. One of the most comfortable beds I ever was in. The first time I had been on a bed since 26th August! One really appreciates a bit of rest these times.

14th September 1916 – No. 257 answering 272, 273 & 274 – Laviéville

I am awfully sorry that you have been so short of letters old dear but times have been rather strenuous & I've done my best. I can quite see that Migwig will want a little discipline. Darling mine you are really very naughty tearing up that letter. You might at least let me hear some of your troubles & you are never to do such a thing again. I don't want letters written for my benefit only. If you are down on your luck, I can at least write & do my best to cheer you up. We can at least share thoughts if we can't at present share anything else. I used to tell you everything when I was down on my luck & now you haven't reciprocated. It's most unfair & I won't have you do it again, or I shan't have the implicit trust in yours that I have had.

The flysprayer arrived by mail today and it has helped a lot. The room is now comparatively free, that is to say there are certainly very many less flies than there were before. My darling, the aching is by no means on your side alone, I can tell you. Stick it a bit longer & then perhaps we may be together again for a bit.

15th September 1916 – No. 258 – tent at Albert

I am not in a writing mood at present old dear so you must forgive a short note but the date is my excuse. I could tell you a good deal if it wasn't for that. It's a pity one can't write fuller these times but I see in General Orders that a fellow was tried by Court Martial the other day for saying too much, so I'm not risking anything. Very fit & well.

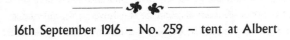

16th September 1916 – No. 259 – tent at Albert

Have seen a lot of German prisoners these last two days, which is always an encouraging sight. I got the Chugs a few rotten little presents & if I have time I will send them off tomorrow.

I am badly wanting inspiration as I have so little news that I can tell you. The infantry soldiering is a sort of compromise of two extremes. One time you are getting far more than you want then the next you don't quite know what to do for a job & today I have been rather that way. I hope it won't be long now before leave starts again & as soon as it does I shall take a short trip to England, home & beauty once more & feel I've earned it this time alright. Only two months to go now to make a whole year since I saw you & it's far too long for me.

Give my love to the dear little Chugs & tell old Bobbo how awfully sorry I am at not getting home to see him during his holidays but that I will come & see him alright when I come on leave. It sounds too good to be true. However, everything comes to those who know how to wait.

18th September 1916 – No. 261 answering 275 – Franvillers

When I wrote you the letter you call the '1.30 a.m.' I was in a little dugout in a trench not a thousand miles from the place where Martinspuich once was, there's not very much more than a few bricks lying among the shell holes in those parts just now. High Wood lay just on my right and in full view, & on my left the Albert–Bapaume road, Pozieres windmill and Mucky Farm & Thiepval. What you might call right in the limelight. It's most amusing to hear some of the blokes laugh when I tell them that that was my very first experience of the trenches.

Our Brigade Major & old Temple were only screaming over it a few minutes ago. You are quite right old dear over the mental worry of the show – it is a bit of a trial when one thinks what it would mean if one was to lose a trench or two. Anyhow it keeps one from falling asleep which is always something. No, the six days doesn't apply to the razor, I have not gone a single day without shaving. You see in the trenches one can always dig in to the side and make a bit of a roof & a small sort of room & so one lives alright. We had a mess, & a good kitchen, & I had my own private bedroom. They were all sort of summer rainproof & really one was quite comfortable. I had a bed made by my pioneers & a table to write on & was really very comfortable. I went to see the big crater that you saw on the film. It is by far the biggest in France. It is 300 feet from lip to lip and from 80–100 feet deep. I wish I had seen it 'go up' it must have been colossal.[181] I've seen some craters out here but I simply stood & gazed at this with my mouth open.

At breakfast this morning I got a surprise packet of letters & your 277 & 278 so everything is rosy once more. I got the candles & they are very good.

I have for the moment given up the 'Brock life'.[182] The cakes arrived yesterday but I haven't seen them yet. What about some grouse?!! 2 brace at a time!

I don't know where old Mac got his idea that I didn't want him because I never wanted him more. I'll write to the old stupid, but I expect it's all part of his 'pessim' at being put back with his arm. The lamp has just come & Buckin is unpacking it now. It's fine old girl, and just what I wanted. I like the burners too, they are alright. Am sending the kids things off by this post too. I tried hard to find old Bobbo a decent battle souvenir but just because I wanted one I couldn't.

My love to you my darling.

19th September 1916 – (2nd) No. 262 answering 279 – Franvillers

I've simply loved your letter tonight old dear, & it answered one that I wrote you from my little dugout. As you say, it is much the best not to think. It does no good & you are better without it. Anyhow for the present I cannot even hear the guns. It was somewhat tiring at times & 48 hours

[181] This refers to a mine explosion before the battle began.
[182] In the trenches.

out & then not out of range of heavy shelling wasn't much of a rest. One has certainly taken one's part now & tho' I have not been 'over the top' myself yet, I've done as much as one can without doing so.

I'd love to be able to tell you all about it & I somehow think it won't be long now before I can come and tell you in person. I told you what my feelings were. It's no good saying that one likes it, no one does, but one's ear gets tuned to the sound of shells and instinctively one classifies them as dangerous or otherwise.

local the effect of even an eight inch shell is – It goes into the ground about 12 feet & then explodes – The result is a hole some 8 feet

← 15 feet →

Ground level

8 feet

deep and about 15 feet across the top – Well the upward angle of the burst is roughly as shown above & consequently if it strikes eight or ten yards away you are as safe as a house from everything except the concussion which may or may not result in a certain amount of shell shock – The blast of the thing alone is pretty strong, you can't get over that but the more one sees of it the more one realizes how very local the effect is – Now in shooting at a given target there enters into the thing

You would be surprised how extraordinarily local the effect of even an 8 inch shell is. It goes into the ground about 12 feet & then explodes. The result is a hole some 8 feet deep and about 15 feet across the top. Well, the upward angle of the burst is roughly as shown above & consequently if it strikes eight or ten yards away, you are as safe as a house from everything except the concussion, which may or may not result in a certain amount of shell shock. Now in shooting at a given target there enters into the thing what is known as the 'error of the gun' that is to say that with a new gun with perfect rifling there is a constant error of a certain amount & that with the same aim you can only guarantee that the shell will fall some-where inside a square having sides of 50 yards.

Hence the value of trenches. If you are aiming to get your shots into a ditch 4 feet wide you can see that tho' you have the range exactly it is quite possible that out of 100 shots you may only get, say, one or two in & quite possibly not that and if they are, say, 10 yards short or over the result is nil except what moral effect it has. If one even got 20% in, under modern conditions of fire both sides would have been wiped out ages ago. You ask about our 'joining up', yes, it did mean that the trench had to be marked out in the open & dug down & that to start with the men were fully exposed, & under heavy fire too, but here again what I tell you of the shell bursts, unless it falls actually among the men, tho' it's perfectly damnable, it does little or no actual harm so long as it's 10 or 15 yards away. On a new bit like that it isn't registered & consequently the Hun has to find the new range exactly. In all probability the telephone from his F.O.O.[183] is bust & so there's really lots in one's favour.

Of course during a show of this sort I don't go right up there as I have to sort of hold the strings behind, as one must be in touch with one's companies & the brigade too. If a C.O. goes messing about up in front on occasions like that, he is quite out of touch with his command & the result is chaos. There are times when one's presence in front is absolutely essential but in the majority of cases one is far better with all the strings in one's hand behind. You keep the show together then & the companies rely on one for direction. There's nothing more disconcerting for the Companies in front than to find the director away from where they expect him.

Buckin was with me all the time but he was never in the front line with

---

[183] Forward observation officer.

me. His duty didn't take him there & I won't allow 'joy-riding'. My dear old girl, as I told you I was perfectly all right & the more one sees of it I think the more sure one becomes, not that you ever can enjoy it but simply that experience soon teaches you what to look out for. I am sure enough of myself now, I merely wanted to be tested & it was a bit of a test. I walked up through Contalmaison day before yesterday & just arrived in time for the Huns' morning hate, & I certainly felt far surer of myself than I had done before. I mean to say I wasn't fussed at all & felt that one's instinct was keener & one realized so much better where they were all going somehow. The old Hun is very systematic in his shelling & very accurate & consequently one can gauge things pretty well once he has begun to shell, the chief danger of course, is the first one of the bunch, if you are unlucky enough to be on the spot before it arrives. Thank the Lord the Hun didn't deliver a strong counter-attack that morning & the relief passed off well. He made a small one the previous evening but it came to naught & was easily driven back. I'm awfully glad to hear old Bobbo is better.

Well Lass dear, as this is your second letter today I shall to bed.

21st September 1916 – No. 263 – Condé-Folie (near Abbeville)

Just at present I am in a very comfortable little shop, far from the madding crowd. I hope after lunch to get some letters as we have been moving about a bit the last day or two. I find that I dated my letter 262 the 18th & it should have been 19th. Anyhow it's better than some of yours which have had no date at all on them lately!! I suppose writing 'Thatched House'[184] has had to take its place!! I find it takes 8 months to become a Brigadier even if you are real good so perhaps the war will end before my chance comes. However, let us hope for the best.

I have just had a very pleasant evening's boating on the Somme. Hereabouts the Somme forms a sort of chain of large lakes & reminds one exactly of Wroxham Broad in miniature. We fished without success, so then

---

[184] A rented holiday house.

I paddled the old box about. It was a lovely evening and really most awfully jolly, about half way between Amiens & Abbeville. I'm going to Merville tomorrow. I hope to get a letter from you today but so far no luck.

My love to you old dear.

22nd September 1916 – No. 264 answering 281, 282, 283 – Estaires

Darling mine, I had many qualms as to whether to let you know where I was as I felt it would increase your anxiety, especially as I was really taking so minor a part in the show. Folk at home, of course, think one is spending one's whole time fighting whereas one really does not do so, as it's so very strenuous while it lasts that you have to have rest & really one is less in the line than out of it.

Troops have to be constantly relieved by both sides so you mustn't get it into your head that one is always at it. I wasn't in any actual attack myself tho' I saw several going on pretty handy. Just fancy the family getting that new bus and just the one I want!!

I'm hoping you were able to let old Bobbo go back up to time tho' if he were genuinely seedy I think you would be right to keep him, but if he was up & about & doing alright I know you would have sent him. I am so sorry not to have seen the old lad but I hope I shall soon now. Yes, Temple has got four kids, the eldest girl being 14, I think, but she has had to be sent to school as she was a bit wayward & uncannily artistic & wanted a rather firmer upbringing than the Governess.

I don't mind what you call Ken in the least. Edward is alright but not Teddie!!

You say you wish you could see what I am doing tonight, well I'm writing to you in a very comfortable bedroom indeed with a large double bed (for one!!), several good hanging wardrobes and a full-length glass that I've had a good look at my boots in & the general 'tout ensemble'!!!

I'd love to tell you of all my wanderings this last month old dear, but I can't & it must wait till we meet. The 'tanks' are some weapon & were in a number of instances most useful, but again I can tell you nothing as a full description would no doubt be very useful to the Boche.[185] They certainly are on the lines that you suggest but less vulnerable. I was fortunately able to thoroughly inspect four of them the day before they were used & they were top-hole things. I quite longed to go & drive one. It's the very first thing in which we have gone one better than the Boche & I hope it won't be the last.

My dear old girl the flysprayer is absolutely immense. I did my room out only the other day & as it was a polished wood floor you saw the result. It seems to absolutely clear the room right out. Thank goodness the ground isn't so foul in these parts.

The General told me tonight that leave is in the offing so perhaps it will come along one of these days shortly. I'm quite sure it will seem like a second honeymoon, but when did the first one end! You call it 'the second' but *I* wasn't aware the first had ended. I'm sorry !!!!!!!!!! I'm sorry old Bobbo didn't get his rabbit or pheasant!!

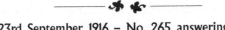

23rd September 1916 – No. 265 answering 280, 284 – Armentières

I got a letter today from the C.O. of the Canadians thanking me for the work of the Battalion[186] & I will send it you when I have answered it. We haven't had much rest so far old girl but things look like settling down a bit now for us. Yes, old Temple is a real good fellow & I like him awfully. He & I are working together & his Battalion relieves mine & vice versa. I'm sure you will like him & he's such a good soldier too. We have another fellow here who is a cavalry man. Richardson, 20th Hussars. A first-chop fellow. He's alright to become a brigadier & a jolly good one he will make.

---

[185] The invention of the British tank had been largely at the urging of Winston Churchill, with the idea of lessening the wholesale slaughter on the Western Front. Its effectiveness would not be fully realized until the Second World War, owing to constant mechanical failures and the difficulty of operating in entrenched battlefields, pockmarked with shell craters.

[186] Lt Colonel Swift, 2nd Battalion, Canadian 1st Division, wrote expressing 'sincere thanks . . . for assistance rendered us by your Battalion on the 9th inst. It was necessary to have strong support on our right and you certainly gave it to us.'

He is only just back after being wounded & he & I were in riding school together!! My dear old girl don't you worry about that D.S.O. they are not won quite as easily as that so if you pin your faith to Bibby, you will be disappointed.

You have done marvels over the car & the petrol & I heartily congratulate you!! I am so sorry you have lost your little son old dear, & I know it must have been a great wrench.[187] I'm so glad tho' that he was able to go back up to time.

Well darling mine, I must to bed now. All my love my dear.

O
n 24 September the battalion relieved the Gordon Highlanders in the front-line trenches. The period proved to be quiet, with little shelling, though one officer died of wounds and four other ranks were wounded.

26th September 1916 – on a scrap of paper – front-line trenches, Armentières

I am frantically busy, so busy that I haven't a moment hardly that I can afford to lose and have been waiting from 10 a.m. until now (noon) for a General & the Brigadier wasted my whole morning yesterday. Half, or rather $^7/_8$th of one's time in the army is spent waiting for some other bloke. Simply damnable!

I hope my friend Temple will get home next week & if he does he will probably come over & see you. I hope to be with you about Oct. 24th!! Hardly dare mention a date as it always seems to fall through.

---

[187] Their eldest son, Bob, had just returned to prep school.

27th September 1916 – No. 267 answering 286 & 287 –
front-line trenches, Armentières

Two nice letters today. I see you are enjoying yourself at Catsclough[188] as usual. I'm sorry your Ma feels so in the dumps but if she will live at that damned place, I don't wonder. Many thanks for sending me the knife, I expect it will be alright when it comes. I was extremely busy on the 15th & 16th & pretty handy tho' never closer than a mile so had no real hand in the show. We have great news today of Combles & Thiepval. The poor old Boche is getting it fair & square in the neck these times. I only hope he'll get some more. Lass dear, I propose if the fates are propitious to come home on Oct. 23 or 24 or thereabouts if that will suit your arrangements!!

I hadn't seen that Harry Cubitt was killed. I am so sorry. I had a very good lad killed yesterday. Poor boy died of wounds. I saw him into the Ambulance, & he held my hand & asked me, did I think 'anything would happen to him' & I assured him he would be alright as soon as he got to the Ambulance. It was no good saying anything else, tho' I knew he was done, I am afraid.

Best of love old dear.

30th September 1916 – No. 269 answering 289 & 290 –
subsidiary trenches, Armentières

As you say old Bobbo's letter sounds really first class & the old boy seems to be doing fine. Your suggestion as to his coming home for a couple of days if I get leave meets with my entire approval. I'm awfully glad he has gone up so very well in the school. I loved your letter written in the train old dear, it was a topper. You see it does make a difference who you go to bed with!

I haven't got my Adjutant back yet, I am sorry to say, but am expecting him any day now. My darling old girl it's no use your worrying about me.

---

[188] Ethel's widowed mother's home in Cheshire.

I've told you that you get short doses of concentrated essence punctuated by long periods of comparative quietude & if anything happens you would get a W.O. wire long before the actual show was in a paper, so just don't trouble trouble before 'troublie' troubles or doesn't 'troublie'. Old Temple, lucky beggar, goes home for a bit day after tomorrow & it is quite possible that he might go over and see you with his Mrs. Temple & I are living together just at present. We had a nice house to live in, but it was a little too conspicuous and yesterday we decided it would be perhaps wiser to occupy a more unpretentious residence in view of certain possibilities. Now I live in a ditch, a nice writing table, a comfortable bed, with my air mattress on it. The walls are hung with canvas & in fact it's a very comfy little shop indeed! It's a little bullety of an evening, but if one doesn't play the ass it's all right here.

Well darling mine, adieu.

1st October 1916 – No. 270 – Armentières, subsidiary line, Epinette Sector

That damned Searton girl, how dare she run down the soldiers & to you too. Damn it, she's not fit to live in the same country with them. Does she realize that because these men are giving up their lives, hundreds a day these times, that she's able to go on living in the lap of luxury? Really it's almost heartbreaking to think that there can be anyone at home so utterly callous to what's going on. I wish to God you had ordered her out of the house.

The absolute magnificence of the men is beyond all praise & every man seems the same. If you hadn't seen it you couldn't believe it. A fellow said to me only the other day 'it makes you proud to belong to the race that produces these men'. Only last night I stood & watched old 'Buckin', standing outside the cookhouse washing up, smoking a cigarette while certainly not more than six feet over his head there was a perfect stream of machine-gun bullets from a Boche M.G. that fires over our Mess. He certainly was perfectly safe because of the parapet & it was impossible for him to be hit, but it was the whole sort of 'air' of the thing that impressed one, not that Buckin is particularly brave, but just as an instance of the total disregard that the men pay to what is going on – they just go steadily on & if they're hit they're hit & that is all there is to it. I don't know what it is that does it but the men are all the same. Simply wonderful.

The battalion now returned to the front line, having relieved the 25th Battalion. This time, however, the enemy were more active, principally with *Minenwerfer*, which caused several casualties and damage to the trenches. The War Diary records that whilst in the front line from the 4th to the 9th, three men were killed, and nineteen wounded, of whom three died of their wounds.

4th October 1916 – No. 273 – Armentières, front line

We've got a real soaking day today which makes everything rather miserable especially as in this damned flat country there's more water than one can do with in the finest summer weather. It looks now very much as tho' we have done with summer alright & the winter is setting in.

Anyhow we're not in the trenches here, which is something, as it's too wet for trenches & we live on the top of the ground behind breastworks & so keep as dry as possible, but only moderately dry at that. I wonder if Temple has rung you up yet? I hope so. I got three officers back last night which has eased the situation, one of whom I am making Adjutant on spec, as I hear he is a good fellow. So far I have only gathered that his best pal is a retired policeman whose present job is doorkeeper at the town hall at Newcastle!! Oh dear, o' dear, this is a ragtime army these days but still a damned good one at that. I sit down & laugh so at times, & wonder what the old Regiment would think of it all.

However, it's odd that I believe I am happier here & now than I have ever been soldiering before. After all, the old life was chiefly one of amusement with little or no real objective & now one is doing something & doing it with only very moderate tools which keeps one constantly on the go. The material one has to deal with is real good really, only soldiering isn't acquired by the mere donning of a khaki suit, but what they lack in knowledge they make up for in keenness & the whole ball keeps rolling along somehow.

Best in the world to you old Lass and may we meet soon.

5th October 1916 – No. 274 answering 294 – front line, Armentières

I had my extra hour in bed & was in a very cosy little hole dug into the side of the ditch. Just like a yacht's cabin. Rather low tho' & one couldn't stand up in it very well. However, it was quite comfortable.

I'm sorry the car ran so badly. Have you tried petrol for her? I found she ran very well on it, much better than on slightly smelling air! Yes, I did get the knife old dear, very many thanks. I am awfully sorry to hear you have a cold but it seems pretty general & everyone seems to have it here too. All my lads have got it. Sort of influenza. I'm in the front line now. We stir the Hun up & then he retaliates & stirs us up & so it goes on day in day out, not very exciting. There's a good deal of sameness in the 'daily round, the common task'.

They still go on well down on the Somme & by the papers it looks as tho' the Romanians were going to score off old Falkenhayn.[189] Hope they will. I'm awful worried to think K.E.H. is declining but I expect really it is alright, just other methods. Lass dear, I must stop now. I've got a biggish problem to settle & must tackle it at once.

7th October 1916 – No.? answering 295–7 – front line, Armentières

The main piece of news is that my C.O. has rolled up out of the blue today, 'all of a sudden Peggy', without any warning whatsoever. He is at present acting Brigadier so I am still in command. I don't think really that it will make very much difference to me as I have got to know a good many folk of the right sort lately & I don't think they will let me go back into obscurity any more. Anyhow things are a bit uncertain for the present & I hardly quite know how things will turn out yet, but I don't anticipate very much trouble in keeping my end up. Anyhow it looks as tho' it had made leave a certainty so it isn't altogether an ill wind.

[189] Erich von Falkenhayn, Chief of the Imperial German General Staff.

Your talk of your 'talk with the usual Sunday folk, the usual Sunday beef, & the usual Sunday walk' makes me quite homesick!! I don't know what time the leave train gets in but will let you know in lots of time. Any arrangements you make will suit me. All I want is you & as long as we are together I don't much mind where it is. I daresay, old dear, Mac's nerves aren't just quite the thing, & if you were to examine us all I expect you would find a very large percentage pretty much the same.

I think old Bob's letter is splendid old dear, it's so awfully well written too & your question paper most amusing. He has gone to the front of the class too which is also fine. Hope he will stay there.

------------ ✤ ✤ ------------

9th October 1916 – No.? answering 298–9 – billets, Armentières

At last, after sleeping in my clothes for eighteen days, I have got a really comfortable bed & a pair of pyjamas on. As a matter of fact I am in bed now and writing to you as I sort of feel like writing tonight, old dear. The Brigadier, as I told you, is on leave so my fate is not yet decided but at present I am to get the Battalion now commanded by our mutual friend the Commercial Traveller who is to be outed. I saw the Div. Commander yesterday & he is very keen about my getting it & as you know the Corps Commander won't put any spoke in my wheel. Anyhow I'm not at all alarmed at my prospects. They've found out that one isn't an absolute fool & having got one they're not going to lose me.

A Battalion Commander nowadays has a price above rubies & one can almost dictate one's own terms. Certainly I have dictated mine & that is that the present C.O. who is to make way for me isn't reverted to 2nd-in-command. If you subtract 3 from my present Battalion, that will give you the number of the new one.

I am afraid that I shall not have as good a lot of officers, but one doesn't really know till one gets there. Their idea is to send me on leave till things are settled & then get me back as a Battalion Commander, so I won't have to revert. The Battalion came out into rest today & I think everyone was pretty glad, we've had a very hard time indeed now for some time & rest, like jam, is one of those things which are always tomorrow!

We don't look like getting much sleep, it will be all 'chatter' all night & I shall be quite glad to get back to the trenches for a rest!!!! I'm fearfully busy now old dear, even tho' I am supposed to be resting, there's an awful lot to do. There is no doubt that a Battalion Commander has just about the hardest time of anyone out here. Tremendous responsibility, an absolutely colossal amount of orderly room work, far more than I ever had as adjutant in peacetime. I have never in my service seen so much paper as there is now.

I have recently been living in a house about a mile behind the line. The other night the old Boche set about us about 11 p.m. Fortunately he didn't hit the house, but he dropped a heavy shell into a long building in the yard that I used as a workshop for my pioneers, as it had a bench in it & I also kept all my trench stores and reserve of ammunition in it. The door was in the middle of the side & it just blew exactly half the shed to atoms, the door remained hung on one side & was swinging in air on the other, amidst absolute ruin. Well it set the ammunition on fire & we had to turn out with buckets & put the damned thing out. The ammunition was popping off like Xmas crackers & we had a bit of a job with it during which time [Captain] Bibby managed to throw most of a bucket of water over me!

Alas! They ate my grouse while I was out last night & I didn't even see them!! More please! A pot or two of cream & some Devonshire ditto wouldn't come amiss.

Steward is a topper & I like him most awfully. A real soldier & I now see where Temple has got most of his ideas.

10th October 1916 – No. 278 answering 300 – billets, Armentières

The town I'm in is well in the shelled area & there is an order that we are to wear our steel hats in it.

Tonight as I was walking home, in the glorious moonlight & absolute stillness I met three loving couples strolling along concerned with nothing but just their two selves. It was in the Church square with the battered church looking down on the scene, all smashed to bits, no windows left, the spire knocked off & huge gaping holes in the roof & walls. The incongruity of the whole thing was really most striking. The house I am living in now is really a beautiful house, you turn in from the street through large carriage doors & the car pulls up in a marble sort of porch, marble steps lead up to a remarkably fine hall & staircase, it reminds me inside very much of 51,[190] but is a very much more airy & finer house.

It's only when you open certain rooms upstairs that you find that there's a floor & that the outside wall doesn't exist. However my room is very comfortable & there's a bathroom & tho' one has to carry the water up from the kitchen it's really a very presentable imitation of a bath.

What I hate seeing is the number of kids that play about in the streets. Perhaps they're too young to realize but it's rather awful the kids getting killed, as I'm afraid they too often do. There is no doubt that war has nothing to recommend it at all.

As you say old dear, 300 is an awful number for your letters. How have you managed to keep it going so long? Lass dear, I'm heartily sick of having been away so long too. Let us hope the year won't close without another meeting. I really think that they will want me out of the country for a bit just to tide over an awkward situation – anyhow I shall have a real good try to get as much leave as I can. Don't expect more than ten days. I am afraid dearie, it will be very many weary months before we can do things together once more. Things go very well, but the end is not in sight. The beginning of the end has come, but the end is not yet.

I'm awfully sorry to hear that Mary Ann[191] kicked the Chugs off but it was undoubtedly due to them both being on her. I do so hope that it won't have made them lose confidence, but it can't be helped. I shouldn't let them take liberties. Even the quietest of mokes may one day resent a liberty & one doesn't want to frighten them if it can be helped.

On the 12th, a raiding party made up of six officers and a hundred other ranks entered the German front line at the Railway Salient. Artillery had success-fully breached the wire on the left and a Bangalore torpedo,[192] placed unobserved on the right, had been exploded to make the second breach. Three parties entered the salient, working down both sides. Three dugouts were bombed, killing a number of enemy soldiers and a shoulder strap was brought back for identification. These

---

[190] 51 Cadogan Square, a friend's house in London.
[191] Their donkey.
[192] A portable 'torpedo' about 1.8 metres long, designed by British forces in India, and used to explode barbed wire entanglements.

raids were not accomplished without cost: three officers were wounded, one dying later, two other ranks were killed, eleven wounded and four missing.

14th October 1916 – No. 280 answering 301–3 – billets, Armentières

I shall leave here on Monday night 16th and arrive some time on the 17th. I can only have the 10 days' leave but even that is something. I'm sorry that I didn't manage to write to you yesterday, but I had a couple of my lads wounded the previous night & was running round the hospitals seeing them, which took me longer than I expected.

This leave business has thoroughly unsettled me & I don't feel at all like writing to you my old dear as with actual conversation in view in the very near future it seems to be too futile. I can't follow the wandering of your very low mind in the Paris reference. I don't know what you mean at all & should think that Paris was one of those places where a wife was hardly necessary!

My love dearie mine,

Ever your Robert.

Robert's two weeks in England were spent mainly with his family at Brook Hill, but he and Ethel had their last three nights at the Berkeley Hotel in London together before he returned to France on 25 October.

CHAPTER THIRTEEN

CO, 24TH BN, NORTHUMBERLAND FUSILIERS, THE TYNESIDE IRISH

As winter 1916 approached, the two major battles of the Western Front were drawing to a close, their dying moments proving as savage as their beginnings. The Battle of the Somme was brought to an end in mid-November by snow and bad weather, though not before the British had taken Beaumont-Hamel, Beaucourt and St Pierre-Divion on the River Ancre, but with little ground gained to compensate for such terrible losses. Verdun, the longest battle of the war, ended the following month after almost a year, with the French retaking Douaumont and Fort Vaux, denying victory to the Germans, the initiators of the offensive. Allied perseverance had prevented the Central Powers from making a decisive breakthrough.

On 25 October, Robert returned to France, crossing the Channel in the transport ship the *Queen*. The following night the ship was sunk by an enemy destroyer. Colonel Hermon immediately took command of the 24th Battalion, Northumberland Fusiliers, in front-line trenches at Armentières, close to the Belgian border, resuming once more the onerous responsibilities of an infantry commanding officer.

27th October 1916, 7 p.m. – No. 2, Series 3, Vol. XVI!! – front line, Armentières

My own brave Lassie,

Darling mine, the candle has gone out alright this time & it's very dark. What a contrast was last night to its predecessor & how I loved your dear sweet note & the thought that prompted it, my love. I am so glad you love your ring dearie mine. I've had that ring, exactly as you've got it, in my mind for *so* long now & have often wondered if I should ever have the chance to put it on. Anyhow now you have it & I put it there, & I can hear the censor say 'Betrothed'!

We had a capital journey down, good breakfast on the train and went straight on board, underway almost at once and in Boulogne hotel at 1 p.m. Had tea in the Brigade office at 4.30 p.m. I then heard that I was to assume command of the 24th Battalion. I had to go & see the Divisional General after tea & get myself to the trenches afterwards & take over command of the Battalion on arrival. I picked up Buxton & some kit, got back to the Brigade office, dined with them & motored up to the trenches, walking the last couple of miles. Fetched up about 10.30 p.m. & took over from my commercial friend 'well known in the North' who immediately went on leave.

If he cannot get another job he is to come back to me as second-in-command but he is doing his best to find something. I should be more than glad if he did. The Battalion, so far as I have seen it, I like very much indeed. There is just a chance that I may have to get another Battalion later on, I hope it won't happen, but I have told the Div. Commander I will do anything he wishes to help.

Have had dinner & am now off to bed. Not a bad little bed – not as good or as nice as one I have known lately.

My love to you my own darling.

28th October 1916 – No. 3 – subsidiary trenches, Epinette Sector[193]

I'm pleased to be able to report that your husband's health is very much improved. All yesterday & the previous evening he felt as tho' he had a severe attack of typhoid combined with acute dysentery, and with influenza supervening, while his body felt as if it had been run over by a tank. I was certain that my temperature was at least 103 if not 105 & was quite disappointed to find that I could only raise the thermometer to 96!! I am taking a real good pill tonight and hope by tomorrow evening to be completely restored to health.

---

[193] During this period in the subsidiary lines the battalion supplied working parties to the Royal Engineers, repairing trenches in the front line.

My love to you my darling & don't worry as I am now perfectly well & happy. Go & see Mrs Temple one of these days & tell her that her good man is fit & well.

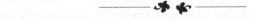

30th October 1916 – No. 5 answering 1 & 2 – subsidiary line, Epinette Sector

Two lovely letters rolled up at lunch time & I was so very glad to see them, old dear. They are, as you say, very poor substitutes for what we have had lately, & yet they are everything now. Lass dear, as you know I was absolutely happy all the lovely time & it was just glorious. I loved the first week with the Chugs, & seeing them ride & old Bobbo's first shoot was topping but what will always remain with me will be our last three days together when the world held just you & me & I long for the time to come when it will hold you & me only again. You say you enjoyed this honeymoon better than the original & have no qualms. Well I have & it is the only worry I have, however it's in the lap of the Gods & until such time as one is sure it's no good worrying!!

My darling you don't know what a pig I felt at going off and leaving you all the packing up to do as it must have been rather a beastly job after all the fun we had had during the time those selfsame clothes had been in use & I so wished I had done it all myself the night before but the last hours were all too short to be wasted packing a damned bag! The hotel bill was very much cheaper than I expected. Are you sure that the car was included in the bill? I enclose you a cheque as my share of the beano & very cheap at the price.

You ask what I was doing at 9.45 p.m. on the night I returned, well Buckin & I were trudging our weary way along a very wet & slippery communication trench on our way to Battalion H.Q., it was raining & blowing, inky black & about as big a contrast to a stall at Daly's [194] of the same hour the previous night as you can well imagine.

All the love in the world to you, my own.

[194] Daly's Theatre, off Leicester Square, London.

31st October 1916 – subsidiary line, Epinette Sector

My dear, I do feel very much better for my holiday really & truly & not only for your comfort. It was the *Queen* that I crossed in, so glad they didn't come a bit sooner!! You seem to have had a very successful sale indeed. Will you have the bacon sent only once a fortnight instead of once a week, as we are a very small mess at present.

I like my Battalion very much but there is a good deal that wants altering and I shall not want for a job, I'm thinking. It's apparently never had a regular C.O. in its life, & if it's true, it is wonderful that it's as good as it is. I have had a very happy day building a new mess which Temple started & it's going to be fine when it's finished.

Thank the Chugs for their nice letters.

1st November 1916 – No. 7 answering 4 – subsidiary line, Armentières

The pheasants & sausages arrived safely & I hope to have some for dinner tomorrow. Very many thanks.

I saw the account of the Salcombe lifeboat accident in the paper, really awfully sad. It is the only time I remember a whole crew going since the St Anne's boat were all drowned.

Well, well, like Hindenburg[195] I wish the damned war was over and done with, but what on earth to do for a job when it is over beats me. I shall have to remain a soldier I think, & become a general.

Goodnight my old dear & I wish you would send me another copy of that little paper book of prayers that was on the Jane stand by your bed.

---

[195] Field Marshal von Hindenburg.

O n the night of the 3rd, in retaliation for the British bombardment, German artillery and *Minenwerfer* caused considerable damage to a communication trench. The battalion sent out two patrols and located and dispersed an enemy wiring party. During periods in the front line, when patrols went out nightly, losses were inevitable.

4th November 1916, 5.20 p.m. – No. 9 answering 6 & 7 – front line, Epinette Sector

I could only send you a service postcard yesterday as I am in front line again & was very busy. However, I have a few minutes tonight & can answer your lovely letters that I got a few hours ago. You lucky old thing, I expect that you are with old Bobbo now & I do so wish I was too, instead of having a damned German machine gun playing on my dugout. The doctor has just shut the door (½ matchboard) to keep it out!! One is really perfectly safe because the dugout is safe from bullets so it's not very heroic, but merely annoying. My nice doctor went home yesterday for a spell of leave & I shall be glad when he is back as I have got a very lousy substitute. The proper man is really a topper by name Svensson, a Yorkshireman whose Pa, I think, in some long gone age was a Viking. You would like him I'm sure.

The glasses and air cushion haven't rolled up yet but will probably come with the transport & rations tonight. I will tell you the truth, the whole truth & nothing but the truth about the air pillow. I AM ABSOLUTELY SURE ABOUT THE MOTH IN MY SUIT!!!! Probably they liked that suit best & concentrated on it.

I don't think the Commercial[196] will come back as I hear he has been given extra leave until Div. Commander has settled what to do with him, but I expect he will become Town Major somewhere. The thing is that he has a very strong 'hail-fellow-well-met' sort of personality, an unlimited capacity for whisky, and isn't altogether an asset in a Battalion. I hope that they will find him something & I am sure the Div. Commander will do all in his power.

[196] The temporary CO.

Your remarks re my memory I treat with scorn! I am top-hole, the pill I had was a real nailer & has fairly screwed me up. Never felt better in my life.

Love to the Chugs.

Enclosed with his letter of the 4th was a newspaper cutting about the wife of the Mayor of Quebec giving birth to her twenty-eighth child. Underneath Robert had written in red pencil: 'Why, you're only just beginning!!?'

5th November 1916 – No. 10 – front line, Epinette Sector

We got a couple of prisoners this morning, very tame Huns of the 17 Bavarian Inf. Regt. They had been out on patrol and I think got lost & being glad of the excuse, surrendered at once, as soon as they were found.

Getting two letters today, I expect I shall have to go without tomorrow. I simply hate the letterless days & am heartily sick of the damned war.

My love to you all my darlings.

8th November 1916 – No. 12 answering 11 & 12 – front line, Epinette Sector

We have had a wretched time these last few days & the water is awful.[197] There are two streams running over the mess floor as I write, flowing gallons to the minute. I have just got up to bid Buckin 'Bon Voyage' & he starts for home tomorrow. I have given him a cheque for his 'amusements' so there is no need for you to do anything for them in the way of trips to London or the like. Have them into the house or anything of that sort if you like. He is going to get us some Mess things which you might pay for,

---

[197] In the War Diary it is recorded that there were 18 inches of water in several of the trenches.

if you will. I think my leave has made me want another more than ever &
I do fairly envy old Buckin. Thank old Bet & Mairky for their nice letters,
but I haven't time to answer them I am afraid. Tell the Chugs they must
write to me out of school. I don't like their copybook letters, they're too
neat & formal.

We've got a stove in the dugout & the temperature is about 100 and
together with an acetylene lamp with a hole in it the fug is priceless!

10th November 1916 – No. 13 answering 13 & 14 – Armentières

Last night I slept between sheets for the first time since an ever-memorable
night at the Berkeley!! I hope to have a bath tonight. I have no time to
write more now as I have a fearful lot of work to do and have to meet the
general & discuss some things with him. One comes out of the trenches
for a rest & one certainly gets one's nights in bed & the relaxation from
anxiety & responsibility is great, but the work has got to be done all the
same & as it accumulates a bit in the trenches one has to do it now. It is
a miracle!![198]

10th November 1916, 11 p.m. – No. 14 (second effort) –
Armentières

We have had two top-hole days lately old dear, & it makes things so
much nicer. The only consolation however, is that the old Boche's trenches
are much wetter than ours, you see them hopping out and running along
the top & it's better fun than rabbit shooting. The other morning I was
down in the front line just before daylight & the men were having a fine
old shoot.

I was watching an old Hun plodding about in the mud through my
telescope & you could see him so plainly. It's rather amusing seeing them

---

[198] His reaction to news that his wife was not pregnant again.

hating the water like poison. I'm sure they are jolly wet. I was looking at an air photo tonight & it shows a deuce of a lot of water in their trenches.

12th November 1916 – No. 15 – on pages from a notebook – Armentières

I hear that I am to be confirmed in my rank which means that I get the Battalion permanently. Anyhow, if I was to be wounded or go sick I should come back to this Battalion. I was interviewing candidates for commissions today & asked one what he was in civil life. 'Ladies & gents hairdresser Sir'!! It was so very funny, I nearly burst out laughing.

I am thoroughly Berkeley sick but one month has gone dearie & it probably won't take long now to get through the other two. I should love to have a few hours with you tonight. I've no fellow spirit here & I'm a bit disappointed at old Mac not coming as he would have had a fine influence on the Battalion & I want someone with his soldierly ideas most awfully badly. However, I mean to make the show go, I've got good men & good N.C.O.s & two or three really good officers but the rest are no class at all. I shall have to do something rather drastic I expect shortly.

13th November 1916 – No. 16 – on pages from a notebook – Armentières

My dear I quite forgot my youngest son's birthday! Please apologize & start his banking account with the enclosed. Thank the Chugs for their nice letters which I got today. The prayer book turned up today & I hope to open it & read some when I go to bed in a minute or two.

All my officers seem to be down with diseases of sorts & I am pretty badly off at present. There is a sort of influenza running round & everyone seems to have it. I don't know if it is a new sort of Hun frightfulness & he is sending us 'Snishoo' germs down the many brooks which run from him to us. I expect I shall have it shortly as all the other members of the Mess can hardly see out of their eyes.

Goodnight my old love.

14th November 1916 – No. 17 answering 17 – Armentières

You are quite right about the officers; they are very like the curate's egg. There are some really good ones & I like them very much. There is one called Allison who is an exceedingly nice fellow & his brother is a Lewis Gun officer & he's very nice too. Then there's a bloke called Blott who's nice & most capable. There's a funny little man called Crichton, a Wesleyan minister, who is also a good bloke tho' nothing very much socially. My Adjutant, Brady, is a nice fellow & our proper doctor, Svensson, is a most charming fellow. You would like him & Allison I'm sure.

You know the British soldier is a most wonderful person. We have recently taken some prisoners and during the night these blokes, had they met, would have killed one another & enjoyed it. When morning came, they surrendered & came in. No sooner had the men got them than they gave them a tot of rum & cigarettes, & when I got back to Battalion H.Q. they were sharing their breakfast with them. It's one of the finest traits in the national character the way the men treat their prisoners. In a real fight there's no doubt a great many somehow do get killed that perhaps mightn't but the moment they surrender, when there is nothing on they might almost be an honoured guest. They look on them as sort of pets!! They really are rum blokes but there's no doubt it's fine.

Just been handed a G.H.Q. wire saying that total prisoners taken on Somme is now 5,400. Real good, isn't it. Just when the old Hun thought he had fixed us for good!! We are all awfully pleased as it is a good reply to the French success at Verdun. Make the old Boche think a bit too. I wish to goodness we could break him.

I enclose you a bit of a medal ribbon the same Boche gave me. I don't know what it is but Spinks would tell you & some time I should like to know.

17th November 1916, 9.30 a.m. – No. 19 –
front line, Epinette Sector

Somehow I didn't manage to get you a letter done yesterday in spite of the fact that I was up & out in my front line before daylight broke. It was a glorious day & same today tho' it froze like Hades last night & I was plunging about in water up to my knees with half an inch of ice on the top going round the line last night.

My unfortunate runner fell down twice. If it's true that the Boche has no rubber boots now I don't know how he will get through the winter. We have all got thigh waders, which tho' by no means proof against frostbite, are very much better than wet feet.

I somehow can't write letters now, since that lovely time dearie they seem so rotten but I seem to want yours more than I did before.

18th November 1916 – No. 20 answering 20 & 21 –
front line, Epinette Sector

It is now nearly II p.m. & I have got to wander down & look round the front line. It's raining & beastly & I would far rather be at home in bed!! The last time in the trenches we were simply flooded out. This time I have been walking round on ice and this morning where the water was less than a foot deep, the ice was thick enough to bear me walking carefully. The poor men I am afraid had a terrible thin night.

I'm awfully glad old Buckin is pleased with the cottage and things in general.

20th November 1916 – No. 21 answering 21, 23 & 24 –
front line, Epinette Sector

I feel again that I have neglected you too shamefully these last few days, but I haven't had a moment. I have been organizing a minor operation of sorts & have not had a moment in which to write to you. It merely remains to sit & wait until the hour strikes for action. I take no part myself beyond the control of the operation & it's a great anxiety & rather damnable waiting.

It's fine the progress on the ANCRE.[199] If Romania could only hold her own now for a bit, it would snooker old Hindenburg. I don't think the bit the Huns got back was of much account & they probably lost pretty heavily in getting it.

Now I must stop & write a line to the family as I owe them some letters & have got six very anxious hours to get through somehow.

My love to you old dear. Will you post me my long waders please.

The 'anxious hours' were because a raiding party from the battalion had entered the enemy trenches under darkness. The trenches had been damaged by artillery fire and were deep in water and no sign of the enemy was found. Whilst these patrols were out the commanding officer needed to remain awake.

22nd November 1916 – No. 22 answering 25 – subsidiary line, Epinette Sector.

My folk entered the Boche trenches a few days ago & did pretty well tho' the Hun had evacuated his front line where they entered and so they didn't get a prisoner. Anyhow it's caused great satisfaction all round & done the men worlds of good. I was very pleased too as they have attempted two raids before & both have been hopeless failures. I think it was the last fiasco that got me the Battalion.

The cups & teapot turned up today. Many thanks.

Well dearie I must go to bed as I find it is already tomorrow.

[199] On the Somme.

23rd November 1916 – No. 23 answering 26 – subsidiary trenches, Epinette Sector (Marked 'Examined by Base Censor')

I am afraid I am very late tonight as I see it is already tomorrow again but I am having another little venture with the Hun in the early hours & so I do not expect to get to bed much before 6 a.m.

I am glad you & the Chugs enjoyed yourselves at White House. How are you getting on, on Standard bread? Are you able to get no flour for puddings? I hope the pony will come alright again, as it suits old Mairky well.

Well dearie I must be off as I am preparing a very hefty bomb for brother Boche & my party starts soon.

24th November 1916 – No. 24 answering 27 & 28 – subsidiary trenches, Epinette Sector

My little show last night was a great success in that my folk entered the Boche line, stayed there for an hour & 50 minutes & when they left destroyed a dugout with gun cotton. They never saw a Hun at all & I think there is so much water in his line at this point that he doesn't occupy it. Anyhow it has done the men a most awful lot of good, bucked them up like anything, & the Battalion in general benefits no end by a successful show of this sort.

I am awfully sorry little Mairky has been seedy. I should shut her & her pony up together & leave them till they get well!! Send the socks to the Central Depot as there are most probably hundreds who are more in need than we are. We have got a very good system running here. Each man possesses 3 pairs of socks & has one on, a dry pair in his pocket and one pair at the Div. Laundry.

Darling mine, I'm so damned tired I'm going to bed. Tomorrow I am on a General Court Martial to try an officer, so may not have time to write you more before this post goes.

26th November 1916 – No. 26 answering 27, 28 & 29 – subsidiary trenches, Epinette Sector

Did you see in the casualty list that my nice doctor man Guthrie had been killed? I was so awfully sorry. The world is very much the poorer for his death. I was awfully fond of him, he was a man after my own heart. Yes, old Prior has behaved magnificently & does at once anything I ask him & does it in a really nice way. I will tell you if I hear whether I get confirmed in my rank but I understand that it is so & that I shall appear in the Army list with the Battalion, tho' also in K.E.H. as seconded.

29th November 1916 – No. 28 answering 31, 32 & 33 – Fort Rompu [200]

At last I have got a rest & am back behind the line with a prospect of ten days before I go into it again, which is simply topping. The only crab is my cold & the fact that our billet is very poor indeed. However there's nothing else, so there's no use grumbling. We are now enjoying low ground fogs, bitter damp and cold & the whole outlook is very far from pleasant, I can assure you, but the men have nice little huts & are clean & dry which is always something. My darling old girl, I am terribly cut up about poor old 'Medicine Man' Guthrie. He was another Mac of the finest possible type. It's too sad for words, but he must have died finely as I hear he was killed whilst bandaging men in the last attack, right out on the ground they had won.

You have fairly mystified me over the little present & I am anxiously looking forward to its arrival. My second-in-command[201] was ordered to England today and I am genuinely sorry to see the last of him. I wouldn't have believed that a man of his class could have been so loyal or behaved as finely as he has done under the circumstances. I know many folk who

---

[200] An army camp '5 km west of Armentières'.
[201] Major Prior.

wouldn't know him in civil life & who couldn't hold a candle to his behaviour. I admire the old man more than I can say. There's no doubt that a lot of our social ideas are rot.

As you say the Romanian business doesn't look well & I am afraid it will put another year on to the war, but one never knows, the more line they have to hold the weaker they must be. There is no doubt that the Huns have got some goodish thinkers at the top.

My head, old dear, is far too cotton-woolly to write you any more now. My love my darling.

3rd December 1916 – No. 32 – answering 35 – Fort Rompu

I can't remember what was in my number 22 but I think that the Censors do dive at very fat envelopes in case of finding unauthorized enclosures. You say why was I strafed, well it was merely because I went out to see my wiring parties at work one night & I didn't know that C.O.s weren't allowed between the lines.

Your nurse sounds nice old dear & I hope you will engage her. After all one can't get everything these times & she sounds quite alright. I don't think her age matters & you can hire a small boy to push the pram. I hear from the family that you were in town when the aeroplane came & that Nell was covered with bricks from a beastly bomb?

6th December 1916 – No. 35 answering 40 – Fort Rompu

I'm going to have a covered car tonight & I'm going off to an Old Etonian dinner in the hopes that I'll meet someone I like better than myself. The weather is still damnable, cold & cheerless & looks like remaining so for the rest of the winter.

7th December 1916 – No. 36 answering 40 & 41 – Fort Rompu

Well, I went to the dinner last night & had a really very pleasant evening. Nicholson said I wasn't fit enough to go in an open car so he sent a covered one for me & four of us went off from these parts to Cassel. The first soul I saw in the room was Wally & I was so pleased to see him & I sat next to him & on my other side was an Eton master who knew Dick. He had a staff job somewhere & was a Grenadier Guardsman. His name was Wilkinson & he told me he knew Pa, who had invited him to go yachting with him & to meet him at Cowes in 1914!! I could so well see the old man doing it, can't you?

There were 73 of us sat down at dinner but very few folk that I knew. My circle of acquaintances being a few folk met hereabouts and Wally & old Trotter Carter!! The latter was the oldest Etonian present, having gone there in 1869!! Amongst the rest were a few odd folk like Vivian Nicholls, & Bill Pawson. General Plumer was in the chair.

Coming back our car ran out a big end bearing half way between Cassel & Bailleul, but luckily an empty car came along and we commandeered it & got home again alright. I think it did me good as I certainly am much better today, I am glad to say.

10th December 1916 – No. 39 answering 43 & 44 – Fort Rompu

Things certainly do look bad just at present but they will come right in the end; there was one December in the S.A. war when folk thought all was lost. We are all right here & if the folk will really buck up at home & play the game & chuck all the damned foolishnesses till the war is over, it will be alright. We are bound to win in the end so long as the navy remains top dog in the North Sea. It all turns on that.

No, I didn't exactly design these stables tho' I gave them a plan of my last ones with measurements, but these are better still. I've told you already I am moving right-handed a bit. Unfortunately I am very unlikely to see my mess hut again or my own nice fireplace.

13th December 1916 – No. 41 answering 46 – front line, Rue de Bois Sector

Short note tonight as I am just off round my line & would give worlds to be going to bed instead. I've got a damnable sore throat today & it's beastly having to run the show when one is not really feeling quite the thing. However it's got to be done. We are all most frightfully excited about Lloyd George's reply to Bethmann Hollweg[202] – 'K' said the Huns would offer peace on their terms in November 16 & that two months later would have to accept ours!!

16th December 1916 – No. 43 answering 48 – trenches, Rue de Bois Sector

Many thanks for the Xmas things, which I expect will arrive tonight or tomorrow. The rats have eaten two cakes in my bedroom. We found an old 'Jane' cupboard which is doing duty as a meat safe in my bedroom & the cakes were in it. The old bit of wood we had over it for a door got left off & of course the rats had it in no time, there are lots in my bedroom.

It doesn't matter about the marmalade, old dear. As a matter of fact what we have been having lately is so unlike the original article that it is unrecognizable.

Well dearie, I've just got another nice letter from you (50) but I'm going to bed. Will answer it tomorrow if possible. Don't worry I'm mending alright.

18th December 1916 – No. 44 answering 48, 49, 50 – Rue Marle

Last night for an hour after going to bed I simply coughed my soul out, but I think it was because I painted my throat with some glycerine &

---

[202]On 6th December, Asquith had been replaced as prime minister by Lloyd George, who, according to Winston Churchill, had more 'aptitude for war'. Hollweg, the German Chancellor, had offered to open peace negotiations with the Allies.

carbolic that was rather too strong. However I'm much better today in fact very much better, but this country is dampness itself, with beastly cold foggy days one after the other & it's not much weather for getting better.

The plums & raisins have arrived alright & are much appreciated. The little diaries are fine dearie & just what I wanted, thanks. Wasn't Mrs Lloyd George's letter amusingly put? Hardly the parliamentary language one expects from the Prime Minister's wife, & hardly the personality whom the ordinary man in the street would go very far out of one's way to specially please.

My love to you old darling.

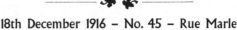

18th December 1916 – No. 45 – Rue Marle

I have been sending Xmas cards to all my friends today so I thought that before going to bed old dear, I would write you a line too. I wish I could be there to provide the rails for old Bobbo's engine & play with it with him, but perhaps I may be back in time to have some days with him before he goes back to school.

Darling mine, I should so love to be back with you all & have everything as it used to be just for a bit, but it's no good wishing tho' I must say things look to me as tho' the Boche is breaking up. There are all sorts of wild rumours going round tonight that the French have brought their prisoners up to 14,000 & that we have made another advance on the Somme. Also that the Hun has proposed a 28 day armistice to discuss peace terms. Of course any question of the latter is too ridiculous & if he thinks we are idiots enough to do that I hope he is wrong. I think that this question of peace is the greatest sign of approaching failure that he has shown yet & I think that the hope that we may see a termination this next year is very bright. I'm very optimistic tonight, I suppose it's because I have got a fairly comfortable bedstead & a fire in my room.

Thank goodness I don't go back to the trenches for another fortnight, I don't think, so I ought to be well shut of my cold by then.

Give my love to the dear little Chugs & I hope you will all have a 'nice time'.

20th December 1916 – No. 46 answering 51 & 52 – Rue Marle

I'm glad to say that I am very much better old dear & very nearly myself again. I've got a damned Review Parade in a day or two which means standing for hours in the cold, which I don't fancy very much I can tell you.

The sun is actually shining now, isn't it wonderful!

My love & blessings to you all.

21st December 1916 – No. 47 answering 53 & 54 – Rue Marle

I am afraid my beastly cold isn't gone yet & I'm feeling pretty rotten tonight which is a bore. However perhaps it will improve in a day or two. We are all frightfully bucked over old Lloyd George's speech, it's a really fine effort & will make the Hun think a bit. We have him beat I believe now, tho' it will be some months yet. I talked to the Brigadier about my leave today & I think all will be well.

Will you send me the mouth organs as per enclosed. Last night we had a concert & one of my men played a mouth organ. It was a very cheap one we raised here and he was simply wonderful. I never heard anything like it in my life. My runner sang too. The finest bass voice you ever listened to. Absolutely untaught with the most immense power – simply ripping. There's a gold mine in it if he was trained, you would have loved it.

22nd December 1916 – No. 48 answering 55 – Rue Marle

I went to bed last night feeling an awful worm & not at all pleased with the idea of having to take my Battalion some miles[203] today to be reviewed by my late brother officer, in the most beastly cold wind. I liked it even less when the day was simply pouring with rain as it was today & I got all my knees wet en route.

---

[203] The parade was taken by Douglas Haig, at Erquinghem.

However, the rain stopped soon after we got to the place of parade & it cheered up & the sun shone & was quite nice. D.H. recognized me alright & I rode along with him while he passed my Battalion & he was most complimentary & very pleased with their turnout.

Dearie mine I very much doubt if I get home for some time now. Today they have put all C.O.s & staff officers on the ordinary leave roster, & not supernumerary to it as they used to be. The consequence is that I come a long way down the list now & I fear the 17th is dead off. I'm awfully sorry as I had so looked forward to getting home again & seeing old Bobbo. I don't know that it is hopeless, but if it's to count as one of the Battalion allotment, then I must take my turn with the rest.

Darling mine there's a prayer in the little book I should like you to teach the kids. It's one that starts about 'the sentry on watch this night, those who command that they etc.' There are a couple of lines in the middle that you might eliminate.

In Time ✝ of War

"The LORD shall give strength unto His people : the LORD shall give His people the blessing of peace."

℣. Give peace in our time, O LORD.

℞. Because there is none other that fighteth for us, but only Thou, O GOD.

O GOD,
the strength of all them
that put their trust in Thee,
Whose power
no creature is able to resist ;
we flee to Thee
for succour on behalf of those
who are now struggling in the war.
Prosper our armies,
protect those who are in danger,
give help to the wounded,
recovery to the sick,
rest and refreshment to the dead,
comfort to the mourners,
and in Thine own good time
restore unto Thy people
the blessings of peace.
Grant this, O FATHER,
for JESUS CHRIST'S sake our LORD.
Amen.

AT EVENING

"What meanest thou, O sleeper? Arise, and call upon thy GOD."

℣. Therefore will the LORD wait that He may be gracious unto you.

℞. He will be very gracious unto thee at the voice of thy cry.

O GOD, Who never sleepest, and art never weary ; have mercy upon those who watch to-night : on the sentry, that he may be alert ; on those who command, that they may be strengthened with counsel ; on the sick, that they may obtain sleep ; on the wounded, that they may find ease ; on the faint-hearted, that they may hope again ; on the light-hearted, lest they forget Thee ; on the dying, that they may find peace ; on the dead, that they may have rest ; on the sinful, that they may turn again ; for JESUS CHRIST'S sake. Amen.

From *The Dial of Prayer*, Longmans.

I would love to think that the kids were saying it, or had said it when I go round the front lines at midnight & it appeals to me awfully as I see so much of the sentry & know what he has to go through, with no protection against the weather bar what he can put on his body. He wants all the help one can give him. Well my love, good night.

24th December 1916 – No. 49 – Fort Rompu

There's a special dispensation leave going now of a fortnight for all C.O.s who specially require it & who have been in the country 2 years & as I'm nearly that, I think there is a very good chance that something can be done but don't set too much store by it.

Tonight we are all going to have our Xmas dinner in the town & tomorrow we spend most of the day with the men. I've managed to get hold of a big room where I can get the whole Battalion in & we have got two nice pigs killed & hope to give them a fairly decent dinner & tea & concert. I've been having a very quiet time lately & am now back in reserve for a bit.

26th December 1916 – No. 50 answering 59 – Fort Rompu

We had quite a nice Christmas dinner on Christmas Eve for the officers & we all went into the town to a little place where a certain lady of the name of 'Lucienne' provides for hungry officers. It's wonderful how these women carry on, it was only a short time ago when every window in her house was smashed by a shell; since I came to these parts.

The table was very nicely decorated & by the menu card you will see that we didn't do so badly in the food line & when you consider that it is exactly 4700 yards from the Boche front line & easily within field gun range it is marvellous. We had a most cheery evening & I thoroughly enjoyed it. We all had to sing or do something so I read them your poem 'If'.[204] The only crab was a 4-mile walk home at 1 a.m.!! We were very lucky to be out of the front line for Xmas.

[204] By Kipling.

Christmas Day, I started by going to early service at 7.30 a.m. Then I took the Battalion to Church at 10.30. We had got a big room where we could get about——men in at a time and by having two sittings we got the whole Battalion in for their dinner. Then we gave them tea there and a concert to follow & finished the day at 8 p.m. thoroughly worn out as we all waited at the two dinners.

I must stop now old dear. The pudding & galantine & a parcel from Bassingtons has just arrived. Very many thanks.

My love to you all my darlings.

30th December 1916 – No. 53 answering 60 & 61 – trenches, Bois Grenier Sector

The worst has occurred. An edict has gone forth tonight that no one is to go on leave until he has done twelve months in the country or since last leave. That rather busts our little holiday doesn't it, but you must cheer up old dear, it may be rescinded before long & I have great doubts whether the blooming old war will last half the time.

It was rather odd you sending the cutting about the virus because tonight we got a brochure on the subject of setting about the rats. The virus, however, is not to be used as I fancy they are not absolutely certain about its action. You see we are living under conditions that folk don't know much about really & there are so many odd complaints that have arisen that they don't want everyone suffering from Liverpool Virus as well & until it was discovered exactly how it got on with present conditions. I must say I shouldn't care to risk it.

I've just lit the stove in my bedroom & as it is about ten times too big for the room I'm nearly roasting! They are instituting a leave for tired C.O.s who have been two years in the country so I may get tired shortly! The Brigadier tells me today that Temple goes on leave at once. My poor Adjutant should have gone yesterday only got a note to say he was to prosecute on a General Court Martial on the 3rd & the edict arrived tonight.

The heat has reached such a pitch now that one of my candles has had a serious relapse & fallen on the floor.

As you will have gathered old dear, we were at Church together Xmas morning alright. I should so have loved to have seen the Chugs' Xmas Tree. The old stick[205] is very well known. Heaps of fellows say to me 'I saw the stick coming & I knew it couldn't be anyone but you!'

Both last night & this morning it rained like Hades & I shall be jolly glad when the spring weather comes, but I believe the wet is preferable to frost. It doesn't knock the men about so much.

1st January 1917 – trenches, Bois Grenier Sector

I've got several nice letters from you these last few days old dear, but am feeling too seedy to answer them now. Perhaps I'm going to have three weeks leave to try & pull round. There's nothing radically wrong with me dearie, but I just can't get well again. Temperature about 96 & doesn't seem to go up. My love to you old dear & will write you a better letter as soon as I can.

3rd January 1917, 2.30 p.m. – trenches, Bois Grenier Sector

First & foremost I'm coming home in a day or two for three weeks. I'm rather knocked out just at present so I hope you will have plenty of beef tea etc. Just to put me on my legs once more. You needn't worry old dear as I'm quite alright really & only want a bit of nursing.

My love to you old dear.

4th January 1917 – 2nd letter – No. 55 answering 62–67 – Bois Grenier Field Hospital

I feel an awful beast old dear, that I have written you so seldom lately & with the mails being as uncertain as they have been, it makes news seem further off than ever for you. I'm just beginning to sit up & take nourishment & most thoroughly enjoyed a poached egg I had for tea. Buckin just

---

[205] His wife had given him a thumbstick.

asked me what I would have for dinner & I said 'a really nice fried sole'. He said he was very sorry he couldn't do that but if I had spoken a little sooner he could have managed a kipper!!

My darling if you could only see my hospital! It would make your hair curl. The Temperance Hotel was the very essence of hygiene compared to it. When I got back from the hospital yesterday the mattress looked so filthy that I couldn't lie down on it even with my fur coat on until Buckin had got some of our own damp-resisting, smell-obscuring, G/S [General Service] blankets on it!! Yesterday things were so very miserable here that I decided to go into the Officers' Rest House but to my horror after driving some way I found myself landed at a C.C.S.[206] which wasn't at all what I was after, so I flatly declined to leave the Ambulance & after taking a dish of soup off the C.C.S. told them they could just take me back where they found me so I came back & crept into bed again.

I'm awfully glad the Chugs enjoyed their Xmas. I wish I could have been there – it's a rotten life, this. Well old dear, so long. I wonder if this or I will get home first.

6th January 1917 – No. 56 – Officers' Rest House, La Motte

I have now come to the officers' rest house as I wasn't fit enough to go back to the trenches. This is a lovely place & is run rather as an officers' residential hotel & Club, only everything is free!! I had the swell room of the château last night & was most comfy indeed. I don't feel like writing somehow, when one expects a car to come & fetch one off any day or hour.

Undated, postmarked 9th January 1917 – lettercard – Officers' Rest House, La Motte

My darling,
I should arrive Victoria about same time as before on Tuesday next.
Robert (Sunday)

[206] Casualty Clearing Station.

On 9 January, Robert went on home leave to Cowfold, to recover from his illness, with Buxton in attendance on the journey. Meanwhile Major Wallace took temporary command of 24th Battalion. Robert and Ethel spent their final few nights together at the Berkeley Hotel, before he returned to duty on 6 February.

CHAPTER FOURTEEN

PREPARING FOR THE SPRING OFFENSIVE, 1917

During February 1917 the fortunes of war continued to fluctuate between the Allies and the Central Powers. Allied morale was bolstered by the arrival, on the 3rd, of the Portuguese Expeditionary Force in France, comprising 50,000 men. The following day the Kaiser ordered the withdrawal of his troops on the Western Front to the recently fortified trenches of the Hindenburg Line, reducing the length of the German front line by twenty-five miles. Several of their divisions were now released into reserve, and as the troops retreated, everything between the lines which could afford cover to attacking troops was destroyed.

On 4 February, President Woodrow Wilson broke off diplomatic relations with Germany after the interception of an encoded telegram from the German Foreign Minister, Zimmerman, to their Minister in Mexico, offering to unite with Mexico and Japan against the United States. As U-boat attacks on American shipping continued, it seemed increasingly likely that the USA would enter the war.

On the Western Front preparations were being made for the spring offensive. After returning from home leave Robert resumed command of the 24th Battalion at Tatinghem: 103 Brigade was now on the move eastwards towards Arras, training for the impending attack.

6th February 1917 – Series III – No. 1 – en route for Tatinghem (near St Omer)

My own darling,

Well done my dear brave lassie, your last cheering smile was everything in the world to me as was your nice cheery note. It has been the most lovely day, simply glorious tho' most bitterly cold & the snow is pretty thick over here & it's freezing hard now.

The car wasn't here & so I have to wait for the train which leaves just after midnight. I was a bit cold last night but not half what I am going to be tonight & I shall miss the cup of Ovaltine, or should be very glad of it in the train.

I was rather amused this morning as the train didn't leave in the end till 7.20 & there was a captain in R.A.M.C. talking most awful rot to a friend & was rather annoying me. When the train started he took off his coat & had a V.C. & a Military Cross!! Can't always tell by appearances & oddly enough reading *The Times* a few minutes later I saw the account of his investiture.

Darling mine I'm sitting in the Club & there are such dozens swarming about that I can't write decently or as I should like to but the quicker that fourth honeymoon comes along the better.

My love, my whole love, & nothing but my love to you my own dear, dear, love.

Ever your Robert.

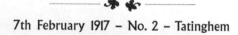

7th February 1917 – No. 2 – Tatinghem

The day has been glorious sunshine & on the sunny side of a building was like summer except for the snow, of which there is quite a lot. I've got quite a lot of new young officers since I left and everything seems to be going top-hole. We've got a very nice house for H.Qrs tho' it's a bit cold as like all these small French Châteaux it's only one room thick with windows on both sides.

The enclosed little brooch is for Mairky as I subscribed to a soldiers' charity some time ago & if you gave a certain sum they sent you a gold brooch as a memento & as old Bet got the grenade I thought it was Mairky's turn for a 'pres'. I'm sorry I had no 'pres' for you dearie but I didn't quite know what to give you.

Lass dear, we had a ripping time, hadn't we & I don't think I ever missed you quite so much as I did last night, sitting in the club, packed with folk I didn't know, & was feeling very sad but now I'm back I am as right as rain & quite happy once more.

It was a topping time old dear & I loved our last days together but they went so terribly quick. I don't know that I've any more news for you old dear, & each time I come back I feel it harder to write – it all seems so thin & poor & yet one simply lives for one's letters.

Give my best love to the dear little Chugs & my all to you, my own darling.

8th February 1917 – No. 3 answering 1 – Tatinghem

I got your first instalment today & was very pleased to get it too. The whole Battalion practically is down with inoculation so I have had a quiet day. I am going to have another of old Juckes' doses as soon as I have finished this letter.

Today has been again glorious and the roads are in fine condition for sleighing & I wish I had the White House sleigh here now as with a couple of mules in it we could have rare good fun. Your old horse looks very well & Harry & Saxon are both looking top-hole.

I got a nice letter from old Bet too today. I am glad to hear that the doggies are out once more. Give old Spoot a kiss from me as I shirked saying goodbye to her, somehow it was the only one I felt I couldn't just manage. I know it was very silly but I couldn't, with the goodbyes to the Chugs coming on top of it & I didn't feel I should be quite sure of myself when the time came. I don't know why, but somehow the fact she didn't quite understand sort of tickled one up & it was much harder saying it to Ken than any of the others. However it's all over now & let us hope that we shall not have to do it again.

10th February 1917 – No. 5 answering 2 & 3 – Tatinghem

I see by the paper today that you are not going to be allowed to drive the car so you will have to drive the new pony in the cart. It's a pity we bought it now tho' I do not really regret it, but I never thought that you would get cut down so very soon. I see too that they now object to our car standing outside the Savoy?!! However the more drastic things are the sooner the show will be over.

I have simply loved your two letters old dear – they were ripping. I laughed like anything over the canary hunt because I was sure they were bound to get out. I'm so afraid that even when they clean the hut[207] they will, but perhaps it won't want much cleaning. I should just put more sand in!

I am sorry to hear you have got to cut down your rations so much but there it is & it's no good worrying & if it helps to win the war it's everything.

My love to you old dear.

11th February 1917 – No. 6 – 2nd Army School, near St Omer

Well I've gone back to school again and am in about the coldest shop you ever were in in your life. My bedroom is a little wooden hut and the mess and sitting room is an old Monastery. The dining hall is a magnificent hall but it is about 150 feet long and certainly 80 to 100 feet high, all stone. Cold beyond words but it's thawing very slowly so it isn't as bad as it might be but it's pretty bad nevertheless.

A cake & marmalade rolled up today and also prayer books and undies etc. Many thanks. It's so cold old dear I'm going to bed as I can't write in the cold. My Spanish blood isn't warm enough to write you a really nice letter, but I could do with my last Berkeley pillow well tonight.

13th February 1917 – No. 8 – 2nd Army School, near St Omer

To my great delight the thaw seems to be firmly established now & since about midday it has been really very nice up above tho' the conditions underfoot are really beastly. We have had a poor day again today & I am afraid unless things brighten up a bit more the course won't have done one very much good. I had hoped that I should have picked up a good deal from the other members of the class in conversation but they don't seem to be overflowing with ideas.

[207] During leave he had built an aviary for the children's canaries.

One's movements etc. are taboo, as with most other bits, so it is very difficult to say much. I hear today that Temple has been given a 'Croix de Guerre' & that Richardson has got a Légion d'honneur & I am so glad, tho' I suppose it will stop Temple from getting anything in the next honours list which is perhaps rather bad luck.

The thaw hasn't lasted very long as it is freezing like anything now & I am shying off getting into my pyjamas but I shall be Spartan, I think. I asked the Brigade to let me chuck the course & go back to the Battalion tomorrow but I don't know if they will let me. I think as a matter of fact these next few days will be far the most interesting.

I'm far too cold to be in a writing mood as the servants have let the stove in the passage go out. Anyhow I'm very lucky really not to be in the line.

My love to you all my darlings. I must hurry to bed as there is a very nasty draught blowing over my ankles!!

14th February 1917 – No. 9 answering 6 – Tatinghem

I have returned from my class I am glad to say. I pointed out to the powers that be how very stupid it was to send me there just now and so got off it.

I got your old 'pessim' today and I am sorry for you old dear that you are so very short of grub. I can't help thinking that the submarine campaign has been a failure as they will have to get a lot more ships than they have if they are to gain anything out of it. I know it is very serious but it will have to be very much more drastic if it is to accomplish its object. You must cheer up old dear, things will have to be very much worse before we pull too long a face.

I very nearly sent you such a nice 'pres' the other day, a really nice 'Nitie'. Pink in colour and French!! I saw it in a shop and I am sure it would have suited you well. The Chugs wrote me three such nice letters & so awfully well written and expressed. Their writing is really very good & Mairky writes almost as well as Bet which I think is awfully good.

My 'bête noire' while I was away went & refused to obey an order and so has got to be tried by C.M. It is really a damned nuisance and gives one a lot of trouble. I am sorry for the fellow but really he is an awful nuisance in the Battalion & I wish he would go. However life is full of little worries and this is really only a little one these times. I enclose you two small presents.

16th February 1917 – No. 10 answering 7 – Tatinghem

The weather is so jolly now that I am certainly picking up well & feel quite fit tho' I can't say that I am absolutely free from cold altogether.

I am glad that old Mairky liked her little brooch. You will never get those pearls old dear, you're not made that way!!! Poor little Ken it was nice of him to be looking for me. I must be off now to see the army old dear, as it is footling about in a field.

My love to you all.

Saturday 17th February 1917 – 10 a.m. – No. 11 – Tatinghem

I have been having a drastic overhaul of my kit & am sending you a lot of stuff back (5 parcels) as I have far too much & even by doing this I have not in the least inconvenienced myself.

Yesterday we had quite an amusing afternoon putting the Battalion through gas. The Div. Gas officer arrived with all his boxes of tricks and it was really very amusing.

It is nearly a fortnight now old dear since our ever memorable time at the Berkeley & in bed last night old dear I could see your dear old face smiling so bravely as we parted just as if you had been there yourself. I shall not forget those last minutes old dear & the splendid send-off you gave me. I've got many memories still & it is a huge help when one looks back to the times we've had.

My love to you my darling & the Chugs too.

The 34th Division, of which 24th Battalion, 103 Brigade, was part, had now been transferred from the Second to the Third Army and had begun their march towards Arras via Wardrecques, Thienne, Valhoun, Chelers and Béthonsart where they carried out further training until moving up to Ecoivres on 1 and 2 March.

21st February 1917 – No. 15 – on pages from a notebook – Valhoun

Tonight I am in my old billet at the vicarage where I was last June. It really was rather like coming home again. Everyone in the village recognized me & were so genuinely pleased to see one. I was most awfully bucked too by the way they spoke of the old regiment. They simply loved it & the men & said they were the best men they had ever had & I was so pleased. I really had a splendid welcome. The Padre is putting me & my Adjutant up & we are messing here too which is very good of them.

We have invested 15 francs in two chickens which are about to appear. Rather expensive but as we've had nothing but beef at every meal since I came back it is well worth it. I hope, old dear, that you & the poor Chugs aren't starving under the new food rules? You must tell me some more about it. I daresay when you have got the thing figured out it won't be so bad. I haven't seen an English paper for nearly a week now & so we are all anxious to get one if we can.

My love to you my darling & I hope you are now nearly fit again.

23rd February 1917 – No. 16 answering 12 – Chelers

I got your No. 12 last night & was very glad to see your old fist again, tho' 10 & 11 are still to arrive. I expect however they will arrive alright today.

I got three top-hole Chug letters too last night & was very struck with the neatness of old Bet's. She seems to be frightfully bucked at the canaries having made an effort to nest. I am sure that the nesting compartment should be covered with brown paper or else you will find that the hen won't sit. However I know they will want to look at the nest so often that that in itself will stop any possible success!!

Will you send me the English equivalent of my old chair as I miss it awfully & must have another. You can get them at Harrods or Wilkinsons. You might ring them up and tell them to send it direct. It's the Indian pattern – original made in Sappers & Miners workshops in Rorkee.

I wish we could see some of that 'Spring' of yours. We have had thick fog for days now, cold & chilly in the extreme. Poor old Spoot, it is rather a nuisance if she is going to bite folk, tho' it's rather nice the way she won't allow any interference with anyone who has to do with her. Thank all the Chugs for their letters.

My love to you my darling.

25th February 1917 – No. 18 answering 10 – Béthonsart

You needn't have worried about the photos as I never for a moment intended them for you nor did I look on them in that light when they came & I saw them. As you say there is nothing in a photo. No warmth, no love & they can never, never convey anything like the impression one carries in one's heart. That is why I have never bothered about one of yours. It would give me little pleasure to look at as it would never represent truly what I value, so we are quite quits on that point.

Old Wallace[208] was riding out on a horse to do a job for me the day before yesterday & the old beast stumbled & fell with him & has, I am afraid, bust a small bone in his foot. It's an awful bore as I can ill spare him now. However it may not be as bad as one thinks & I am going to see him this afternoon & hope to find him better than I expect. I am just off to the kirk such as it is, I expect a very draughty barn.

My transport officer too has now developed a temp of 103 so he's got to go into hospital too which is another beastly bore. However I have old Heath & also another K.E.H. boy one Donnelly who knows a bit about horses so I am really luckier than most folk.

My love to you my darling & to the little Chugs too.

---

[208] His second-in-command.

25th February 1917 – No. 19 answering 13, 14, 15 & 16 – Béthonsart

My dear old thing I never really took your 'pessim' seriously, tho' I am cheered to think you are not exactly starving. The men have not had their ration reduced since the introduction of the food laws & tomorrow if I can remember, I will tell you exactly what they get a day. They get a magnificent ration & have no cause to grumble at all. Occasionally there is a slight shortage of potatoes but it is nearly always made up in a day or two afterwards. Parcels of food are always acceptable because they make a little change but they are not necessary at all.

I was very pleased with the photo of you on the old horse, I like that one very much. I'll pay you the compliment of saying that it looks as if it wasn't the first time you had been for a ride!!![209] I'm awfully pleased that you are really feeling better old dear, as it is wretched being seedy these times. I enclose old Bobbo's letter.

All my love dearie mine.

28th February 1917 – No. 21 answering 17 & 18 – Béthonsart

I wonder if you remember the name of the place where the big towers were and where I was when I left the Old Corps. Well I am now some 8 miles due south of that place.

I am so glad to hear that Pa is so much better. Will you ring him up & thank him for his letters and cigars & tell him I will write as soon as I can but I am fearfully busy just now. Wasn't it luck your keeping fit until after the honeymoon! It would have been too hard if you had been seedy then, especially if you had had to go to bed at the Berkeley.

Give my love to the Chugs & thank them for their nice letters. I am glad to hear that the 60 hens are laying better now.

My love to you old dear, it's fine getting Kut[210] back, & it will be very interesting to see what this German withdrawal[211] means.

[209] His wife rode side-saddle.
[210] Kut, in Mesopotamia (Iraq), was recaptured by General Maude in February 1917.
[211] The German withdrawal to the Hindenburg Line.

2nd March 1917 – Ecoivres (X Hutments)

I wish too, dearie, that I could tell you more of what I am doing but of course it is impossible. I am some eight or nine miles further east than I was, with a shade of south in it. I know it must be rather beastly not knowing one's doings but of course it is quite out of the question to tell you, I am afraid.

We are still all very interested in the Hun retirement & how far he has decided to go and over how great a front. I suppose we shall know soon.

Do tell me who it was who made the flattering remark on your appearance at 'Houpla'? I have paid for our man Scholey and I have also subscribed to the Eton Memorial £100 in year instalments of £10. In case of need it might help old Bobbo or even his boy!

Well darling mine au revoir.

4th March 1917 – Ecoivres

Far from being disappointed I got a clinking good letter from you & also the photos with which I am delighted & congratulate you on the top-hole job you have made of them. Exactly what I wanted.

The Padre asked me to bring you to see him après la guerre. Our weather isn't good yet tho' we have had no rain for some time, but thick fogs & still bitter cold. There was no church today so this evening I went to our Padre's service. He calls himself 'united Board'. It merely means that he combines Non Com, Methodist, Primitive Methodist & Wesleyan all in one!! Service very simple. The only prayer we had was the Lord's prayer & he had one long sort of conversational prayer – seemed to me just what came to his mind to meet the actual circumstances. Several hymns and a sermon. It was really rather nice & after all one was only out for one object, & it was all so odd in a big hut, with some men in bed & others sitting about & then those who were joining in the service. Bits of old candle stuck in fellows' equipment & in jam tins on the floor. I don't know about Methodist but it certainly was primitive!!

Will you thank Mimi & Nell for their letters. The mac turned up alright thanks. I am awfully glad to hear old Bobbo talking about his football as he seems so thoroughly keen about it and sounds as tho' he is coming on well.

It's rather amusing but now I have been confirmed in my rank I believe I rank senior to old Temple. Anyhow he tells me so. He lives only a few huts off & I have seen a lot of him the last few days and we went for a walk together this afternoon.

Well darling I must to bed. My very best thanks for your topping letter old dear & the photos.

Ever your Robert.

CHAPTER FIFTEEN

ARRAS

With the advent of spring, the joint offensive planned by the French general Nivelle, and agreed by Field Marshal Sir Douglas Haig, was about to begin. German defences were to be attacked in three places, with British and Canadian forces concentrating in the Arras area and the French further south near the River Aisne, with the aim of pushing the Germans further east so that the Allied armies could link up in a pincer movement. Unfortunately this had been made more difficult now that the Germans had retreated to the heavily fortified Hindenburg Line.

Expectations that the United States would come to the assistance of the Allies were finally realized when President Wilson declared war on Germany on 6 April 1917. In Russia, however, the rumblings of the revolution which would erupt in October were already creating political turmoil.

On 7 March, the 24th Battalion left Ecoivres for the town of Arras, around which the forthcoming assault was to take place. While Robert was careful not to overtly mention the build-up to the assault, his wife would have realized from those letters she received – mostly written in pencil on pages torn from a military notebook – that a major offensive was about to begin. The following day, the 24th Battalion relieved the 20th Battalion in the front-line trenches. From hereon the pattern of life for the battalion would be days in the trenches punctuated by rest periods in the town of Arras, itself under constant bombardment.

8th March 1917 – No. 28 answering 25 – Arras

My darling,

Your letter about the lovely weather is most encouraging but as I happen to be sitting in a house without any glass in the windows & as it is snowing hard, I fail to see it!! I am in the big town close handy to where I was. I didn't get a letter yesterday so hope for two tonight, with luck.

I can't say that snow is much fun under these conditions & I wish to goodness it would go. The sun keeps peeping through every now & then so perhaps it's going to cheer up. I rode down here yesterday in the most biting cold wind I ever remember. It blew clean through one.

My darling old girl, you are not getting the least prosy & I love you 'rambling on' as you say. The length is one of the nicest parts of your letters & I wish I could write you more. Give my love to Ken & thank him for his interest in Father.

Ever your Robert.

9th March 1917 – No. 29 – front-line trenches, Arras

Dans le premier ligne once more. Life rather strenuous.

I think you did perfectly right about old Bobbo, dearie, & I certainly should have done the same so you need not worry. With all the boys down [with measles] the chief thing of school, i.e. the mixing in the crowd, is gone. If Stanford[212] wished it, it was the least you could do.

Dearie mine, I've been worked to death the last 30 hours & must stop. I'm very fit. Weather damnable, snow falling all day in showers.

Love to you all.

11th March 1917 – No. 30 answering 28 & 29 – front-line trenches, Arras

I'm very weary old dear & so you must excuse a somewhat short letter tonight. I've had an awful lot to do lately & life is pretty strenuous. I've had two very nice letters from you & the photos too tonight. Meggie is very good but riding a hole or two too long. Pookie's position in the one by herself is ideal & good enough to print in the Cavalry drill book!! I never saw a kid sitting like it. If I had posed her I couldn't have put her

---

[212] Stanford, headmaster of St Aubyn's prep school.

in a better position. Make old Bet keep her heels down a bit more. Do you know, I couldn't for the life of me think who it was standing by little Meg till I see the one of you with them all!!!

Darling mine I can't write you any more I'm too tired & must be up at 4 a.m. I'm rather in the dumps tonight as I've lost a few men these last few days & my friend Duncan the Padre was killed today. He was actually conducting a service at the time & a shell came in & killed him.[213]

My love to you my darling.

12th March 1917 – No. 31 – front-line trenches, Arras

This is a pretty lively spot as both sides do a good deal of shooting at one another. However it's all part of the game. I've got quite a good dugout here but the fire smokes something awful & you can't see across the room.

This snow & frost & now the rain makes the mud pretty bad I can tell you. I never saw the mud much worse than it is now. Richardson came in & had lunch with me today. Poor old Temple had a very hot day yesterday but he is alright himself tho' I fear a bit shaken up & I don't wonder as the same shell that killed Duncan killed two of his officers too.[214]

The Huns brought down three of our aeroplanes yesterday. Just got a wire I must go & see to.

15th March 1917 – No. 32 answering Nos. 30, 31 & 32 – Arras

Out again once more after a very bad tour so far as weather conditions were concerned. We went in, in a hard frost & the trenches were like a pavement. Then we had snow & rain with the result that the last four days

---

[213] Captain the Rev. E. F. Duncan MC had gone to the assistance of some men wounded by shelling whilst taking a service in Arras near 27th Battalion HQ, but was killed as he ran across open ground.

[214] The War Diary records briefly: '8th–14th March, *Trenches*. Shelling normal on both sides. We had 18 casualties, 6 O.R. Killed, 12 O.R. Wounded.'

of our tour were really terrible. The mud was in evidence to a degree that I have never seen before, men literally up to their knees in it. One morning I got absolutely stuck going round the line & looked round to see my runner stuck too about 10 yards behind. There we were, quite immovable. After a most frantic struggle I managed to get on to the parapet & got to my runner & took his rifle, then got him out.

That will give you some idea of what one means by mud in the trenches. However, we got out alright & I was well cheered up on getting in by finding three lovely letters from you. With regard to the scale of rations – what I sent you is for infantry in the front line. Folk further back have a trifle less but very little. As for picking up crumbs from the French – well no Frenchman wastes anything & there are no crusts to pick up!!

At this point Jackie dropped in to see me. He tells me Algy went home 'returned empty'. He's got a bit too old for the job. My poor horses are now standing up to their necks in mud & he is going to have them in his stable I think. Anyhow, I hope so. There's not much more to tell you now, old dear. I'm very well.

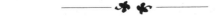

16th March 1917 – No. 33 answering 33 – Arras

I am in no mood for writing dearie as I'm beastly cold & the damned guns make such a beastly noise, & one has one ear sort of listening for 'arrivals' all the time, which as we have no cellar is most unpleasant. No windows in the house & a shortage of coal today doesn't help much. Poor old Peter, I'm sorry he's dead, but he was a real tiger. I wish I had the same courage as he had.

I had two nice letters from the Chugs today for which please thank them.

17th March 1917 – No. 34 – answering 34 & 35 – Arras

The Huns are hardly ten miles from Bapaume yet, tho' I hear that they have set it on fire today which looks as if they wouldn't be long before they were a decent way back. I saw little Rory Dickens had been hit & I hope he isn't bad.

I think our bit of line is quite good & I like the trenches better than breastworks, but of course it is a bit more strenuous. The great objection to trenches is that they are most difficult to drain & consequently one gets a lot of mud & water at the bottom of them in wet weather. They are however, in my opinion, far safer than breastworks. One can make a good dugout under these conditions which of course was quite impossible without cement & a very great deal of labour further north.

There's been some wonderful air fights here today. There is a Hun who flies a bright scarlet machine & it is real hot stuff. He seems to be a sort of star flyer & does most of the fighting. He is a real gallant fellow & we all admire him.[215]

They have got some of the fastest planes you ever saw here – go two feet to our one & their tactics are wonderful. Four or five of them fly about together at an immense height & when they see one of our planes that they know they can catch, they simply nosedive right down on it & then a real battle begins, sometimes ours falls, sometimes theirs.

Thank old Bobbo for his very nice letter. Wallace is in England & has a bone broken in his foot.

Sunday 18th March 1917 – No. 35 – Arras

It's a rare noisy place this. Old Temple had a house in one part of the town where we should have relieved him but last Sunday they had a shell through

---

[215] The 'gallant fellow' was Baron Manfred von Richthofen, the 'Red Baron', credited with shooting down eighty Allied planes. When finally shot down himself in April 1918, he was accorded a full military funeral by the British out of respect for his gallantry.

both houses on either side of them, so they thought it wiser to find a new home & I am glad they did as I hear the house has since been demolished!

I want both fields on either side of the drive offered to any farmer who cares to plough them up rent *free*. Will you please let Grantham or Jones know or Arthur[216] can have them if he will plough them. I don't want them broken up & then not cultivated but I do want anyone to have them who will make a genuine effort to raise a crop.

The old Boche seems to be on the homeward journey alright down on the Somme & tonight we hear we have Bapaume. Last night we could see it burning, the whole sky being lit up. Things grow most absorbingly interesting you know. Whether the old Boche will do us in over the ships or whether we shall have him beat first, it's a regular race at present. Anyhow I really believe that one side or another will have to chuck it before long. I don't believe it will go another winter tho' it's only my poor little opinion.

I heard that the Hun had got a hospital ship, but I'm glad they did so well & saved everyone. We went for a walk tonight but there's so much gunning these times it's not much pleasure. Both sides seem to be influenced by the spring & are getting quite active.

My love to you my darlings.

20th March 1917 – No. 36 answering 38 – Ecoivres

Back once more in our little wooden hut & jolly glad to be back as our town dwelling wasn't as healthy as it might have been. Shells are beastly enough in the country but I hate them among the houses & just before we left & during tea we had one good one about four doors off & I think we were all glad to say goodbye to the place for a bit.

It was the most awful evening you ever saw, blowing half a gale or more with torrents of rain & we all arrived soaked. Thank goodness my Q.M. had a good fire so we undressed & sat round it waiting for the transport to turn up with our kits.

Today is still blowing hard but the sun shines very brightly between the showers which are snow & sleet. I suppose one of these days we shall have some fine weather but it's high time it came along.

[216] Hodgson.

We are not doing quite the same tours in & out as we were when I came on leave last & you will have to sort it out from the scraps you can glean from my letters. It's splendid getting Bapaume & Péronne & the old Hun is going back between Arras & Bapaume I hear. I expect he doesn't mean to stop till he has reached the Hindenburg Line which runs from Arras to St Quentin in a fairly straight line. It's all most awfully interesting now, trying to picture in one's mind what the old blighter is about. Read through German eyes p. 7 *The Times* of 19th very good. There seems nothing more to tell you dearie mine.

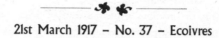

21st March 1917 – No. 37 – Ecoivres

Spring commences, so I see in my diary, today. Result, biting wind & snow showers punctuated, however, by bright sun. I expected to move today but in the end I was left behind & so am still in my little hut. One end is the pantry, then a couple of blankets hung on a wire makes the dining room door & wall. At the other end we have six bunks, really quite comfortable & we are very happy & contented.

I haven't had time to go and see the horses since I came out & as it has been so wet & cold & they are standing up to their eyes in mud, I have put it off till they are likely to look a bit better!

The old Hun still retreats south of Arras but remains where he was to the north of the town. If he went back there it would mean his giving up Lens I expect, & I don't fancy he wants to do that as he probably gets a good bit of coal from there & thereabouts. He is an old beast as I hear he has gone so far as to hack down even the fruit trees in the gardens in Péronne & leave them lying on the ground. Pure wanton destruction. Didn't even want them for firewood.

The worst of it is that even if we got into Germany we should never do the same & he knows that well. I'll bet the civilians in Péronne were jolly glad to get shot of him. It will be rather interesting reading their accounts of the time of occupation.

Our huts are called 'Nissen' and are like this: they are made of tin & lined with matchboard & they put them up in a couple of hours, almost. They are about 30 ft long by 15 wide & really very cosy & warm.

My best love to you all.

3

their accounts of the time of ceahtahin
our huts are called "Nissen" & all
like this

They are made of tin & lined with matchboard
& they put them up in a couple of hours
almost — They are about 30 ft long by 15
wide & really very cosy & warm —
I've no more to tell you old
dear — my best love to you all

Ever your

Robert

22nd March 1917 – No. 38 – Ecoivres

Heavy snow all day in showers & now 6 p.m. it is falling fast. They are only frozen April showers but very unpleasant.

Yes, it was very bad luck about poor Duncan. There were three of them [who] all ran to help the sentry and Bibby who was close behind was blown right across the room. He is quite knocked out I am afraid & looks very bad. Only a few days before Duncan had given our Padre a little sort of prayer book & written in it:

> *Self is the only prison that ever can bind a soul.*
> *Love is the only angel that can bid the gates unroll:*
> *And when he comes & calls thee, arise & follow fast*
> *His way may lead through darkness, but it leads to light at last.*

They are all such nice lines that I thought you might like them. No, I was in the line when it happened or I should most probably have been there. I wouldn't allow any services the Sunday I was in the town, much to one Padre's annoyance tho' the others were in agreement. I wasn't going to risk my men. It's the height of folly to go & collect a huge lot of men together in a town that is constantly under shellfire. It's quite bad enough to have to live in it, let alone collect in bodies.

I should have your governess if I were you as I like her shoes & stockings!! Good boots are always a good sign!!!!

Give my love to the Chugs.

23rd March 1917 – No. 39 answering 39 & 41 – Ecoivres

We had a very heavy fall of snow last night but it's all gone now & has been a lovely day & I'm hoping that we shall have a bit of fine weather.

I seem to remember some very dusty Easters in the old cars. I wish I saw the prospect of another. I should love to take on old Arthur in his 'Henry' with our cheap American!! I fear those old days are gone for ever now & somehow one never seems to contemplate going a trip with old

Arthur any more. Let's hope our next trip will be one here to see the result of the war with the Chugs.

Of course, by now you know more about the German retirement than I do really, as you have had one more *Times* than I have. The Hindenburg line runs north from St Quentin to Bartouzelle where it turns westwards & runs by Marcoing, Inchy, Mercatel to the scarp at Arras.

According to the papers he is retiring there so that, if any preparations have been made by us for the much-talked-about spring offensive, we may have to start again & [take] them all over again some miles further on & in the meantime his submarines will sink all our ships. However the best-laid plans often go wrong & as he has been so very wrong often before, perhaps he will have miscalculated again. War is one of those delightful uncertainties that a very small thing may completely upset. It is all *most* awfully interesting & I hope I shall see the end. I often long for the time when one will be able to read the history of the early phases & know why he didn't do some of the many things that he ought to have done.

I got three delightful letters from the Chugs too, today. I wish I had more time to answer them. Thank dear little Mary for her nice message & her letter too. I am so pleased to hear she sat on her pony so well when it fell down!

Goodnight my darling.

24th March 1917 – No. ? answering 42 & 43 – Ecoivres

Things have been pretty lively in these parts lately but we have been fairly fortunate I am glad to say, & I only hope it will last. As you have gathered I haven't seen anything of this last beano as it is south of me mostly. Don't think, old girl. It's a bad habit & it's all in the lap of the Gods.

You are quite right this is a damnable game, the more you see of it the less you like it & some of the scenes with the civilian inhabitants of the towns & villages that the Boche has evacuated must be beastly. It was bad enough having the women & children in Loos but they hadn't been there so long as these have.

I am glad you are having the Governess as she seems to have many things one wants & I expect the rest will come if she has a nice inside, as you seem to think.

Our mud is awful after the snow & frost – carts up to their axles & one is over one's boot-tops when one steps out of one's hut & off the duckboards.

25th March 1917 – No. 41 – Ecoivres

It seems astonishing that I can only write '41' at the top of my letter. It seems years my love, since I saw your dear smiling old face as I left you. Darling mine, that smile has simply lived with me ever since. It's my last memory of you & whenever I think of you it's there to cheer one up. I'd give worlds to hold you in my arms once more my love, but I am afraid that there's a long, long trail to be trod before that happens again.

Tonight I went to church in one of the church Army Huts close here & we had such a nice little service, ending with a celebration[217] for which I stayed. All the time the service was going on the Hun was throwing some very heavy shells into the village about half a mile off & what with the church being lit up & it dark outside & the whistle & crash of the shells it made the whole thing very weird & also impressive & I'm afraid that my voice was not particularly strong as I sang the third verse of hymn 322.

> *And then for those, our dearest and our best,*
> *By this prevailing Presence we appeal;*
> *O fold them closer to Thy mercy's breast,*
> *O do Thine utmost for their souls' true weal;*
> *From tainting mischief keep them white and clear,*
> *And crown Thy gifts with strength to persevere.*

However, it was all very, very nice in spite of the surroundings being a bit odd & I was very glad of the opportunity. This afternoon Barber motored over to see me as a full-fledged staff officer, G.S.O.3 of a Corps. He looked awfully well & was very well turned out & quite a credit to the old corps.

I can't help thinking that they have lately been actively engaged in operations against the Hun as I understand that they are S. of Péronne

[217] Of communion.

somewhere. It will be rather an irony, after all, if they [K.E.H.] get in the first blow. Jimmy will have quite another crow over officers who desert their regiments.

I had two letters from you yesterday dearie & so I drew a blank today. However, I can't complain as I have got them most regularly & when you come to see figures like those in the papers today, 11,000,000 letters & 800,000 parcels a week, it's rather wonderful how they turn up at all, let alone punctual to the minute 19 days out of every 20. I got the nominal roll book from Gale & Polden today. Very many thanks. The other parcels too.

Well dearie mine I'm busy these days and must to bed now, especially as we started summer time last night & I lost an hour of sleep, not to mention the fact that the padre, who sleeps just under me, dreamt that he saw a man cutting the rope of one of the observation balloons & jumped up shouting at the top of his voice to stop him & nearly flung me out of bed in the process, & I felt rather as tho' a mine had gone off underneath.

27th March 1917 – No. 43 answering 45 & 46 & Chug letters – Ecoivres

I wrote you a very scrubby letter last night & I am afraid that this will be even scrubbier as I have little to tell you beyond the fact that the Hun woke us up by throwing a few shells into the camp just to let us know he was still there. However he did no harm to anyone so it didn't matter.

It's funny, old dear, how our letters have crossed again with almost exactly the same words in them. You are quite right, a dugout is by far the most preferable place.

I quite understand about the fields & felt all along that such was the case, but I wanted it known in the village they were there & could be used by anyone who would properly cultivate them. I should be quite willing to let any folk in the village have allotments in them, starting on the piece behind Miss Payne's if any cottage or village folk want a bit of ground to grow anything in. Mind, don't cut yourself with the hay knife. Look out when you have cut a truss that it doesn't slip & down you go with the knife, onto the floor.

My love to you all, old dear & to the Chugs & a thousand thanks for their dear letters.

29th March 1917 – No. 45 answering 47 & 48 – Ecoivres

I am glad to hear that Mary is still riding the new pony & likes it. Keep her at it as that pony will teach her far more than old Mary Ann. I read Buckin your letter & he was awfully pleased, especially with the flattering reference to his own flowers!!

I've had a very happy day today carpentering, building a framework over a water cart to carry some more water in petrol cans. It's very handy having it in cans like that. The pioneers did the work & I just chipped in with advice!! You know. Beyond my carpentering I have hardly done anything today except deal with a mass of correspondence & some urgent military matters. I am going over with some folk to see old Trevor tomorrow, who is about 9 miles off with Temple & Richardson and another.

The visit to Brigadier-General Trevor was to receive instructions for the forth-coming attack: Temple, Richardson and Colonel Hermon being the commanding officers of the Northumberland Fusilier battalions involved.

30th March 1917 – Ecoivres

We've just settled that the vote should be given to the women! Most heated argument but carried 'nem. con.'. Well I had my bus ride today & had quite a pleasant day. Saw Richardson & Temple & old Trevor lent me a horse. Met the Corps Commander and the Div. Commander. The former a most charming old gent. Perfect manners & most pleasant. The day was alternate bright sun & ice cold & very heavy showers, but tonight is fine with a newish moon & everything looks like a fine spell. I wish we were together for just one night as I could tell you so much more than one could write & lots that would interest you, but if speech is silver, silence is golden.

1st April 1917 – No. 48 answering 49 & 50 – billets, Arras[218]

I sent you an unnumbered letter of surpassing shortness last night which should have been No. 47. I got two lovely letters, old dear, this morning. Before I forget it, you remember that I promised old Buckin that his wife should be our special case should anything happen to him. Harry I haven't paid for a long time & I don't know what I owe him, but he could tell you alright.

We've got a lovely day today – coldish but still bright sun. I am just going to take up my residence at my town house. We are all rather sorry to leave our little hut as we have got to look on it as home. The Padre who replaced Duncan had one look & didn't like it. Felt his nerve wasn't strong enough & has had to be evacuated. Thank goodness they aren't all like that.

I think, old dear, that for the children's sake you must keep on with the bread & potatoes. If they want to reduce things they should put you on compulsory rations. So long as you are below the ration scale I should rest content, because I do not see why you should give up rations in order that those who won't accept the scale should have more. Stick to the ration scale & if you can keep below it, do so.

My love to you my darling, now and always.

2nd April 1917 – No. 49 answering 51 & 52 – Arras

Life is full of little worries, my house has no windows, it's damnably draughty, there's nearly two inches of slushy snow on the pavement outside & the dirty Boche put a shell through the house next door this morning & woke me up. However, we're bearing up & wonderfully bright & happy & your nice letters help & crown the lot of the soldier. I'm sorry to say one of my boys, young Wright by name, was killed today, but it is no good moralizing these times.

---

[218] The War Diary records that the 'enemy shelled Town', and on 1 April one officer and four other ranks were killed and ten wounded on a working party in the line.

There's little news for you old dear, as I hear or know little beyond what I read in the papers. I am so sorry about those beastly measles, it is bad luck & just as you thought you were clear.

I am very glad indeed that you offered Bram the car as it will be a little return for what he did for me. I know the old bus does eat petrol tho' I was perhaps a bit shy at confessing it before you when I was at home!!! I do like still getting the bits from the men. I would far rather have the regard coming from below than above, as the former always knows best.

My love to you old dear.

3rd April 1917 – No. 50 – answering 53 – billets, Arras

A lovely bright day today but bitterly cold and the snow still deep in the back yard where the sun hasn't touched it. Old Begbie has just been in to see me looking splendid as a Highlander in full rig-out. I was awfully glad to see him – it is so nice how any of the old folk when they hear one is near, always come round & see one. It makes life well worth living.

I got a ripping letter from you, old dear, today & have simply loved it. As you say old dear we have got beyond appearances when we are alone, but I still like to hear of you described as the 'best turned out woman' in public!!

I am sorry to hear of old Betsy's sprained ankle, but I hope it's better. You might tell her I thought I heard her voice but wasn't sure.

My love to you my old darling.

4th April 1917 – No. 51 – trenches, Roclincourt Sector

I had a long walk round the trenches this morning, most unpleasant as the snow has made them very bad going indeed. Our old guns have been fairly pooping off today & the old Boche has got a bit angry about it too & the air hasn't been very balmy in consequence.

I met another K.E.H. fellow here today and he tells me that three of my original lads are close here & I hope to see them one of these days soon. I am hoping to hear all about the doggies & their work when I get your letter this evening.

There is such a damned din going on that one can hardly hear anyone speak. However, I am feeling very fit & there is something rather exhilarating about it all. The feeling that one [is] rising above all the clamour & sitting very tight on one's natural inclination to rush out of the door & hare away into the back of beyond where one could sit down & be away & quiet for a time.

Anyhow, one does rise above this inclination alright & feels a better man for it. You simply can't help it because the men are so proud. If you had told me that you could lay hands on every man you met in the street, clap a uniform on him & send him out into this & that he would behave like a stoic & not only in crowds but as individuals and small parties, I should have said the whole thing was absolutely idiotic. That any nation in the world could do it. Anyhow we have done it & one is proud that one is a member of a country that produces men like the men out here.

One does find some who can't stick it as I had a man who threw himself out of a third storey window today, in order to avoid it & tho' he landed on the pavement he has little or nothing the matter with him & so he will only get tried by C.M. for a S.I. [self-inflicted] wound.

The last letter home

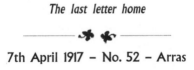

7th April 1917 – No. 52 – Arras

My darling,

I've had rather a strenuous time in the line these last three days & so beyond a postcard I haven't been able to do much for you, old dear.

We have been in for three days during which time our guns have been most particularly active. The result being that one hasn't known a moment's peace. The bottom of the trenches has had water & mud over it to the depth of the top of my field boots. Last night I was relieved, thank goodness, & the Adjutant, the Doctor and I walked back here together getting in at 6 a.m. (My town residence.)

Three more weary, mud-bespattered officers it would have been hard to find. I just flung myself down on the bed & slept as I never slept before with guns blotting off in all directions close to me without ever hearing a sound till Buckin woke me about noon. I hadn't had six hours' sleep in the three days, been damned nearly killed once & was what you call pleasantly weary, but it's a wonder how very quickly a few hours' sleep revives one & I'm as right as anything now, tho' looking forward to bed.

The guns make life quite unbearable in the house & now I'm down in a cellar where I've got my orderly room & a nice brazier of coke & am really quite warm & comfortable tho' it sounds hardly so. The erring stockings are really useful now as I've got them under my breeches with my field boots over them & they keep me nice & warm.

You certainly manage to put in a strenuous day when you go hunting. Your letters were a great 'pick me up' today as they were on the table when I got in. I'm so glad that old Bobbo got on so well with the pony – it seems to suit him fine. You have had just the same weather as we had, by your mentioning the big flakes of snow. It snowed yesterday again too. I go in the line again tomorrow. Your son certainly seems to be a helpful lad & I hope your younger one will be the same when he gets a bit bigger. Will you please thank Mimi for her letter and the Chugs too.

My own dear lass, I must go to bed now as I must store up what energy I can, as I shall probably need it these next few days as I'm likely to be pretty busy so far as I can see. Give the dear little Chugs my love & a kiss from Dad & with all my love to you old dear, & your dear old face to love.

Ever your Robert.

O n 8 April at 5 p.m., the battalion left Arras for the trenches in preparation for an assault, launched at 5.30 the next morning by the 24th and 25th Battalions. Colonel Hermon was killed shortly after 6 a.m. as he crossed open ground to follow up his troops, possibly by fire intended for a tank bogged down in the mud.

He was shot through the heart, one bullet slicing through the papers in his top pocket, including photographs of his family and the four-leaved clover his wife had given him for good luck. His final words to his Adjutant were 'Go on!' before he sank to his knees and died almost instantaneously.

Carried from the battlefield by his faithful soldier servant, Buxton, he now lies in the Commonwealth War Graves Cemetery at Roclincourt, three miles from Arras.

Tragically, the news of his death did not reach Ethel Hermon until she received the official telegram from the War Office on 13 April. The only letter to her husband which survives was written on 12 April, three days after he had been killed, in reply to his final letter: her concern for his safety is obvious however much she tries to conceal it. Her letter was returned to her in an official brown envelope, marked 'Killed in Action'.

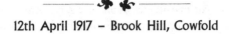

12th April 1917 – Brook Hill, Cowfold

Laddie my own,

I got a lovely letter this morning, 52, written on the 7th & doubly appreciated as you must have been feeling far more like going to bed than writing to me. You must be having a desperate, strenuous time, so laddie, do spend your spare minutes in a bit of rest & not in writing.

I know, of course, now that you must have been in the front line when the show started on Monday, tho' don't know whether this necessarily means you were among the first to go over the top . . . All surmise is quite useless, I know, & yet one simply can't help thinking & picturing things. It must be awful never getting a moment's peace from the noise of the guns, but I'm thankful you were able to fix up a cellar for your town residence last time as that might relieve the strain a bit tho' it could hardly lessen the noise. [The letter continues with home news about the children, how they had rigged up a tent to protect the goats from a snowstorm but in the morning it had collapsed and had taken them half an hour to disentangle the goats again.]

I went & had a bit of talk with Mrs Buckin today. She tells me you tried to persuade Buckin not to go up with you the last time you went up into the line but that he said 'rats' or its equivalent in language more in accordance with discipline! She said she would have a very small opinion of him had he taken you at your word & altogether was very nice & rather splendid about it. She has been awfully good in that sort of way all through.

Laddie mine . . . I could read so easily between the lines that you knew big & strenuous things were in front of you & I do so hope & pray you'll come thro' them safely laddie my own, & to your own satisfaction too. I wish the Germans would collapse like a pack of cards & end the whole thing, it's all too damnable for words.

My best of everything to you dear, dear laddie.

Yours ever, Ethel.

On the same day Buxton wrote to Mrs Hermon in his despair at the loss of his 'master', whom he often referred to as 'Father' in letters home to his own family.

Thursday 12th April – near Arras

My dear Madam,

It is impossible for me to express in my letter my deepest and heartfelt sympathy for you in your terrible loss. I have prayed to God to comfort you. I have thought of you night & day since I found the poor dear Colonel, oh dear it is too awful. I feel broken-hearted and I don't know how to write this letter, if I could only come home I could explain everything so much easier. I am going to try for leave, if it is only for a few hours just to have a few words with you. I wanted to go 'over' with him but he wouldn't let me, he thought it much better for me to stop in the dugout until he was settled down in the new line & then he would send for me to bring along the rations. He was in good spirits & very anxious to get away. When he started he said nothing to me and I didn't like to say anything to him, now I wish I had, if it was only to grab his hand for one second. He hadn't got very far before he was shot right through the heart & couldn't possibly have lived only a few seconds. The Adjutant ran to him but only told him 'to go on & not wait for him' – they were his last words for he was quite dead when they found him. I went to the Brigade in the afternoon and saw the General to arrange for the Colonel's burial. The General was very upset & expressed his deepest sympathy with you and the children & it was comforting to hear the warm tributes of praise & sympathy from everybody on the Staff & in the Battalion. We buried the dear Colonel in the military cemetery in the village close to the trenches yesterday afternoon at 3 o'clock. The General was unable to attend but the Staff Captain was there, also Major Campbell (senior Chaplain) and two other Chaplains. We had a nice little service & after everybody had gone I lingered by the grave of my dear master & friend. Oh dear Madam, my thoughts were of you, so far away it seemed so cruel to leave him there. I feel I have lost everything. Oh! It doesn't seem true it is like a dream, 4 days ago he was with us so full of life & hope. I never thought I should lose him but it is you & the dear children that I am thinking of all day & night. He died a brave soldier's death. I have got the gold disc & chain which the Colonel wore round his neck. I hope I didn't do wrong in taking it off but I thought you would like it. I have a lock of hair which I have put inside his watch and I will send them to you as soon as I have received instruction from you. All the Colonel's kit is at present in my charge & I will take care of everything until they are sent home. The Brigade is sending all his papers that were found on him. Colonel Richardson's brother is buried next to the Colonel. He was killed the same morning. I came down from the lines last night and am staying with the Quartermaster until the battalion comes out, but I am sorry to say there won't be many of them. So far I know at present we lost 11 officers killed & wounded. They say the casualties were not heavy considering the nature of the fighting, & the whole thing was a great success. Oh dear this attack has cost us a lot of fine officers & men. The Cavalry have suffered too. I am writing this letter on an old *Times* & the first thing that caught my eye in the died of wounds list was the name of Capt. Robin Loder – how awful it all seems.

Well dear Madam I am afraid I haven't explained things very well but I feel lost, I shall never be happy until I have been home to see you, then I could come back to try to be a brave soldier like my dear Master who was always so good & kind. I don't know what to do without him. I miss him so, but what is my loss compared with yours. I have never forgotten my promise to you 'to always look after the Colonel' and have tried to do my best & I feel I can't come back without him. Poor Mr & Mrs Hermon will be terribly upset too. The Adjutant is writing you & will explain the actual facts better than I have. Madam please forgive me for any mistakes I have made & anything I can possibly do that will be of any comfort to you I will do, if it costs me my life. I couldn't do too much for you – you have given more to the country than my insignificant life is worth. Oh! I know how you feel so well. I tried to get Mr Heath[219] & Harry to be present at the funeral but I am sorry to say [it] proved impossible. Harry and I may go back to the regiment if we like but we want to do whatever would please you. If we stop for a few days I am going back up to the Colonel's grave & plant some shrubs round it, is there anything you would like me to do? If so, I would love to do it. Harry wished me to 'express his deepest sympathy with you & the children'. I will now await your orders.

---

[219] The former Sergeant Heath who had been commissioned by this time.

Please accept my very deepest sympathy in your great sorrow. I do hope they will grant me leave.

I am your obedient servant,

Buxton

Buxton wrote to his own wife, Marie, on Friday 13 April, signing himself 'Freddie', the name by which he was known to his family.

My darling sweet Marie,

You have heard the sad news by now, poor Mrs Hermon whatever will she do, it seems too awful for her, oh my darling I feel so sorry for her, it is impossible for me to express how I feel, it doesn't seem true that he has gone for ever. Your words have come true, Marie love. He went over on Monday morning in good spirits & very anxious to be at them but he hadn't got very far before he was shot right through the heart & must have died in a few minutes. The Adjutant who ran to help him was the last man he spoke to, told him 'to go on and not wait for him'. I wanted to go 'over the top' with him but he wouldn't let me, he told me I should be no use to him if I got wounded or anything, so I remained in the dugout. The arrangement was that as soon as they had taken the German second line he was going to send a runner for me to come forward with the rations. But he hadn't gone long before I was over the top myself & I hadn't gone far before I met one of our men who told me the Colonel had been killed. I looked around for a long time before I found him, he was then quite dead, oh my darling, I did not know what to do, it upset me so. I feel I have lost a good Master & Friend. My heart is broken & I feel I can't write about it. I want to come home & try to comfort Mrs Hermon. I can't rest, I am thinking about her all day & night. I am going to make a special effort to get leave but I don't suppose I shall be successful. I had quite a long talk with the General, he was very nice. He is going to let Harry & I go back to the old regiment. We buried him on Wednesday afternoon in the cemetery amongst the ruined village close to the trenches where he was killed, nobody touched him but me. I did him up in two groundsheets & made him look as nice as possible. I buried him in his uniform just as he died. I tried to get Harry there but there wasn't time, it was such a pity. We had quite a nice little service, there was 3 Chaplains & the Staff Captain from the Brigade. I lingered by his grave after everybody had gone & prayed

that God would comfort his dear Wife & children & make me as good
and brave as my dead Master & my thoughts were of poor Mrs Hermon
so far away. I had to have a good cry Marie love, I couldn't help it. Oh,
everything seems so changed now, there seems nothing to work for. We
had had an awful time but the whole thing was a great success but at a
terrible price! I mustn't say much here but if I ever get home I can explain
things better. The weather has been awful & the poor men have suffered
terribly. Harry & I are going back to the regiment unless Mrs Hermon
would rather we stopped here. Well my darling I mustn't stop for more
now. I did my best to write Mrs Hermon a nice letter but I am afraid I
didn't express myself very well. I hope you are all well. We are off again so
I will write again first opportunity. I am all right but very sick at heart.
Goodbye my sweetheart.

   With my fondest love & kisses to everybody,
   Ever your loving Freddie.

On 17 April Ethel Hermon replied:

Dear Buxton,
   Your letter came this morning & I can never thank you enough for your
loving care of him & for your sympathy & prayers. I knew you would be
heartbroken & that I should have all your sympathy as you probably knew
as well as anyone could know how much we were to each other.
   You will by now have had my other letter telling you that I have asked
Gen. Trevor & now Gen. Nicholson to let you come home if it is possible
as I simply long to talk to you even tho' you have told me so much in
your letter. I can never thank you enough Buxton for that letter as though
I seem to know all that pen & paper can tell, one just longs to talk to
someone who was there.
   I am so more than glad you have kept the chain & disc for me as I
longed to have it. I don't know what to say to you about sending the things,
if you get leave it will be all right & you can bring them, but if not I think
perhaps you had better post them tho' I hate trusting them out of your
hands. Still the post always has been reliable & I think you must risk it.
As far as the kit is concerned I would be pleased to give the air bed, chair
& everything *not personal* to Capt. Svensson or Lt Jolland or the Adjutant
or Major Downie if they care for them but I would like the old basin &
cover & its contents to come home if possible.

Buxton, do they mark the graves with the name of the person buried there because I shall never rest now till I've seen where he lies & I must go out after the war & I trust you will be spared to go with me & show me? Who can be asked to care for it after you have left? I don't know how to answer your question about what you & Harry should do. I daren't take the responsibility now of choosing for you both. Gen. Nicholson wrote me that he was arranging for you to go back to K.E.H. I don't know what to do about the horses. I think they must take their chance of who gets them. They belong to the Government tho' if it can be worked that Mr Jackie Ashton could have them (he was an old Cheshire friend & is A.P.M.[220] & had been in to see the Colonel several times) I should like it. He wrote too this morning & asked whether I would like him to try & get them. I *should* as he is a fine horseman & they would be well ridden & cared for, tho' I don't know that I could ever have them back, I feel I should never hunt again, nor do I want to. I enclose you Mr Ashton's letter & then Harry will know that I should like this arrangement if it is worked. I will write to Mr Ashton about it tho' things may have been settled by now & if the horses have gone elsewhere, I must rest satisfied. Once more thanking you from the bottom of my heart & hoping if you can't get leave that you will be able to write again if you go up to the grave, also that you will tell me where you go to.

Yours most gratefully,

Ethel Hermon.

Brigadier-General H. E. Trevor, the Brigade Commander, also wrote twice to Mrs Hermon. These letters were found in her diary for 1917. The first letter from Brigadier Trevor was written in pencil and was dated 11 April 1917. The attack at Arras was still in progress and yet the brigade commander found time to write to a commanding officer's widow.

[220] Assistant Provost Marshal.

'103 Inf. Bde.'

Dear Mrs Hermon,

You will know that you have the very deepest sympathy from all ranks in the Brigade concerning the death of your husband. He had established himself as a very able & gallant commander in the Field & was recommended for promotion to command a Brigade.

On the morning of 9th inst. about 5.30 a.m. an attack on a very large scale was launched on the German lines from 7 miles south of Arras to north of Thebes (Vimy Ridge) by the army to which we belong. The 24th Bn North. Fus. was one of the leading Battalions of this Brigade. The attack succeeded & about 6 a.m. your husband decided to move his Hd Qrs from our own trenches to one in the German line & follow up his Battn. This is the usual procedure with Battn H.Q. in an attack nowadays.

The enemy were not shelling us very badly & we hadn't suffered many casualties at the time your husband crossed no man's land with his Adjutant. An enemy shrapnel bullet caught him as he was walking forward. It appears to have gone through the papers in his left top jacket pocket & killed him instantaneously. I am sending you the papers in a small parcel. His medical officer took charge of the body & brought me the papers a few minutes afterwards. He was buried at ROCLINCOURT as shown on attached map this afternoon about 3 p.m. I've seen his servant and he is looking after your husband's kit. I also saw General Nicholson, the Div. Commander, this afternoon & gave him details.

We are fighting a big battle which is going successfully for us but it is impossible to say who will come out alive. None of us have had sleep for 3 nights as there is so much work that I feel I cannot do justice or express to you all I feel concerning your very gallant husband.

I know that nothing I say can be of any use to you but I should like to say that I had the very highest respect & admiration for him. He never spared himself & knew no fear. His ability was considerable & it is cruel that he should have been cut off from a great career. Beyond all this personally, I had a real affection for him which was shared by many of the officers in his Battn & the Brigade.

I hope you may be given strength to bear your sorrow which I feel acutely (as I once told you) because I am responsible for his becoming an infantry C.O. I hope to write to you again later & you will of course let me know whether I can do anything for you. With deepest sympathy,

Yours very sincerely,

H. E. Trevor.

The last words your husband said (as stated by his adjutant who was behind him) was 'Go on' to his Battalion.

A second letter from Brigadier-General Trevor was dated 17 April 1917:

Dear Mrs Hermon,

I'm sending this note by Buxton who goes on leave today to report to you. He will bring the papers etc. found on your husband & handed me by the medical officer of his Battn.

Allison, the adjt of the 24th Bn N.F., tells me that when the Colonel and he went forward the enemy's artillery barrage had considerably slackened. Apparently a tank was caught up on the German front line (I saw it myself – The CAREFUL) by running into a concrete m.g. emplacement & the Boches were firing at it. Allison says that three bullets came over from the direction of their left. The Colonel was just in front of him & there seems little doubt one of these rifle bullets hit your husband just below the heart or in that region, penetrating the papers in his left hand top pocket (as you will see). He went down on his hands & knees & told the adjt to 'Go on' but almost immediately sank. The medical officer tells me he thinks a big blood vessel below the heart was severed & that death was almost instantaneous.

Your husband's horses are being sent to Div. Hd Qrs with the groom. General Nicholson has promised to look after them & they will be better cared for than with an Inf. Bn Hd Qrs. I can only repeat how much I feel for you in your irreparable loss.

Yours very sincerely,

H. E. Trevor.

Your husband's kit & valise are being sent home to you through Cox & Co., 1 Charing Cross. There is a 100 franc note in the pocket book found which Buxton is bringing. Allison is writing you concerning some money (about 50 francs) advanced by your husband to the Battalion which he is to settle.

Among the papers in Colonel Hermon's pocket was one from General Trevor himself, who had sent him a note before the battle:

Dear Hermon,

Just a line to reiterate my best wishes to you & your Battn. I know you will get your fellows as far forward as possible in the assembly trenches.

No good altering anything now that the men have been taught & trained. Apparently there may be some dugouts found to be intact. I think the best way to deal with them is to shoot down at any men in the trench before getting down into the trench & doing any bombing.

The last wire forwarded you on this subject was a copy of a 34th Div. wire. You had better not bother to alter anything you've already taught your fellows.

Yours ever, H. E. Trevor.

1.20 a.m. 9/4/17

One of Robert's fellow officers from King Edward's Horse, Lieutenant (later Captain) Donald MacKinnon, wrote a letter of sympathy to Ethel Hermon from Dublin, where he was with the Reserve Regiment. 'Mac' had served with him when he was commanding 'C' Squadron and still referred to him as 'the Major'. His words might well serve as an epitaph for Colonel Hermon. He wrote:

The Major was right about those below knowing best. The men just adored him: nobody outside the regiment can imagine what absolute faith they had in him. He had an extraordinary moral influence over them which I have never seen another instance of. You get it among boys, & you find a kind of blind devotion among the Regular Tommy class, but with the Squadron it was more than that because the majority were well-educated folk & mostly above the average age. He was so absolutely above everything that was mean & crooked, in fact he could hardly believe it to exist in others.

You may say this is a commonplace virtue, but in the Army you see it is not. Most of us every now & again do show a little spite or mean-ness especially in soldiering, but he never could, he was too generous & too sympathetic with everyone.

And then the greatest of all he helped everyone he had under him to avoid spiteful things & mean things. And in this his spirit will never leave me I know, nor the rest of us.

AFTERWORD

The First World War would continue, with its appalling human toll, for another eighteen months before the Armistice was declared on 11 November 1918, finally bringing the terrible slaughter to an end.

Initially the attack at Arras had been successful, in part due to the rolling artillery barrage, as on this first day of the battle the German trenches were overrun and over 5,000 prisoners taken, but it later developed into a stalemate although the Canadian Corps, at terrible cost, achieved their objective by capturing Vimy Ridge. Once again the losses to both sides were unacceptably high: the 24th Battalion alone lost four officers killed and nine wounded with scores of soldiers killed, wounded or missing.

When Ethel Hermon received the telegram from the War Office on 13 April telling her that her husband had been killed in action, the news affected her deeply and her diary entries end abruptly after this date. She kept his dressing-room at Cowfold untouched, just as he had left it on his final leave. Despite her grief, she continued to be a dedicated mother to their five children. Robert's father, Sidney Hermon, undertook the cost of educating them and the two boys followed in their father's footsteps to Eton whilst the three girls were educated at Abbot's Hill, Hemel Hempstead. Brook Hill remained the family home until after Ethel's death in 1930.

During the last years of her life Ethel suffered from a heart condition described as a 'tired heart'. She died at the early age of fifty, when Ken was just fifteen years old. Her daughter Mary was with her at the end and firmly believed that her parents were reunited in death: in her final moments, her mother had opened her eyes, smiled, and murmured her husband's name, as if she could see him standing beside her. Ethel's obituary in the *Cowfold Parish Magazine* described her as having 'a real enthusiasm for anything that aimed at a high ideal'; however, 'the trait by which she would be most remembered was her most splendid capacity for motherhood: she gave her whole forceful character to this as a vocation'. Her coffin was borne from the house on a wagon covered with evergreens and at every house in the village the blinds were drawn.

After Robert Hermon's death, Buxton and Harry Parsons returned to the old regiment where they continued to serve until the end of the war, when Mrs Hermon wrote to the authorities stating that Buxton had previously been in her employment and that she was happy to offer him work 'as a motor driver *immediately* on his return to civil life'. Buxton did go back to Roclincourt, to care for Colonel Hermon's grave, just as he had pledged. In 1917 Ethel Hermon wrote to him, expressing her thanks: 'It is the greatest comfort to know that you were able to do so much. I am *so* grateful Buxton, for all your trouble. I know you spared no pains. I do so hope the little box shrubs will live & that some day I shall see it for myself. I am so intensely glad that the primroses, the one little bit of home, are there as it were to keep him company.'

Buxton remained with the family at Brook Hill until after Mrs Hermon's death. He and his wife Marie had six sons and when at last a daughter, Jessica, was born to them, the church bells in Cowfold were rung in celebration. Nigel, the sixth and last son, obtained a bursary through his father's old regiment, King Edward's Horse, to attend the Imperial Service College, Windsor. He obtained a commission in the Royal Artillery and was Mentioned in Dispatches for his bravery in Normandy soon after the D-Day invasion.

Colonel Hermon would have been proud that his sons, like him, fought for 'King and Country', in the Second World War, though he would doubtless have been deeply saddened at the onset of another world war – a conflict that he had predicted if the German war machine had not been totally annihilated by the end of the 'war to end all wars'. His elder son, Bob, was commissioned from Sandhurst into the Royal Dragoons in 1926 and in July 1942 took command of the King's Dragoon Guards and fought with them in North Africa. In March 1943 he was wounded during the attack on the Mareth Line in Tunisia, and, like his father before him, awarded the DSO. Promoted to full colonel in April 1944 he became deputy-commander of 23 Armoured Brigade. By the end of the war he had been awarded the OBE, and received a Mention in Dispatches.

Of the three girls, Mary was the only one to have children. Betty married Luke Leslie Smith and lived at Nuthurst in Sussex, where Buxton worked for them after the death of Mrs Hermon, until well after the Second World War. Betty died in Yorkshire in 1975. In 1929 Mary married John McKergow, who had spent five years in India with the Royal Scots Greys. They lived at Shermanbury in Sussex until going to New Zealand to farm in 1935 with their eldest son and daughter. A second son was born in 1938. With the advent of the Second World War, Mary's husband, John, joined the New Zealand army as a captain, and was badly wounded in Italy in late 1943, whilst commanding the 20th Armoured Regiment. Mary ran the farm in Canterbury, New Zealand, with great determination and success for the four years John was away and after the war they had two more children, a daughter and a son. John died suddenly in 1961 whilst the two post-war children were still teenagers, and Mary, like her mother before her, was left to bring up children on her own. However, she lived for another thirty years, to enjoy her eighteen grandchildren and even some of her thirty-two great-grandchildren, before she died in 1991 at the age of eighty-three – the matriarch of a large dynasty spread over five continents.

Meg, the youngest daughter, became engaged in the early 1930s to Anthony Gilliat, a brother officer of Bob's in the Royal Dragoons, who died in India a few months later after being attacked by a tiger. Meg travelled to New Zealand with Mary and her family in 1935 to recover from this tragedy, and on the voyage home the following year she met and subsequently married an Indian Army officer, Thomas Atherton, of the Deccan Horse. She died in London at the age of fifty-one. Meg is buried in a grave beside her mother's in the churchyard at Cowfold. On the night of her funeral her husband, then in his sixties and in poor health, returned to the Cavalry Club in London and took an overdose, as he could no longer face life without her.

Ken, the younger son, joined the Durham Light Infantry after Eton and Sandhurst. During the Second World War he volunteered to serve with the Commandos, and was captured in Crete in 1941. Having escaped from Eichstadt POW camp, he was recaptured and sent to Oflag IVC – the infamous Colditz Castle – from where he corresponded with Buxton. After the war he married and had two sons. He died in Cumbria in 1978.

Ken once wrote that Buxton had been 'an example to us all from our youth upwards', and on his death, Mary wrote to his widow Marie that he had always been 'a very great friend & counsellor to me all my life. His passing seems to have severed the last link with my old home, my parents and all my childhood.' For the Hermon children, 'Buckin' – or 'Buccy' as they called him – had proved to be an unbreakable and enduring link with the father they had known so very briefly.

SELECT BIBLIOGRAPHY

ARCHIVES

The National Archives, Kew: War Diaries of King Edward's Horse
Imperial War Museum, London: Photograph Archive
Northumberland Fusilier Museum, Alnwick Castle: War Diaries of 27th
  and 24th Battalions, Northumberland Fusiliers
Queen's Own Hussars Regimental Museum, Warwick: papers

BOOKS

Gilbert, Martin, *The First World War* (Weidenfeld & Nicolson, 1994)
Holmes, Richard, *Tommy: The British Soldier on the Western Front,*
  1914–1918 (HarperCollins, 2004)
James, Lionel, DSO, *History of King Edward's Horse* (Sifton, Praed &
  Co., 1921)
Keegan, John, *The First World War* (Hutchinson, 1998)
McCorquodale, Colonel D., OBE, *History of the King's Dragoon Guards,*
  1938 1945 (Caxton Works, *c.* 1946)
Sheen, John, *The Tyneside Irish* (Pen & Sword Books, 1998)

INTERNET

firstworldwar.com

ACKNOWLEDGEMENTS

In preparing this collection of my grandfather's letters, I am greatly indebted to Gordon Buxton's only daughter, Jessica Hawes (Members Secretary to the Montgomeryshire Genealogical Society), who has provided me with invaluable material relating to the Hermon family, including photographs, letters from members of the family to her father, extracts from his diaries and newspaper cuttings. She has cheerfully responded to numerous emails, and answered endless queries. Amongst the items are postcards from Colditz from Ken Hermon, wartime letters from the Middle East from Bob Hermon and news of life on the farm in New Zealand from Mary McKergow.

Michael Meredith, the Eton College librarian, initially suggested the transcription of the letters so that they could reach a wider audience, and it was thanks to him that the whole project began. The collection will eventually be donated to the Eton Library for safe keeping. I am indebted also to our friend and neighbour, James Holland, the military historian and novelist, for introducing me to Trevor Dolby of Preface Publishing; between them they have given me the encouragement to publish the letters.

My thanks are also due to Kate Johnson, the publisher's editor, for her endless patience in receiving and attending to frequent emails during the final cutting of the text. Mel Haselden too, of the Loman Street Studios, has been a pleasure to work with whilst choosing the illustrations. I would also like to thank the archivists of the museums of both the Royal Northumberland Fusiliers at Alnwick Castle and the Queen's Own Hussars in Warwick, who have been most co-operative in my quest for information. Finally, I would like to thank my husband Ian for his help and support, particularly on military matters, and for putting up with his wife spending endless hours at the computer.

Anne Nason